Obligatory Blathering Blurbs

"I guarantee you've never read a business book like this one. The scathing insights, sarcastic humor, and steamy sex scenes all make for one hell of a read."

Karen Phelan

"If I were alive, I would encourage everyone to read this brilliant book by my brilliant daughter, who is also good-looking and a very nice person."

Karen's mom

"I strongly recommend you buy this book. In fact, you should buy lots of copies. We could really use the money."

Karen's husband

"Mom told me to say how terrific her book is. How terrific her book is."

Karen's teenage son

"She promised she would redo my website if I gave her a blurb for her book."

Semi-famous author acquaintance

"It's amazingly brilliant."

Karen's friend

"I find myself telling everyone that the book is amazingly brilliant."

Karen's other friend

"I can't stop telling all my friends how amazingly brilliant this book is."

An acquaintance

"Did anyone notice that Chapter 5 makes you go around telling all your friends that the book is amazingly brilliant?"

Karen's hypnosis teacher

Other Books by This Author

BLANK: THE POWER OF NOT THINKING

We don't think rationally, so why bother? This step-by-step guide will give you the power to approach each decision and task as if it were brand new!

OUT-AND-OUT LIARS: THE TALL STORIES OF SUCCESS

Learn how the very rich and infamous became that way by creating an alternate reality and partaking in that reality with others. From third-hand accounts of Bernie Madoff, Jeffrey Skilling, Dennis Kozlowski, and many others.

THE SEARCH FOR ELUSIVE GRAY MATTER IN THE CORPORATE UNIVERSE

Learn how to apply the thinking of the greatest scientific minds to the workplace. See how Heisenberg's uncertainty principle shows you that you can't know what you are doing and where you are going at the same time, learn from Einstein when to say "It's all relative," use M-theory to discern the strings attached to new proposals, and discover tips to manage that black hole in the center of your desk.

WHO MOVED MY HOLY HAND GRENADE? II

This time Monty Python and the Holy Grail teaches you everything you need to know in life. Learn the most important lessons for having a fulfilling life, such as heroics can be harmful, inner conflicts make us our own worst enemies, there are some people you can't win over, and remember that it all ends in blankness.

I'M SORRY I BROKE YOUR COMPANY

Karen Phelan is sorry. She tried to do business by the numbers—the management consultant way—developing measures, optimizing processes, and quantifying performance. The only problem is that businesses are run by people. And people can't be plugged into formulas or summed up in scorecards.

Who Moved My Holy Hand Grenade?

Who Moved My Holy Hand Grenade?

Everything I needed to know in business, I learned from
Monty Python and the Holy Grail

The Corporate Drone's Handbook

Karen Phelan

Copyright © 2013 Karen Phelan
All rights reserved.

Library of Congress Control Number: 2013923033

ISBN: 0991213807
ISBN-13: 978-0-9912138-0-1

Lineson Publishing
New Jersey, USA

Cover art: Rae Monet, Inc.
Editor: Susan Lang (Editcetera)
Author Photograph: Lightroom Studios

Contents

ANTILOGUE — xi

INTRODUCTION — 1

CHAPTER 1: YOU'RE USING COCONUTS
How About Some Kool-Aid? — 5

CHAPTER 2: HE'S NOT DEAD YET
Sacrificing Long-Term Health for Short-Term Expediency — 21

CHAPTER 3: WELL, I AM KING
Ensuring Leadership Is Aligned with the Rank and File — 35

CHAPTER 4: IT'S ONLY A FLESH WOUND
Knowing When to Cut Your Losses — 49

CHAPTER 5: IF SHE WEIGHS THE SAME AS A DUCK
Logic and Decision Making at Large Corporations — 57

CHAPTER 6: ON SECOND THOUGHT, IT'S A SILLY PLACE
Having the Right Song and Dance to Communicate Your Vision — 77

CHAPTER 7: OH, DON'T GROVEL
The Proper Way of Sucking Up — 89

CHAPTER 8: NOW WE LEAP OUT OF THE RABBIT
The Perils of Poor Planning — 99

CHAPTER 9: CUT YOUR OWN HEAD OFF
The Dangers of Corporate Infighting — 115

CHAPTER 10: LET ME HAVE SOME PERIL
Sometimes Good Opportunities Aren't in the Plan — 119

CHAPTER 11: WE ARE NOW THE KNIGHTS WHO GO "NEOW WUM PING"
Keeping Up with the Latest Corporate Initiatives — 131

CHAPTER 12: AND MAKE SURE HE DOESN'T LEAVE
The Current, Confusing State of Corporate Communications — 147

CHAPTER 13: LET'S NOT BICKER OVER WHO KILLED WHOM
Stuck in a Competitive Paradigm — 161

CHAPTER 14: BEHIND THE BUNNY?
It's the Little Things that Bite You — 173

CHAPTER 15: THOU SHALT COUNT TO THREE, NO MORE, NO LESS
Making Simple Things Complicated — 187

CHAPTER 16: THE GRAIL IS IN THE AAAAAARRRRGGGGGHHHHHHH
How to Leave Behind a Concise, Understandable Message — 199

CHAPTER 17: WHAT'S YOUR FAVORITE COLOR?
Attitude Is Everything — 205

CHAPTER 18: I UNCLOG MY NOSE IN YOUR DIRECTION
The Graceful Art of Negotiation — 225

CHAPTER 19: MOVE ALONG, THERE'S NOTHING TO SEE
The Utter Futility of Grandiose Journeys — 239

ANSWERS TO EXERCISES — 247

FEEDBACK SURVEY — 249

Contents

APPENDIX A: OVERVIEW OF LIFO (LIFE ORIENTATIONS)	253
APPENDIX B: STRATEGY DEVELOPMENT TOOLS	257
ACKNOWLEDGMENTS	261
BIBLIOGRAPHY	263
OUTTAKES (If Movies Can Have Them, Why Not Books?)	269
INDEX	273
ABOUT THE AUTHOR	277

Antilogue

Once, long ago in a land far away, there lived four little characters who ran through a maze looking for cheese to nourish them and make them happy.

Two were mice named "Sniff" and "Scurry" and two were littlepeople—beings who were as small as mice but who looked and acted a lot like people today. Their names were "Hem" and "Haw."

Due to their small size, it would be easy not to notice what the four of them were doing. But if you looked closely enough, you could discover the most amazing things!

Every day the mice and the littlepeople spent time in the maze looking for their own special cheese.

The mice, Sniff and Scurry, possessing only simple rodent brains, but good instincts, searched for the hard nibbling cheese they liked, as mice often do.

The two littlepeople, Hem and Haw, used their brains, filled with many beliefs and emotions, to search for a very different kind of Cheese—with a capital C—which they believed would make them feel happy and successful.

As different as the mice and littlepeople were, they shared something in common: Every morning, they each put on their jogging suits and running shoes, left their little homes, and raced out into the maze looking for their favorite cheese.

(From Who Moved My Cheese? by Spencer Johnson)

Who Moved My Cheese? is a best-selling business book that recounts a fable about managing change in the workplace. Two mice and two littlepeople who live in a maze awake to discover that their supply of cheese is gone. Although the mice move on as soon as they make that discovery, it takes a while for the littlepeople to realize that they will have to change, and then just one leaves to look elsewhere for new cheese. His journey is long and lonely, dark and depressing, as he finds only bits of cheese here and there, until one day he finally catches up with the mice, who have found a significant supply. He realizes that someday this supply, too, will be exhausted, and he will need to set out, yet again, on a search for more cheese. The parable of the story is that our work life will never be stable, and we should be ready to change whenever needed. All we need to succeed is the right attitude about managing change.

If you loved *Who Moved My Cheese?*, then this is probably not the book for you. Really. I'm warning you. It's probably not. My tale is neither heartwarming nor simplistic, because my experiences in business have none of these characteristics.

SO PUT THE BOOK DOWN AND BACK AWAY FROM THE TABLE!!!

Unless, you prefer a different tale of cheese......

Monty Python's Flying Circus: The Cheese Shoppe

A customer (John Cleese) is looking for some cheese to buy in The Cheese Shoppe and is asking the owner (Michael Palin) for various kinds.

CUSTOMER: Greek Feta?
OWNER: Uh, not as such.
CUSTOMER: Uuh, Gorgonzola?
OWNER: No.
CUSTOMER: Parmesan?
OWNER: No.
(The customer proceeds to inquire about an exhaustive list of cheeses with the same "no" for an answer.)
CUSTOMER: Aah, how about Cheddar?
OWNER: Well, we don't get much call for it around here, sir.
CUSTOMER: Not much ca— It's the single most popular cheese in the world!
OWNER: Not 'round here, sir.
CUSTOMER: And what IS the most popular cheese 'round here?
OWNER: 'Illchester, sir.
CUSTOMER: IS it.
OWNER: Oh, yes, it's staggeringly popular in this manor, squire.
CUSTOMER: Is it.
OWNER: It's our number one best seller, sir!
CUSTOMER: I see. Uuh...'Illchester, eh?
OWNER: Right, sir.
CUSTOMER: All right. Okay. "Have you got any?"
OWNER: I'll have a look, sir.... nnnnnnnnnnnnnnno.
CUSTOMER: It's not much of a cheese shop, is it?
OWNER: Finest in the district!
CUSTOMER (annoyed): Explain the logic underlying that conclusion, please.

Antilogue

OWNER: Well, it's so clean, sir!
CUSTOMER: It's certainly uncontaminated by cheese....
OWNER (brightly): You haven't asked me about Limburger, sir.
CUSTOMER: Would it be worth it?
OWNER: Could be....
CUSTOMER (slowly): Have you got any Limburger?
OWNER: No.
CUSTOMER: Figures. Predictable, really I suppose. It was an act of purest optimism to have posed the question in the first place. Tell me…..(pause)
OWNER: Yes, sir?
CUSTOMER (deliberately): Have you, in fact, got any cheese here at all?
OWNER: Yes, sir.
CUSTOMER: Really?
OWNER (pause): No. Not really, sir.
CUSTOMER: You haven't.
OWNER: No sir. Not a scrap. I was deliberately wasting your time, sir.
CUSTOMER: Well I'm sorry, but I'm going to have to shoot you.
OWNER: Right-O, sir.
(The customer takes out a gun, shoots the owner and leaves the shop.)
CUSTOMER: What a senseless waste of human life.

(Excerpt from Monty Python's Flying Circus skit "The Cheese Shoppe")

My experience of business is much more like "The Cheese Shoppe" than *Who Moved My Cheese?*—idiotic conversations, escalating frustration, pretend professionalism, futile effort, and, in general, collective lunacy. This book is about those experiences and how to handle them.

Introduction

Although mice running through a maze is a fitting analogy for the modern workplace, I offer a different metaphor to symbolize the quest for corporate success: the Arthurian legend. Think about it. We have Arthur as the celebrity CEO who searches for the best talent to fill his leadership team so that they can embark on a quest for the elusive strategic objective, I mean, the Holy Grail. When he gets into trouble, Arthur seeks the counsel of his trusty management consultant, er, wizard. He and his knights seem to hold all the power while the peasants struggle to eke out a living. When you consider it, we haven't progressed all that much since the Dark Ages.

The Dark Ages—Sadlibs Version

The (<u>Early Middle Ages</u>, <u>last few decades</u>) are also known as the Dark Ages due to the lack of advancement in (<u>the arts, literature, and science</u>, <u>finance, economy, and government</u>) during this period. Many people blame the stranglehold (<u>the Church</u>, <u>economic dogma</u>) had on society, and hence this period is also known as the (<u>Age of Faith</u>, <u>Age of Wishful Thinking</u>). The governing structure was a rigid hierarchy, known as the (<u>feudal system</u>, <u>organizational structure</u>) whereby the (<u>nobility</u>, <u>executives</u>) were able to maintain control of the (<u>peasants</u>, <u>employees</u>.) The (<u>kings</u>, <u>CEOs</u>) were in possession of a huge amount of (<u>lands</u>, <u>assets</u>) and could not govern them effectively from a central position. Therefore,

1

the (king, CEO) granted (manors, departments) to his (lords, vice presidents) in return for their homage and fealty. Likewise, the (lords, vice presidents) granted (property, responsibility) to their (knights, managers) in return for their loyalty. The last people in this chain were the (serfs, staff) who usually ended up with only small (plots, cubicles). In return, the (serfs, employees) agreed to obey their (lords, managers), work hard, and follow the rules laid down by (the lord's court, corporate policies).

There were various types of (serfs, employees), each with different degrees of (rights, respect.) A lucky few were (free serfs, entrepreneurs) who ran their own businesses while paying a large commission to the (lord, venture capitalists.) Most of the (serfs, employees) were not free and led miserable lives. Forced to do the will of their (lord, employer), they looked to the wisdom of (the Church, management consultants) for relief. The (serfs, employees) mostly believed that if they worked hard, followed the word of the (clergy, latest management guru), gave their money to (the Church, their 401k), and did the (king's bidding, latest corporate initiative), they would go to (heaven, Boca Raton) in their (afterlife, retirement.) Unfortunately, giving all their money to (the Church, their 401K) did nothing to ensure a better life afterward, but only served to make the (bishops, fund managers) very wealthy.

Kind of scary, isn't it? After all these centuries chock full of enlightened thinkers like Locke, Darwin, Marx, Freud, Gandhi, and Einstein, not to mention the revolutions fought against tyranny in Russia, the United States, France, and elsewhere, we are still living in a variation of the feudal system. Granted, as citizens of developed countries, we enjoy a fair amount of freedom to pursue our own goals; as employees of large corporations, not so much. But I don't want to be depressing. We get enough depressing business books and news. This is why I've chosen to use the Monty Python retelling of the quest for the Holy Grail. Let's face it, people are silly, and people run businesses; therefore, businesses are silly. Plus, most business books are dreadfully dull, and it's about time we had a humorous business book that captures what it's really like to work in a modern corporation with all the silliness that passes for common business practices.

Join me on a journey through *Monty Python and the Holy Grail*, which actually covers everything a person should know about business, from organizational culture and strategy development to communications and thinking skills. On our quest, we will meet such mythical creatures as the ideal leader, the breakthrough strategy, and the perfect plan. We'll counter the tyranny of competitive analysis, corporate jargon, and the improvement initiative du

Introduction

jour. While I cover some basic topics, I try to focus on others that I believe are important subjects usually overlooked in management books, like neurolinguistic programming, complexity theory, and cognitive biases. Mostly, though, I poke fun at our modern business practices, models, management theory, and all those components that comprise today's corporate culture of idiocy.

1
You're Using Coconuts

How about some Kool-Aid?

Monty Python and the Holy Grail opens with King Arthur and his trusty servant banging coconut shells together and prancing around to imitate horse riding. (Actually, the movie opens with several minutes of credits that include fake Swedish, multiple mentions of moose, an apology by Richard Nixon, and, well, you get the gist.) Anyway, the production crew couldn't afford horses so they had the actors bang coconut shells to mimic hoof beats and prance with one foot and one arm forward to simulate horse and rider.

Arthur and his page are "riding" in quest of knights to join them at Camelot. When Arthur comes upon a castle, he tells two guards that he wants to see their lord. However, the guards are distracted by the coconut banging, and the only conversation that ensues is about how on earth he got tropical coconuts in the temperate English climate? Did they migrate? Arthur tries to get the guards to pay attention to his request, but to no avail. Were the coconuts carried by swallows? What kind of a swallow could carry a coconut? Would it be an African swallow or a European swallow? Obviously, a coconut weighs more than a swallow, and a bird couldn't carry a coconut on its own. Perhaps two swallows with a vine strung across their wings... Finally, Arthur gets frustrated by the discussion and "rides" away.

In this opening scene, the king and his vassal look ridiculous banging the coconuts and prancing like horses—quite a hilarious setup. Many years ago, when taking some film classes, I learned that the director sets the ground rules for a movie during the first 10 minutes. For instance, if you are making a musical, you need to have a musical number within the first 10 minutes, and the earlier the better. If it is a shoot-em-up, signal that fact early on with some gut spilling. If not, the audience will expect a realistic portrayal of life. Actors bursting into song, or just bursting, later in the movie will be jarring and out of context. The beginning of the movie sets the context for what we expect and what we notice during the rest of the film, just as our coconut-banging knights set the scene for a raucous comedy. However, if you watched *Monty Python and the Holy Grail*, you probably laughed at the pretend horses for the first few scenes, but as the movie wore on chances are you barely noticed the gag. It eventually became part of the background. We became inured to the joke just as we become inured to blood spilling in action flicks.

A similar development occurs in business. As someone new to a company, you notice idiosyncrasies that no one else recognizes. After a while, you also become acclimated to these quirks and can't remember what you found so odd. For instance, when I joined a particular management consultancy, all the employees walked around saying "how to…" and "I wish I knew…" whenever they voiced a concern, as in "how to make sure upper management buys into this" and "I wish I knew our clients' reaction to this change." The intent was to make action items out of concerns. At first, I thought everyone was brainwashed. After several weeks, I saw the value of speaking like that and incorporated those phrases into my daily vernacular, completely habituated to this strange jargon. A requirement of starting a new job is to acquire the culture, so what I'd like to explore in this chapter is the concept of corporate culture: those sets of traditions and beliefs that shape our thoughts and behavior without us being aware of them. This is what drinking the Kool-Aid is all about.

To shed light on corporate culture, I want to make a brief foray into cultural differences among countries. I do this for two reasons: First, much of the research on corporate cultures is based on findings about regional cultures. Second, how we behave with people of other regional cultures gives us insight into how we behave with people of different corporate cultures.

I once attended a dinner that was a microcosm of culture clashes. For several years I had a job managing information technology for my company in the Asia-Pacific region. At first I was a little daunted by having to work with foreign cultures, but soon I got used to the various Asian cultures and customs. Early on in this assignment, I was present at a weeklong meeting in Hong Kong. The meeting attendees were a mix of people from the United States, the United Kingdom, South Africa, Australia, China, Singapore, Malaysia, Japan, and Korea. All of us were accustomed to working with and in other countries. Unfortunately, throughout the week we tended to socialize in two groups, Anglos and Asians, but in an attempt at team building, one of the locals arranged for us to visit a local fish-trading port and eat at a fish market/restaurant. Part of the experience was picking out the seafood to be served, and we Anglos marveled at the abundance of sea creatures we didn't even know existed, let alone were eaten by humans. I enjoyed watching our hosts haggle with the salespeople and then give brassy orders to the chefs on how to prepare the dishes. All of the transactions involved a good deal of yelling, hand gesturing, and wrangling.

Inside, the restaurant was cramped, and our large group was wedged into a corner. We sat around a large circular table, with the Anglos—two Americans (including me), two Britons, an Aussie, and a South African—on one side. On the other side sat a Korean, a Japanese, and ethnic Chinese from Hong Kong, Malaysia, and Singapore. Immediately upon sitting, our coworker from Korea ordered a bottle of sake, which he insisted everyone share. Because I was sitting on the outside, the waitress, an older woman, needed to reach over me to serve the dishes. Rather than asking politely, she brusquely pushed me out of her way and even spilled food on me. Each time she did this, a chorus of protests and complaints arose from my Chinese friends, and an argument ensued between the server and our hosts, upsetting the Anglos, who complained about the rude service. (Personally, I thought being pushed aside was pretty funny.)

After a few dishes, our Korean colleague began to sing at the top of his lungs, and our Japanese friend soon joined in. They embarked on a recital of patriotic songs and poetry, each in turn disparaging the other's country by recounting his own version of Korean-Japanese wars. As the sake took its effect, they became more and more disparaging. My British colleague, shocked by the insults and afraid that the two would come to blows, tried to stop the singing and poetry, but that offended them. Why was he trying to ruin their fun? And why did he fear that they would become violent? *He* was clearly slighting *them*.

As for me, I was trying to make sure the sake didn't incapacitate me and was drinking water feverishly. However, the water refills were not flowing, and when I emptied my glass, the waitress took it away. The same thing happened to my Anglo comrades. Although the waitress continued to spill food on us, she had no intention of refilling our water glasses, so we drank more sake. The Chinese women were shocked that we Anglo women were downing the sake, because very few Asian women drink. Meanwhile, our Japanese and Korean colleagues continued to get more and more rowdy, the waitress became more abusive, and our Asian friends returned her insults more vehemently. Most of the Anglos were appalled at how our "nice dinner" was unraveling into pandemonium, but none of the Asians seemed flustered.

In the years that followed, when encountering some of the attendees and reminiscing about that dinner, I was amused at how some remembered that night as a nightmare of bad service and impending national hostilities while others remembered it with fondness for the gusto of the evening. Of course, it was the Anglos who had a terrible time because they (me, too) misunderstood several aspects of the culture we were in. First of all, our Korean and Japanese colleagues were practicing "day face" and "night face." During the day they are very formal, reserved, and unemotional. At night they can put on a night face, allowing them to party hard and say whatever they want without penalty of hurt feelings. Insults are taken as good-natured and do not lead to blows, and the next morning all is forgotten. Night face is an excellent way of forming friendships—the rowdier, the better the bonding. We Anglos mistook the rowdiness for a serious conflict. One of the Brits, inculcated with keeping a stiff upper lip, was especially mortified. Another simple thing, completely emptying your glass and plate in China means you are finished.[1] This is why the server wouldn't refill our water glasses. Bad service and barking at the

---

[1] In Japan, cleaning your plate means you want more. I learned this the hard way at a meal in Japan that I thought would never end because I wanted to be polite and clean my plate. My Japanese host incorrectly gained insight into why many Americans are overweight.

bad service is also a cultural norm in China, as well as being pushed out of the way. I've been pushed off the sidewalk in Hong Kong for walking too slowly.

This dinner in Hong Kong showed that, even though most people are aware of cultural differences, we still expect people to act according to our own mores. Everyone sitting at that table was well traveled and knew about the cultural differences, but because of our ingrained sense of social rights and wrongs, we were unable to recognize them for what they were. The waitress was rude. The Korean and the Japanese were unruly. The Anglo women were lushes. The Brit was an arrogant killjoy. We judged behaviors through our own filters. Even when we know we are wearing rose-tinted glasses, what we see really is rosier.

From my experience working in different companies and living through several mergers and acquisitions, I've learned that, boy, do we really misunderstand differences in corporate cultures! Although we expect cultures to vary, we do very little to appreciate and mitigate those differences except write down laundry lists of unique company rituals, jargon, and policies. We rarely consider the differences in underlying values or assumptions. We naturally assume that everyone else holds the same values we do. For instance, most American companies cite "respect for others" as a company value, but what does respect mean? In some firms, respect means never disagreeing or being critical, even constructively. In others, it means not dressing down someone in public. Some companies consider respect for other people's time to be part of that value and expect timeliness from everyone. Many enterprises do not include timeliness in that definition.

Here is how something as simple as a meeting differs widely from company to company. When I left one consulting company to join another, I was not aware of the meeting practices of the new culture and ended up violating some sacrosanct behavior. In this particular culture, pre-meetings, where you met individually with all the invitees before the meeting to get their opinions and build consensus, were the norm. The purpose of meetings in this culture was to agree on action plans with responsibilities and due dates. No one wanted to waste valuable meeting time discussing issues. Silly me. I came from a culture where the point of meetings was to hash out different points of view, and I violated this norm by holding a meeting without the advance work. Everyone attending expected that all the issues would have been resolved beforehand, and the meeting became tense when different opinions surfaced.

Afterward, I was taken aside, instructed in the "proper" way to conduct a meeting, and chastised for not being prepared.

In a similar vein, many years later at a different company, when my division was acquired by another company, we acquirees complained about the numerous meetings we attended as part of the merger. My cohorts bitterly complained that the new company never developed any action plans from the meetings, just consensus on all the issues that needed to be addressed. We were constantly compiling lists of issues and never working to resolve them. When I brought this to the attention of employees of the takeover company, they didn't understand why we were complaining. The point of the meetings was to gain understanding, not to develop plans. Action plans were developed off-line, usually by a few members of the leadership team, once they felt they understood the issues. Neither of these misunderstandings had anything to do with the mechanics of meetings, such as agendas, minutes, and timekeeping, which you would expect to differ from culture to culture, but with the basic assumption about why people meet. It's these hidden assumptions and values that cause the biggest cultural misunderstandings, not the lingo, policies, or practices.

Although there are many excellent models and explanations of culture differences, I prefer to use my own set of dimensions, or factors, to articulate these differences because it is simpler. Bear in mind that none of this is scientifically or statistically sound, but you are reading a book called, *Who Moved My Holy Hand Grenade?* and not *Statistically Sound Hypothesis for Culture Clashes with Umpteen Supporting Examples.* This being a satire, I take the liberty of making stuff up.

Dimensions of Corporate Culture

Collaborative versus competitive culture There are certain organizations in which the word "I" is worse than a four-letter word. In these cultures everyone is a member of various teams, and teamwork is one of the corporate values. When a task is required, the responsible member automatically reaches out to peers and forms a team. Competitive cultures, on the other hand, admire heroes, and operating units or departments may be pitted against each other in friendly competition. Although there is sharing of information, usually it is done after the fact when a group has already realized results. When a collaborative culture undertakes a new or risky project, multiple units are involved and they communicate the lessons gained through that shared experience. In competitive cultures, one unit owns the project and usually keeps it secret until successfully completed. Then it shares the results with the rest of the company through announcements or meetings intended to showcase the success as well as share knowledge. In competitive cultures, it is more important to have clearly defined responsibilities in relation to other groups, because infringing on someone else's turf is not tolerated. Collaborative cultures often have fluid responsibilities that team members determine on an as-needed basis.

Twice I've worked for collaborative companies that were subsequently taken over by competitive companies. In one situation, to address some issues that resulted from the merger, I reached out to various departments and put together a cross-functional team meeting to work on the issues. When I told my new boss about this meeting, she was mortified. Reaching out to other departments to "help" me with issues meant that I was weak and unable to solve the problems on my own. My job was to solve my own issues and not enlist the help of others. In another situation, I freely shared the lessons learned from several projects I was working on with my new colleagues and was surprised that no one else was willing to share their knowledge with me. No one else shared because getting assigned to prestigious projects was very competitive and keeping your knowledge and expertise to yourself was one way to ensure being included. After that episode, I was known as a sucker.

Hierarchical versus egalitarian culture   This dimension is straightforward and usually obvious. Some corporations have very clearly defined levels, and these levels do not mix. Vice presidents associate with vice presidents, managers with managers, and so on, even at lunch time! Note that these companies have director meetings, manager meetings, staff meetings, admin meetings, and meetings to determine which levels are entitled to their own meetings. Hierarchical cultures give themselves away with introductions because individuals announce their titles in addition to their names. Or even worse, there are no introductions because the higher levels assume everyone knows who they are, while lower levels are not important enough to be identified as individuals. These are the companies where people behave in a markedly different manner when they are promoted, and also where hazing the most junior members, like making them pull all-nighters or carry someone else's briefcase, is considered acceptable behavior. Another sign of a hierarchical culture is minute distinctions in titles, like senior analyst and associate manager or even senior associate manager. Each tiny gradation in title means one small step up the hierarchy, and titles are defended rigorously, as in "I'm a *Senior* Associate Director, not an Associate Director."

In egalitarian cultures, asserting your level of position is considered an affront and a sign of egotism. It is not obvious who the most senior person is, and everyone is treated more or less equally. Egalitarian cultures tend to have titles like "team leader" or "project leader" rather than the traditional manager, director, and associate titles. Egalitarian cultures tend to rotate people through different jobs more often and assign responsibilities according to experience rather than position. You may find the most junior person leading a team of superiors because he or she has more relevant experience. It also tends to be harder to move up the ladder because there are fewer rungs. However, in this culture people are usually rewarded in other ways for a job well done.

Allocation of office space is a good indicator of which type of culture you're in when you visit a company, perhaps on a job interview. The bigger the discrepancy between the CEO's office and the support staff's cubicles, the more hierarchical the company tends to be. Also, look to see if you can distinguish a VP's office from a director's office from a manager's office. If so, welcome to the hierarchy.

Process versus people culture Process cultures place a high value on how work gets done. The underlying assumption is that there is a right way or best practice. These organizations may or may not have lots of policies and procedures, but the ones that exist are followed closely and regularly updated. These cultures also spend a considerable amount of time planning, and deadlines are taken seriously. The values exhibited by process cultures are fairness and consistency. Everyone knows and follows the same rules.

People cultures, on the other hand, are more concerned with who is doing the work. The assumption here is that there are multiple correct ways of working. These cultures trust the judgment of people to negotiate each situation as it comes and may distrust processes because they cannot accommodate exceptions. Process cultures distrust judgment because it may not be fair. People cultures may have policies and deadlines, but these are largely considered to be guidelines and not the rule of law. Cultures built around people are also more comfortable operating in ambiguous situations and don't often see the point of elaborate plans. They are obsessed with finding and promoting the "right" people. In a people culture, employees understand if they are on the fast track or if they are not.

I once witnessed an amusing exchange between a process person and a people person. After a merger of the two culture types, we were trying to develop one common performance evaluation form. The company that had taken over was a people culture, and we were using their form, which listed the performance objectives and a rating scale of 1 to 7. One woman at the meeting, a process person, was incredulous that the form did not have any goal-weighting factors, meaning some goals are more important than others, and performance on those should be weighted more heavily. While she complained about the inherent unfairness, the man overseeing the form, a people person, responded that that's why managers get together and discuss comparative rankings. From her perspective, how could managers across the entire corporation be trusted to make consistent decisions when the use of weighting factors would be a fairer approach? His perspective was that he would rather have sentient managers make performance-ranking decisions than have a form calculate rankings. This conflict was never settled to anyone's satisfaction, and the compromise was to include weighting factors that could be overridden by managers. The process person and the people person just couldn't understand each other's values.

Action/results versus thought/wisdom culture You know you are interviewing at an action culture when the interviewer doesn't look at your whole résumé and asks only about your latest project. I think American companies are excessively biased for action (does that sound familiar?). Action-oriented companies hold meetings where the end product is a long task list with aggressive due dates. Thought-based cultures may have meetings in which a thorough discussion of the issues takes place, and attendees walk away with a flipchart full of gaps in knowledge but no assignments. These cultures value experts and often bring in consultants for their knowledge and experience. Action cultures bring in consultants to be the arms and legs of an organization and run projects. High performers in action cultures are known by their recent achievements, whereas experts in thought cultures are valued for their experience. Accordingly, in action cultures people fall in and out of favor quickly. Thought/wisdom cultures maintain an informal network of known experts in different areas. Navigating through this network is critical to success.

My earlier examples of misunderstanding why I was meeting with colleagues were consequences of action versus thought. Action-oriented cultures expect that the end product of a meeting is an action plan. Nothing less than a set of tasks with due dates will make the meeting successful. Even if no one in the room fully comprehends the issues or the consequences of the actions, everyone there will be responsible for completing tasks. Americans working in other countries are often surprised when they try to force actions and accountabilities at meetings where the participants want to achieve consensus or debate the issues for further understanding. No one will commit to a task or a due date because that's not why they are meeting.

Given these dimensions of corporate culture, I've identified four common cultural maladies attributable to excesses in one or more of the dimensions. I've put these in a quadrant chart, not because it makes sense, but because as a management consultant I've been brainwashed into believing everything should be explained with a quadrant chart.

* WARNING! *Prolonged exposure to any one of these maladies may result in loss of self-esteem, loss of intelligence, lack of sleep, and, in some extreme cases, depression. If you suspect that you or a loved one may be suffering from one of these symptoms, remove yourself from the situation right away and call your therapist.*

Common Corporate Cultural Disorders

Amnesiac	Megalomaniac
High action/high competitive **Bias for the same action, over and over**	*High competitive/ high hierarchical* **You better make me look good**
Chronically insecure *High collaborative/ high egalitarian* **Do we have consensus on building consensus?**	**Obsessive-compulsive** *High process/ high wisdom* **What's the procedure for following procedures?**

Amnesiac - High action/high competitive

Welcome to the company that is always buzzing with activity. No, there is no time to put together a plan or discuss anything with experts. For every issue encountered, this company puts together a project or initiative. With such a flurry of activity, there is no time to document meetings, or anything else for that matter. The right way to approach this project? Who cares? Just get it done. Yesterday. Read my email? Hardly. I'd rather send out five more than read the one that explains everything. Research the issue? Research is for losers. The only way to learn is by doing. These employees are doomed to repeat the same mistakes over and over again until they burn out.

Overheard in the halls: Hit the ground running, bias for action, self-starter, take initiative
Emotional state: High drama with a vague sense of déjà vu

Megalomaniac - High competitive/high hierarchical

It's really all about me, isn't it? I've led this company to greatness, and now I've surrounded myself with minions who act and think like me. No wonder I'm always right. And because I'm right, I want things done my way. It doesn't matter that getting things done right requires enormous effort. If I like pie charts instead of bar graphs, I'll hire someone to convert every bar graph in this company into a pie chart. Because I can. I'm the boss. Remember, your performance is a reflection on me. Actually, everything is a reflection on me. Don't let me down. Because you know I'll take all the credit anyway. Mistakes? No one here makes any.

Overheard in the halls: The company way (as in the Apple way), not the right type, make me look good
Emotional state: Bipolar, dependent on the state of the business

Chronically insecure - High collaborative/high egalitarian

This company acts like a teenage girl. (My apologies to teenage girls.) Everyone here wants to be liked and to fit in. Did everyone buy into this proposal? Let's include everyone in the meeting. Do we have consensus on the plan? Do we have consensus on getting consensus on the plan? Our competitive advantage is to do everything well. We need to know what our competitors are doing so we can do it, too. What do the analysts say about our product pipeline? What do the analysts say about our corporate strategy? Is our sweat shop in Guatemala considered outsourcing? Because everyone else is outsourcing and we should, too. We want to be innovative so let's benchmark what other companies are doing in innovation and copy that.

Overheard in the halls: Benchmark, competitive analysis, buy-in, consensus, team building
Emotional state: Worry, worry, worry

Obsessive-compulsive - High process/high wisdom

This company has found the approach that works for it. And it uses that approach. For everything. Typically, a lot of analysis or planning is involved. This cultural disorder manifests itself in the form of a proprietary methodology, perhaps a colorful PERT chart or a detailed decision tree that people rely on to solve business problems. Everybody has one. Pinned to their walls. With a binder that describes how it's done properly. And a little pocket booklet version. And a wallet-sized card. All new employees quickly become indoctrinated in the methodology, typically through mandatory training. When something doesn't work quite right, a team is formed to tweak the process or develop a new one. Gurus or experts in the methodology are called in frequently, and everyone has some sort of certification hanging on their walls.

Overheard in the halls: Methodology, due diligence, green belt, black belt, best practice
Emotional state: The process holds the answers, all hail the almighty process

Understanding and fitting into a corporate culture is key to having a happy career in that company. If you don't share the same beliefs, you will end up like the child in "The Emperor's New Clothes," laughing at the king's nakedness and ruining the whole parade. This is why human resources (HR) departments are so concerned about finding people who are a good cultural fit. People who don't believe won't follow the rules. The downside of everyone buying into the same beliefs and rituals is that it is easy to mistake those beliefs and perspectives for reality. This is how a lot of companies get into trouble. They convince themselves of something that isn't true, like Americans will never want economical cars, people will always want a physical keyboard on their phone, or, on a larger scale, free markets are self-regulating. We all encounter coconut banging at some point in our lives, and I hope this chapter has helped you realize that you do a bit of it yourself.

Let's continue on our quest to find the meaning in all the silliness. Please pour yourself a glass of Kool-Aid and read the following paragraph in a John Cleese-like fashion, British accent a must:

> *We are prancing around, banging coconuts, pretending to be medieval knights on horseback canvassing the shire for worthy knights to join the Round Table. We do this because someone started doing this sometime ago, and it seems like an okay thing to do. So, let's go onto the next chapter, which is the infamous "bring out your dead" scene, and if you remember nothing else from the Holy Grail movie, you remember this scene because it is so memorable.*

Test Yourself!

How do you rate your organization on the cultural dimensions? Read the following statements and select those that most pertain to your environment.

1. We spend a lot of time determining who has leadership ability and then putting them on a separate track. Of course, who they are and what that track is change whenever we have a change in leadership. (People)
2. We spend a lot of time training everyone in how to do business the right way. We even have a detailed description of the seven attributes of excellence. (Process)
3. We have lots of teams and team-building activities. Hey, do you want to do the trust exercise? (Collaborative)
4. We have a lot of contests. I bet we have more contests than you do. (Competitive)
5. A lot of people here get advanced degrees and certifications because you lose credibility if you don't. In fact, I am working on my second Ph.D. as well as project management certification. (Wisdom)
6. We value due diligence and contingency planning. Here's my assessment of the 15 most likely scenarios for the budget next year. (Thought)
7. Plan? We prefer action learning and baptism by fire. (Action)
8. You've got to have metrics. How can you manage anything without measurements? Btw, can you give me our return on the switch to the new staplers? (Results)
9. Generally, everyone knows everyone else's title. You only make that mistake once. (Hierarchical)
10. I use my business cards mostly as bookmarks and coasters and as little Frisbees to flip at my teammates. (Egalitarian)

Chapter Vocabulary

Coll-aberration That rare instance when teams from multiple departments communicate and work together on a common goal.

Developmental alignment Being put in a job outside your normal area under the guise of development, but really as a message from management that you better toe the line or your career is kaput.

High conforming employees Those workers who act exactly the way their boss wants them to so that they get good annual ratings.

Iconomies of scale The transformation of an entire company based on the ego of a famous CEO.

The leaning organization Focus on developing specific organizational capabilities so that everyone has the same skills and knowledge and thus reinforces the biases the culture already has.

New hire orientation pogrom The mandatory multiday training boot camp that weeds out new employees who won't fit the corporate culture.

2
He's Not Dead Yet

Sacrificing long-term health for short-term expediency

The black plague is rampant in the Middle Ages. It spreads rapidly, leaving hordes of dead bodies in its wake and wiping out whole villages. Here's the man with the weekly cart to collect the bodies before they can rot and bring more disease and infection. He stops at a village, yelling "Bring out your dead," and John Cleese brings out a family member. Only, there's a problem—he's not dead yet. Eric Idle as the dead collector objects. He can't take a body that's still living. That's against the regulations. The sick man objects. Clearly, he is not dead. He's feeling better. Perhaps, he may even recover. What do they do? John Cleese is not convinced by the nearly dead man's antics and doesn't want to wait a whole week. Aaah—the solution—a quick hit to the head and the man is now indeed dead. Everybody (except the now dead man) is happy. This is truly a win/win solution.

The "bring out your dead" scene, one of the Monty Python skits most often quoted, inspired this book. (It is kind of hard to quote the fish-slapping dance or the Ministry of Funny Walks.) In fact, not too long ago I was on a bus and found myself amid a group of teenagers, two of whom started reciting lines from this scene. When I stared at them in amazement (the movie is much older than they were!), they became a little embarrassed and said that they were quoting from an old movie they liked. Obviously, this scene resonates with many generations. Is it the absurdity of the dead body collector? Is it the crassness of bringing out a nearly dead person? Or is it the violation of humanity by killing a hapless man for no reason, except that it is Wednesday?

No, no, no, the scene is funny because it captures the biggest problem with American businesses today—the obsession with delivering profits and dividends on a short-term basis often at the expense of long-term health. Let me explain.

> Dead cart pricing:
> Mostly bones   1 shilling
> Maggot-ridden   2 shillings
> Stiff-as-a-board   3 shillings
> Lacking color   4 shillings
> Still moving   5 shillings
> No chance of recovery   6 shillings
> High probability of death   7 shillings
> Not really living   Free

Who can deny that over the last two decades companies have been focusing more and more on quarterly earnings? This has been a major complaint of Warren Buffet, who refuses to issue earnings projections for Berkshire Hathaway and for years has railed against earnings guidance. In the bid for federal bailout money for the auto industry, Richard Wagoner, the former CEO of General Motors, blamed some of the company's financial troubles on the desire to increase profits rather than invest in cars and plants of the future. Even Chrysler was taken private in order to enact the changes needed to return that company to health without the scrutiny of Wall Street analysts (not that it helped).

A survey of 400 financial executives conducted by Duke University reported that 75% of executives would knowingly sacrifice shareholder value in order to report earnings that rise smoothly from year to year. Because of the market turmoil that occurs when companies miss their earnings target, executives would rather pass over positive investment opportunities in order to ensure that short-term performance is consistent and earnings expectations are met. In other words, they are sacrificing the long-term value of the company to give the appearance of steady, quarter-after-quarter performance.

I guess this isn't too surprising. Delaying gratification is a big problem for many, especially when an annual bonus is involved. And really, what's the chance that anyone will still be in the same job five years hence and have to suffer the consequences of short-sighted decisions? Even CEOs these days rarely last more than five years. Although investing in long-term health is an obvious goal, we've created a corporate environment where rewards are geared only toward achieving short-term goals. Does anyone rate performance over multiple years? Unfortunately, performance time horizons are becoming shorter and shorter and shorter. Ten years ago, who heard of a semi-annual performance review? Now, it's the norm. At this rate, in a few years we'll be rating performance quarterly, not unlike quarterly earnings reporting.

On a personal basis, I've never been able to work for one company for more than five years, not because I've hopped jobs, but because the companies either merged or were acquired. My corporate career began in 1987, when I started with Deloitte Haskins & Sells. Two years later, it merged with Touche Ross to become Deloitte & Touche. I took a job in 1990 with the United Research Company, which merged that same year with the MAC Group and became Gemini Consulting. In 1997, it became part of Cap Gemini and then, three years later, part of Cap Gemini Ernst & Young. I was laid off in 1999 and took a job with a dot-com that went bust later that year. In 2001, I joined Warner-Lambert Consumer Healthcare just after it was acquired by Pfizer. In the ensuing three years, Pfizer divested itself of two divisions, Adams Confectionary (Dentyne, Halls, Trident) and Schick (shaving products), and acquired Pharmacia. In 2006, just five years after I joined, it sold my division to Johnson & Johnson. Four job interviews, nine companies! And my career is typical.

The paradox of this merger and acquisition (M&A) activity is that it makes organic growth almost impossible. I've seen the same pattern over and over. Usually, a company pays a hefty price for an acquisition target and justifies the price with "synergy savings." These savings include moving both companies into one office space, thus halving the current cost of offices, combining warehouses and distribution centers, and laying off people with similar jobs. The more a company pays for the acquisition, the higher the synergy targets. Integrating two companies also brings about numerous one-time charges for things like severance packages, office moves, and changes in computer systems. From my experience, it takes two to four years to fully integrate two companies. During this time frame, there is no extra budget for business-building activities. In fact, synergy targets can last up to five years after the M&A, and investment in organic growth during that time is limited until all the projected savings are realized. Because the company is not able to grow organically, it becomes reliant on acquisitions to meet growth targets.

Case in point is GE, which grew wildly under Jack Welch due to nearly a thousand acquisitions made during his command. In order to focus on organic growth, the current CEO is investing money in existing businesses, not buying new ones (and the share price is being penalized for this). Not to say that all acquisitions are failures, but statistics do bear out that only about one-third are successful. Just as important, companies rarely anticipate the negative impact mergers can have on revenue generation, expecting that synergy can take the place of investment and that people who are busy with integration activities can also perform growth-related activities—a multitasking mania. Hence, we have an environment in which M&As are a must for survival, even though two-thirds of the time they fail to meet expectations.

Depending on what statistics you read, the average life span of a corporation has declined from about 50 years in the 1950s to less than 15 years now, a statistic that covers American and European companies. I believe that this life span is not so much a symptom of doing business today, but a symptom of doing business here. Japan, for example, has a completely different set of expectations. Recently, I read that the world's oldest continuously operating family business just went out of business. The Japanese company Kongo Gumi had been in business since 578, a total of 1,400 years! Can you imagine an American company in the same family for even 200 years! My dealings with Japanese made me realize that they operate on a different time scale than we do. When we agreed to implement a plan, as an American I expected it to be done within weeks or even days. I eventually learned that it would take my Japanese counterparts a few months to get it done. It took longer, but the task was always completed with greater care than what I would expect in the United States. My work with other countries helped me realize that there are differences in the perception of time across the world, and not everyone shares our short-term focus. Like the Japanese, the Chinese have a long time horizon and often care little for reaping an immediate benefit, preferring to sacrifice for a long-term greater good, like scrimping on food and clothing to send a child to a good college. China and Japan are on one end of the time spectrum, and the US and the UK on the other. Most of the world takes a perspective somewhere in between.

What I also noticed is that time horizons can differ from company to company and within departments. Why is it that the marketing department can never plan more than two months out? Why does it take someone in research and development a week to answer an email? Granted, R&D usually comes up with a thoughtful and well-composed response, but why so long? When information technology discusses service levels, why is two days an adequate time frame to answer a help desk call? If I called the local hospital's emergency room, would two hours be a reasonable callback time? Why do salespeople need everything this minute? When a CEO wants something tomorrow, doesn't he or she really mean right now?

This led me to discover that perceptions of time can vary by individual. I am impatient, and when I ask for something ASAP, I mean within a few hours or at least by the end of the day. Often, my coworkers interpret ASAP to mean within a day or two. Some (nervy folks!) think it means before the week is out.

To remain sane at work, it is helpful to understand how your coworkers perceive time and what the corporate culture defines as its time frame. (Action-oriented cultures have quicker time frames than more thoughtful cultures.) To get a better understanding of the different perspectives of time, I gathered some thinking on time from physics, psychology, and philosophy.

Physics of Time: Some Basic Laws to Remember at Work[2]

Many of the miscommunications and misperceptions of time in the workplace occur due to the relativity of time, as determined by Einstein. Unfortunately, the physics of relativity is not taught well in schools, and many people don't understand how these laws apply in the workplace. Here's a very brief explanation of how relativity affects time and what you should keep in mind in order to be successful in your career.

Let's start with the classic example of identical twins, Betty and Ann. Betty gets an opportunity to fly in a spaceship at close to the speed of light and explore the galaxy. Ann does not get this opportunity and is confined to Earth. Finally, Betty returns home and is surprised to find that Ann has aged quite a bit more than she has. In Betty's time, she has been on her adventure for 12 years, but Ann's time on earth has been 20 years. You should realize how this applies in business. Let's suppose that the CEO takes a shine to Betty and puts her on a career fast track. Betty's world is a whirlwind of activity and new challenges, and her time expands to fit many activities. Betty remains engaged and invigorated and does not age much. Meanwhile, Ann, stuck in the same dead-end job, ages more rapidly, becoming old and embittered. Her time passes her by.

This is an illustration of the time dilation effect due to relative speed. In general, a moving clock ticks more slowly than a stationary one. If you take two clocks and put one on a train traveling at near light speed and leave the other on the platform, the people on the platform will observe their clock ticking at the same constant rate. The clock on the train will slow down, but the people on the train will think that the clock on the platform has sped up. You can try a similar experiment at work. Take a project plan for a new product launch and give it to the VP of marketing for review. You'll notice while you are there that the department is a flurry of activity, a fast-paced environment. Now take the same project plan to R&D for its review. Here, you'll observe the workers carefully deliberating on their actions and moving more slowly than their marketing counterparts. Once you get the project plans back with the revisions, you'll notice the effect of time dilation. The marketing VP has moved

---

[2] Phelan, Karen G. 2020. The Search for Elusive Gray Matter in the Corporate Universe. New York: Tihslub Press.

all the deliverable dates up, shortening the due dates, while the R&D head has moved all the dates back, lengthening the total time! What takes 20 months in R&D takes only 12 months in marketing!

Einstein also discovered that gravity slows time. Using our same two clocks, let's put one on the top of a really, really tall ivory tower and leave the other one on the ground floor. The clock at the top of the tower will run faster than the one on the ground floor. Hence, the higher up you go, the faster time passes. This explains why, when the CEO asks you to complete a task by the end of the day, he'll call you at 3 P.M. looking for the results. His clock has already ticked to the end of the day! Now, when you bring your project plan up to the executive suite, expect that the due dates will be shortened even more due to the lesser gravity. In short, remember to adjust your clock according to the level of hierarchy with which you are dealing: the higher up, the more you need to shorten time, and the lower down, the more you need to lengthen time.

Philosophy of Time

In philosophy, there are three fundamental ways in which someone internalizes and reacts to time frames: presentism, possibilism, and fatalism. Using this model, I've discovered that there are actually *four* ways in which coworkers get stuck in time.

Presentism   Presentists believe that there is no reality outside the present time. The only time that is meaningful is now. You'll notice that people with this viewpoint are either unable to remember any past events or believe that historic events bear no relation to current events. This is because they are unable to perceive any time frame beyond the current moment. Thus, past events cannot be used as predictors of the future, because each day is brand new. These people are also unable to picture the future and, as a result, are unable to delay gratification and wait for future benefits.

Signs that your coworker is a presentist:
- Inability to recall earlier conversations on the same topic, leading to rehashing the same discussion over and over
- Disbelief that the failures of similar projects in the past have any lessons for current projects, hence the repetition of past mistakes

- Constant checking of email via electronic device or cell phone, unable to leave them for later

There is no way you can convince these people to plan for the future or learn from the past. The past and future simply don't exist. The best way to deal with them is to assign them tasks on a day-by-day basis, and, more important, you can give them the same type of work over and over because it will always seem fresh and new. However, plan your long-term strategy meetings on the days they are absent.

Possibilism Possibilists are keenly aware of both the past and the present but cannot visualize the future. For them, the future is a clean whiteboard on which anything can be written, erased, rewritten, and so on. All things are possible in the future, even if they are unlikely in the present. When you make plans with possibilists, the end objective changes frequently because they are unable to hold a steady picture of future events in their heads. In fact, honing in on one possible future outcome is discouraging for possibilists because it prohibits so many other possible outcomes. They prefer a future where all things are possible.

How to recognize a possibilist at work:
- Indecision on even the most minor courses of action
- Dislike for making firm plans, preferring to keep the options open
- Constant changes in direction

Possibilists are great at finding creative and innovative ways to do things, because to them all things are possible. You will be more successful if you already have plans or decisions made before you approach these people. They tend to become so overwhelmed by all the potential outcomes that choosing one course of action is impossible for them.

Fatalism People who are fatalists can sense the past, present, and future at the same time. They can relate past events to current events and current events to future events. In fact, for them the future already exists, immutable; we just have not become aware of it yet. Both the past and the future spread out infinitely in two opposite directions, already written, with time moving like eyes across a page of an epic novel, slowly revealing the story to come. Making plans with fatalists is a calming experience, because no actions today can effect a change tomorrow. Each day flows beyond our control, out of our hands, making all action ineffectual, making all choices irrelevant.

The qualities of a fatalist:
- Absolutely no sense of urgency about anything
- Capable of wholeheartedly supporting two diametrically opposed plans
- Heavy reliance on the phrase "It is what it is"

Fatalists are great in crisis situations because they don't fear the consequences of their actions. Visit a fatalist when you need stress relief, but don't rely on this person to enact any plans. Pairing a fatalist with a go-getter is vital if anything is to get done.

Futurism Futurists believe that the future is so much brighter than the past or the present. In the future, we will have finally attained our perfect selves. We will be eating right, exercising, catching up on our reading, taking up hobbies, and solving all those pernicious problems we encounter at work, problems like being understaffed and overworked. Our computer systems will work easily and reliably, our customers will have stable demand, our suppliers will deliver on time, our bosses will recognize our inner brilliance, and we will be richly rewarded. That future day will surely come. All we have to do is to wait.

The sure signs of a futurist:
- Preference for short-term planning because issues won't exist in the long term
- Inability to connect long-term goals with present-day actions
- Staunch support of the status quo because there is no reason to change
- Failure to comprehend death, finality, or bankruptcy

Futurists are great at finding quick fixes and temporary solutions to issues and problems. Don't go to them with any lasting problems or long-term plans, because to them everything is temporary. All you have to do is wait for the magic day when problems will be part of the past.

Psychology of Time

Earlier in this chapter I mentioned that Japan and China have a different perspective of time. Actually, the perception of time is often cited as one of the dimensions of culture. When you are catching a 1 P.M. train in Germany, you can be sure that the train will arrive beforehand and leave at 1 on the dot.

On the other hand, a 1 P.M. train in India may or may not arrive that day, but it certainly won't be there anytime around 1 P.M.

Cognitive scientists are studying other factors influencing our perception of time. Recently, they determined that the conventional wisdom that time goes faster as we age is really true. When people of various ages were tested to judge how long it took for 30 seconds to elapse, younger people tended to underestimate the time period, thinking that 30 seconds were over sooner than they actually were, and older people overestimated the time period, thinking that a longer time period was 30 seconds. There is no definitive explanation for this effect, but there is a theory that we use our age to help us judge time. In other words, we judge a time period by the percentage of years we have lived. Hence, the summer months constitute a large fraction of a child's life and seems like a long time to the child. Those same months are just a small fraction of a mature adult's life and pass quickly for the adult. The relationship between age and perception of time is roughly logarithmic, so the rate of time passing you by increases dramatically with age.

Cognitive scientists have also shown experimentally that time flies when you are having fun.[3] Here, they do have an explanation. Our brains have a timekeeping function that helps us track the passage of time. During tasks that are engaging, we devote more of the brain to our activity and thus have less processing ability for our timekeeper. Scientists have shown that people will reliably say that an engaging task took less time to complete than a boring task. You can use this effect to your advantage. If you keep your boss really busy, she won't ask you about the important project until long after it is due.

This leads us to the fact that people actually have two different types of timekeepers—perceived duration and remembered duration—that utilize different areas of the brain. Perceived duration is how we think time is passing while it is passing, and remembered duration is how we remember it passing afterward. Surprisingly, perceived duration can often differ substantially from remembered duration. If a lot happens during a really short time period, we remember that period as longer. If nothing much happens, we remember that time as shorter. A lab experiment to determine if time really does slow down or stand still in a crisis showed that people were not able to perform more tasks during a crisis than they could normally, but they did remember the time as passing more slowly. The "time flies when you are having fun" effect combined

---

[3] Cognitive scientists are also currently proving that a stitch in time saves nine and that early to bed, early to rise makes a man healthy, wealthy, and wise.

with the perceived/remembered durations mismatch can lead to the Unfulfilling Job Paradox. If you really hate your job, keeping busy makes the day seem to pass more quickly, but in retrospect it lengthens the time you've spent in a sucky job. If you do nothing all day, your days drag, but in retrospect you weren't in that job for all that long.

Scientists have shown that our level of arousal also affects our internal timekeepers. When we are experiencing intense emotions, our internal clocks tick faster, taking bigger slices of time than they normally would and giving the illusion that the time period is longer. Painful emotional events seem to last an eternity. The reverse seems to be true for joyful emotional events. They just breeze by. Unfortunately, misery seems to last longer than bliss. Yet this quirk of time does explain coworkers who make everyone around them miserable. They are just trying to slow down time so they can complete their work!

The point of this exploration of time is that the constant ticking of the clock, 60 seconds a minute, 60 minutes an hour, 24 hours a day, does not mean that time passes in an absolute, measured manner. Time is dependent on how old we are, what we are doing, how we are feeling, and what is going on around us.

In business, understanding and communicating time frames is vital to success, yet you've seen that there are many ways to interpret time, and it can get quite confusing. To help you understand other people's time frames and communicate your time frame, I've put together an equation that incorporates age, nationality, position, and industry. You can use this equation to convert your time frame to any other person's time frame.

$$\tau_r = \tau_y * C * A * I * F * L$$

where
τ_r = relative time
τ_y = your time
C = culture factor
A = age factor
I = industry factor
F = function factor
L = level factor

See the following charts for the appropriate conversion factors.

Culture	Factor
American	2
British	3
German	1
French	4
Italian	5
Spanish	6
Brazilian	7
Indian	25
Japanese	10
Chinese	9
Australian	3

Age	Factor
Teens	15
Twenties	0.75
Thirties	1
Forties	1.25
Fifties	1.5
Sixties	4
Seventies	6

Industry	Factor
High Tech	0.2
Financial	0.3
Consulting	0.5
Healthcare	1.5
Manufacturing	1
Construction	5

Function	Factor
R&D	2
IT	1.5
Marketing	0.5
Finance	0.75
Manufacturing	1
HR	1.75

Level	Factor
Staff	1
Manager	0.75
Director	0.5
VP	0.25
C-level	2.50E-05

Let's try some examples.

1. Suppose your boss is Indian, in his forties, and a manager, and he has promised to get back to you tomorrow regarding your request for promotion. You are American, in your thirties, and staff level.

    Using $\tau_r = \tau_y * C * A * I * F * L$

    τ_r = 1 day × 25 × 1/.75 or

    You will hear back in 33⅓ days and the answer is no.

    Notice how you need to invert factors depending on how they relate to you.

2. Consider the same two people, but in this example your boss has asked you to deliver a project plan by the end of the week (three days' time).

    τ_r = 36 hours × 1/25 × .75 or

    He expects you to have it ready in 1 hour 8 minutes, and your delivery dates are way too long.

Now, here's a more complicated example:

3. Suppose you are a manager-level consultant working for the CFO of a high-tech company who asks you to put together a business case for an acquisition. He says he wants it next Monday, one week's time. You are both about the same age, and he is French.

$$\tau_r = 7 \text{ days} \times 4 \times .2/. 5 \times .75 \times 2.50\text{E-}05 \text{ or}$$

You better drop everything and pull all-nighters until you are done because you are already late, and he is going ahead with the acquisition anyway, even if the business case doesn't justify it.

Like corporate cultures, our perception of time is a belief that can be changed. Although we can't keep from aging, or ultimately dying, we can change the pace of our lives. If a CEO has an expected tenure of two to five years, his long-term plan will be only two to five years in duration. If a company measures performance every six months, it will naturally have six-month goals. If Wall Street looks at profits on a quarterly basis, then companies will strive to meet quarterly earnings and not long-term profits. It works just like the "bring out your dead" cart: when it comes on Wednesday afternoon, a lot more deaths occur on Wednesday mornings.

Chapter Vocabulary

Anacronyism A leadership team of old guys living in the past.

Bust-in-time practices The practice of being so lean and short-sighted that every deadline requires a major "bust your balls" effort. *Related:* business as usual

Downseizing The massive layoffs that occur after a hostile takeover.

Eternagrating The unceasing process of integrating companies after mergers and acquisitions, resulting in lower stock price, lost jobs, and tedious work for all involved.

Highly beveraged resources Pumping your work force full of caffeinated drinks so that they work longer.

Intorporated The status of a company when it achieves industry-accepted levels of bureaucracy, red tape, and inertia.

Secession planning A senior leadership retirement strategy, in which the corporate officers plan to sell, spin, or make public the company in order to reap a huge payment that can be used for retirement. *Related:* retire-ease

Spinergies The phony cost savings numbers used to justify a merger or acquisition.

Trance-ition The period between the announcement of the sale and the integration of the companies when employees walk around in a daze.

3
Well, I AM King

Ensuring leadership is aligned with the rank and file

King Arthur continues on his search to fill his leadership team, er, Round Table of Camelot, and passes a group of peasants outside a castle who are frolicking? eating? reveling? (What are they doing?) in a morass of mud. Arthur haughtily questions the peasants about the lord who owns the nearby castle. When the peasants inform him that there is no lord and they are all part of an egalitarian, autonomous collective that makes decisions by committee, Arthur becomes increasingly testy. After all, he is their king. He makes the laws. The peasants want to know who elected him. Arthur begins to tell them about the Lady of Lake and the magical sword Excalibur, which solely the king can bear, only to hear the peasants snicker. I mean, that's no way to choose a government, is it? What if everyone who got a sword thrust at him declared himself emperor? A government should be representative of the masses. One of the peasants, Dennis, continues to press his point about the superiority of democracy over monarchy, but Arthur can stand no more. He loses his patience and, unfortunately, unleashes a bit of wrath on Dennis. The scene ends with Dennis yelling, "Help, I'm being repressed!"

Doesn't this exchange say so much about leadership? Not just corporate leadership, but leadership in general. Don't so many of our leaders seem completely out of touch with their people? I think the leadership gurus have it backward when it comes to leadership skills. Business literature is filled with books and articles about how best to align the rank and file with the leadership vision. Isn't it easier and more effective to align the leadership with the organization? This explains why "savior" CEOs brought in to rescue companies often fail spectacularly, à la Robert Nardelli of GE, who became CEO of Home Depot, only to be ousted six years later after alienating employees, customers, and board members alike. His autocratic, cost-cutting management style didn't fit a customer-focused, entrepreneurial, laid-back organization like Home Depot. Later, he went to Chrysler to turn it around with the result that, two years later, Chrysler received a government bailout and filed for bankruptcy. Yet the business press and Wall Street seem to be enamored of the heroic CEO figure who can single-handedly turn a company around, as if the other 50,000 to 75,000 people employed don't really do anything.

Here, from my own career, is an example of why the leadership team should be in touch with the rank-and-file employees. As a management consultant, I am often amazed at how little time management and leadership spend with employees. Much of the time, the consultants' recommendations come straight from the mouths of staff, who feel

they don't have a voice in the company. On one occasion, I was asked to help a refrigerator manufacturer improve its shop floor productivity and on-time order rate. The first thing I noticed was that this company had several expeditors. The job of expeditors is to take care of rush or high-priority orders by babysitting them all the way through production. An expeditor brings a rush order to the first machine, makes sure the first part is produced, then brings it to the second machine, and so on until the order is complete. Having expeditors is a symptom that a company does not have the right processes and policies in place to manufacture according to schedule. Some of the refrigerators the company made were standard and could be completed in a few days, while others were specialized, requiring custom parts, and took weeks to produce. After years of offering more options and more product variations, the company's order fulfillment rate declined because of the added manufacturing complexity. In response, it bought and implemented very expensive shop floor optimization software.

The company's procedure to create a manufacturing schedule was to require its customers to submit their orders by the end of the month. The orders were then entered into a computer, which spat out an optimized production schedule for the next month. However, the company had several important customers who submitted weekly orders that needed to be filled as soon as possible. At first, these orders were fed into the system and a new schedule created, but the old schedule was already being implemented, and creating a new schedule with every new order became disruptive. So the new orders were kept separate and handled by expediters. Though in theory the schedule was kept intact, in practice it wasn't being followed by workers, who had to halt what they were doing to accommodate the expediters' requests. As more orders fell behind their commitment dates, more orders were designated "rush" and more expediters were required, with the result that the shop floor became less optimized and fewer orders got shipped on time—a typical vicious circle.

I spent a few weeks talking with shop floor workers, schedulers, and expediters, and, although some had little to contribute, others were very frustrated with the situation and excited to have someone listen to them. Their management was so busy trying to address the problems that they never had time to go down to the floor and talk with the workers. Walking around the plant, I saw work-in-process parts and materials everywhere. I should mention that I was 23 years old at the time and had never been in a manufacturing plant before. I needed to listen to the workers because I had no experience of my own to draw from. From them I learned everything I needed to know about the factory's problems.

The biggest problem was that the workers were compensated by the number of pieces produced and not by meeting the schedule. This meant that if a machine operator had to change the tools on his machine, which took about two hours, in order to make five pieces, which took about 30 minutes, he would make more than five parts to compensate for the changeover time. The extras would sit at the workstation and, with any luck, be found when that part was needed again. Making the situation worse, the machine operators would always appease the expediters first before following the schedule because the expediters were breathing down their necks, usually looking for some oddball part for a custom order. Again, the operators would make more than one if they had to change tools. Finally, they would look at the schedule and see how much of that they could accomplish before the end of the day. All of the workers knew that this approach was contrary to meeting their order commitments, but this was how the floor operated.

After four weeks, I wrote a report with my recommendations and presented it to the company's management team. Most of the recommendations came from the workers. Obviously, the first change was to stop compensating employees based on the number of pieces produced and to move to on-time order fulfillment as a collective goal. I also recommended that they get rid of the expediters and move to a weekly production schedule because customers were sending in their orders on a weekly basis anyway. It doesn't matter how optimized a monthly schedule is in theory. If your customers are sending in orders every week and you are incorporating those orders into your schedule, then you are working from a weekly schedule. The monthly schedule is just pretend. I also made some recommendations for changing the order lead times and creating a separate job shop. I wish I could say that the company implemented these changes, increased their order fill rates, and became immensely profitable. However, after I wrote the report and presented it to management, I went on to another assignment. The president and his team seemed pleased with the recommendations, and a year later the company was bought by a larger appliance maker.

The point is that no one listened to the workers, who knew what was wrong. The value I brought to the problem was that I listened objectively to everyone and, as an outsider, was able to question the commonly accepted practices such as rewards for piecework. But did it really take management consulting fees to get feedback from employees? Throughout my career as a management consultant, I have joked with my coworkers that we should be called corporate counselors, because most of our time is spent listening to the complaints and frustrations of the workers and getting the various parties to communicate. In my whole time at that refrigerator manufacturer, I never saw anyone from upper management on the shop floor. Yet this was the crux of their entire business. They were a refrigerator manufacturer, not a paper shuffling company.

This is just one of many, many situations I have seen in which leaders of a company fail to learn about what is really happening and choose not to listen to what they consider to be the gripes of the employees. Instead, these leaders enlist a chosen few to come up with a vision and strategy and then interpret their jobs as motivating the rest of the employees to implement the golden strategy. Sometimes, the chosen few includes an outside consultant, who, if any good, will develop a strategy based on the "gripes" and incorporate employee suggestions. When employees hear their leader finally voicing their opinions in a grand strategy, they feel valued, become motivated, and execute the strategic direction. Another circle, but now all involved—leadership, staff, and consultants who walk away with a fat check—are happy.

Unfortunately, much of the time, no one fills the listening gap when a company's leadership neglects to visit factories or distribution centers or to talk with and listen to employees. I've noticed that many companies now use surveys to check the pulse of their organizations as a substitute for "management by walking around." Since when did an anonymous survey foster candid, two-way communication, relationship building, and trust? In many ways, the formal survey process says, "Don't bother me when I'm busy, use the standard vehicle for your feedback." It's especially a problem when employees have to wait for a survey to voice their concerns about pressing issues. This is just another way management avoids including the rest of the organization.

This listening gap is due in some measure to the time pressures we find ourselves in these days, but a big part is due to the type of people we elevate to leadership positions. One of the most respected experts and authors on business performance, Jim Collins, has written two books that analyze what makes good companies good. In his second book, *Good to Great*, he examined companies that significantly outperformed others in their industries and compared their management styles with those of average companies. One thing he identified was "level 5 leaders," or those who were at the top tier of the leadership evolution. Here's what he had to say:

> *Level 5 leaders display a compelling modesty, are self-effacing and understated. In contrast, two-thirds of the comparison companies had leaders with gargantuan personal egos that contributed to the demise or continuing mediocrity of the company... One of the most damaging trends in recent history is the tendency to select dazzling, celebrity leaders and to de-select potential Level 5 leaders.*

In the rest of this chapter, I'd like to explore the notion of leadership and why egomaniacs who create a gap between leadership and the rest of company are in top positions. Leadership is a very hot topic in the business press and in management training, and I think it is important to understand which notions of leadership are mythological and which have some actual foundations in reality. Let's start with the common definition of leadership abilities.

Leadership Abilities

If you've worked in a large company, you've seen them on posters, on little wallet cards, and most often on your performance review form: leadership competencies. They are all pretty much the same anywhere you go and read something like this:
- Thinking strategically
- Focusing on the customer
- Driving performance and results
- Developing people
- Fostering collaboration and teamwork

However, if you've been working for any length of time, you probably realize that getting ahead requires completely different skills, which are more like these:
- Putting a positive spin on everything
- Taking credit for successes and blaming others for failures
- Dominating every meeting you attend
- Surrounding yourself with people who can make you a success
- Becoming friendly with the people who hold power
- Networking with the levels above you
- Using corporate platitudes liberally (e.g., work smarter, not harder!)
- Volunteering for everything at first and then dropping those projects that won't succeed or enhance your career (and citing your inability to say no as the reason)
- When thanking the team, implying that it was your leadership that caused the team to gel
- Above all, promoting yourself all the time

The truth is that many competent employees who exemplify all the stated leadership abilities never get promoted. In fact, I can say with confidence that the people I've known who are role models for the stated behaviors rarely rise through the corporate ranks, while those who do rise often fall short of some of the stated leadership abilities, usually teamwork and collaboration. People get promoted when promotion is their primary goal. Those who aim for promotions work their networks to find the right opportunities, work hard to achieve high-profile results, seem to put in long hours, and always place a positive spin on their actual results. You know these people because you work with them and wonder how they always weasel their way into high-profile assignments without having any talent or experience. What they do have is driving ambition, and they typically share a type A personality. I refer to this personality type as the domineer. (Please see Appendix A for an explanation of personality types.)

The domineer personality predominates the upper management of most American corporations.[4] It is the domineer—that action-oriented, decisive, confident, bottom line–focused doer—who is depicted as management material in business literature. This makes sense given that these people strive for leadership, work hard to achieve it, and have the confidence needed to advance up the corporate ranks. With an excess of domineering qualities, however, they can steamroll people, hog all the credit, and attempt to win at any cost. Still they are the go-to people when something needs to get done. (By the way, I have strong domineer tendencies in my own profile.) Americans like their leaders this way: strong, decisive, swaggering, and competitive, kind of like John Wayne in the boardroom. We equate forceful direction with leadership and undervalue the less authoritative leadership styles. Although we idolize these doers, having a whole leadership team of the same personality type has the huge downside of everyone thinking and acting in this same manner.

In the following chart, I've listed some of the attributes of domineers that make them successful leaders. Next to that, I show how those traits in excess can combine to become somewhat risky behavior. The last column shows this personality type in the extreme and the hugely risky environment created when a domineer is unchecked by other personalities or outside forces.

---

[4] As a certified trainer in one of the numerous personality assessments, I've seen statistics that show this is true for American companies.

Characteristics of the Domineer

Positive	Excessive	Unchecked
Self-confident Belief in ability to control events Bias for action Focus on bottom-line results Risk taking Opportunistic	Overconfident in ability to handle external events Dislike of analysis and planning, especially contingency plans Bias for stretch goals, aggressive timelines, and big payoffs	External events are irrelevant and unmonitored Overly optimistic forecasts Focus on high-risk/high-reward projects

No matter how ambitious we may be, we cannot climb that corporate ladder on our own. We need the help of higher-ups to get more responsibilities and their recognition to get promotions. Many who successfully climb the corporate ladder do so because leadership recognizes that they have "it"—that special quality called leadership ability. What corporate leaders don't realize is that the "it" quality they admire is really just a personality style similar to their own. Humans prefer to surround themselves with people like themselves. We like people who are like us, who speak the same jargon, have the same tastes, enjoy the same activities, and generally "get" us. We click with people like ourselves. I have seen department heads build a team of people who think and act exactly the way they do, picking these go-getters for advancement while alienating all others, who see that the department head is promoting "mini-me"s.

Rosabeth Moss Kanter coined the term "homosocial reproduction" to describe how this tendency to promote people like us creates glass ceilings for women. It's not a stretch to apply this to minorities, as well. The problem I have with most corporate diversity training programs is that they assume people have biases *against* women and minorities. The truth is that leadership is not biased against women and minorities, but it is biased *for* people like themselves, those exhibiting strong domineer traits, usually white males. If it weren't bad enough that diverse perspectives are not represented in the executive ranks, what's worse is that this phenomenon breeds a culture of arrogance that, unchecked, can bring about the downfall of a company. Does Enron or Worldcom ring a bell? From my own experience, I've seen this arrogance and risk taking devastate two of the companies where I've worked (more on this later). In extreme excess, an environment full of domineers run amuck can ruin whole economies or cause catastrophic recessions, as occurred in the 2008 financial crisis.

Diverse perspectives in a leadership team provide checks and balances for excessive behavior, whereas homosocial reproduction fosters think-alikes. The corporate cultural maladies I described in Chapter 1 result from a lack of diversity and a reliance on one type of perspective in the company. We hear HR departments complain about a lack of diversity, but they are usually talking about gender and race. The diversity that is even more critical is a diversity of thought, outlook, opinion, and beliefs. Without these, a company is doomed to view the world through a warped perspective and will eventually lose its grip on reality.

So far in this chapter, I've shown how ambitious, aggressive people use their skills to climb the corporate ladder, then surround themselves with other ambitious, aggressive people, and collectively create a fast-paced, risk-taking, arrogant, and often self-destructive environment. Interestingly enough, it's this type of environment that also causes the short-termism described in Chapter 2. What I haven't discussed is what the traits of a leader should be. To answer this, I pulled out all the books and articles on leadership that I've collected over the years (straining my back in the process) to assess

what they say about leadership skills. Here's the list I gathered of the qualities of a good leader:
- Visionary
- Adept at communication
- Inspirational
- Able to listen well
- In-touch
- Self-confident
- Humble
- Intelligent
- Strategic
- Down-to-earth
- Collaborative
- Decisive
- Nurturing
- Team-building
- Action-oriented
- Authoritative
- Risk-taking

I'm pretty sure that neither Winston Churchill nor George Washington met all these criteria. How could we possibly expect a CEO to embody all these traits? Perhaps, if we looked to more than one person to lead, then they would collectively possess all these traits? Perhaps, if we had a leadership team with diverse backgrounds and personalities, they would embody all these traits? Perhaps, if we used the collective wisdom and the experiences of multiple employees to lead, we would be covered? Perhaps, if everyone in the company had a voice to lend to the leadership of the company...? Then, perhaps, finding a CEO or any corporate leader with all these qualities wouldn't be so important.

Many of the world's greatest leaders had serious character flaws—for instance, Winston Churchill was a heavy drinker and John F. Kennedy a womanizer—but they were the right people for the right time. Churchill, who willed himself, his people, and his country against great odds through a terrible war, became irrelevant after the war was won. He misjudged the people's desires for social reform and lost the 1945 election in a landslide. Kennedy walked a fine line during the Cold War, needing to show America's willingness to contain communism without starting a nuclear war with the Soviet Union. He did this well in the Cuban missile crisis, but completely botched the Bay of Pigs invasion. His bold objective of sending a man to the moon was both a boost to American morale and a non-military show of force. In summary, these were two flawed men who were great leaders in some situations and not so great in others.

Surely, if leadership is a quality that can be possessed, then it is a quality that can be lost, as well. That is the logical conclusion, but it doesn't seem to make sense. That's because leadership is not an "it," but a confluence of who, what, when, and where. Leaders are able to capture the sentiment of the time and use that to guide their actions and inspire their people: Abraham Lincoln and emancipation, Mahatma Gandhi and nonviolent resistance, Martin Luther King and civil rights. Given a different situation in a different time and place, would any of these people have been great leaders?

This is my definition of leadership:

A leader is someone who is able to articulate the vision and values of the group he or she represents and who uses the shared vision and values to shape actions appropriate for the situation.

What is the critical skill required to understand the vision and values of the group? Listening. Hey, Arthur! You might want to stop and listen to Dennis for a minute. He has a few good points.

Top 10 Signs Your Company Will Implode from Self-Importance, as Overheard in the Hallways

1. That's just not how we do it here. You have to get used to the (insert company name) way.
2. Remember, we work for (insert company name), and we have to live up to that reputation.
3. There's no need to take training courses outside the company. We have our own (insert university, leadership, management development, etc.) programs that are better than what you'll find elsewhere.
4. Our benefits are among the best out there. Of course, I don't know what's out there, but I'm sure what we have is better because everything we have is better.
5. Wow, when I look around the room I count over 100 years of experience with our company. How many people here even remember working for someone else?
6. But the *total* compensation is what you need to look at. There's a huge benefit to having our company name on your résumé.
7. I really don't understand all this whining and negativity. If people just had a better attitude, our company performance would improve.
8. The numbers may be down for the third straight quarter, but that's just a temporary blip.
9. Our strategy is still sound. We just have to ignore the naysayers.
10. What's a contingency plan?

Chapter Vocabulary

Core compretenses Those attributes you need to pretend to have in order to advance your career.

Corporate ego-system The complex system of personalities whose egos you need to assuage before you can move ahead with any decision.

Deportmental The tendency of business functions to exhibit similar behavior, e.g., sales, gregarious; marketers, disorganized; finance, detail oriented.

Executive man-hedgement A group of bald-headed guys who never give a straight answer.

Grandular The core competence of being detail oriented and strategic at the same time.

Leaderchip When it's really obvious a person resents being passed over for promotion to VP.

Team vynamics Group behavior wherein individuals at a meeting vie for dominance.

Vialogue Two people trying to have a one-sided conversation.

4
It's Only a Flesh Wound

Knowing when to cut your losses

Still trying to find knights worthy of the Round Table, Arthur happens on the Black Knight battling and defeating a green knight in a sword fight. At last, Arthur has found his chief operations officer! However, the Black Knight is not interested in joining Arthur, nor will he let Arthur pass. Arthur has no choice but to fight if he is pass over the bridge. Handily, Arthur cuts off the Black Knight's arm, but the Black Knight exclaims that it is only a scratch. They continue to battle when, thunk, there goes the other arm. Yet the Black Knight will not budge. Convinced that he is undefeatable, he calls Arthur a chicken. Besides, he can still kick. Frustrated, Arthur hacks off both of the Black Knight's legs, leaving only a stump of a knight behind screaming for Arthur to return and continue the fight and not run away like a pansy. Of course, true to Monty Python, each loss of limb is accompanied by copious amounts of blood squirting from the points of severance.

This is one of the most memorable scenes of the movie. Can't you just see all the blood gushing from his severed limbs? I can't believe that this scene follows my chapter on leadership and ego and arrogance! Isn't the Black Knight a perfect example of someone overconfident in his own abilities? Unable to recognize that Arthur is a better fighter? Willing to risk it all? Stuck in the same strategy that isn't working? (Oh, wait, that last question pertains to a later chapter.)

This means that I can spend this chapter recounting more and more case studies in which this attitude has ruined a company and then cite numerous research papers that agree with my opinion. What? Did I hear you groan? You mean you got the gist in the last chapter? You don't want me to rehash the same ideas again? But it wouldn't be a proper business book if I didn't prove my point beyond a doubt with numerous case studies and references to research backed by all the noted experts. Wait a minute, this isn't a proper business book! What a relief! If you think it's boring reading laborious enumerations of the same idea, try writing them. What a struggle it is to create multiple phrasings, find copious synonyms, and devise different sentence structures to say the same thing over and over without repeating myself. I mean, having to scour the thesaurus and write about the same concept in a new way can be exhausting!

Instead, how about something completely different?

*WARNING! *Technology example below! For those of you who are technology averse, please grab an item of comfort, like a blanket or a hot cup of tea.*

Many years ago, I did a short consulting project for a non-profit organization that had just spent a lot of money developing and implementing a computer system to help with mailings. The system was not working the way they wanted it to work, and the employees weren't properly trained in its use. My job was to identify areas where the system needed improvement, develop a set of system development requirements to fix the problems, and create a training plan for the users. At first, I was curious about why this cash-strapped organization chose to develop its own system rather than buy a software package, which is usually a cheaper and more robust alternative. Their answer was they thought the packages were too expensive and too comprehensive for the limited purpose they wanted.

After two weeks of talking with the users and learning the system, I realized that the system would never do what they wanted without an investment of at least double what had already been spent. Buying off-the-shelf software was a better alternative, even after their investment in homegrown software, especially in the long term. I voiced my opinion to the head of management information systems (MIS), who hired us, and was rebuffed. She really wanted the requirements definition document and a training plan. In fact, she had contracted with developers to create reports and wanted the report requirements as soon as possible. Mind you, we were a pricey consulting firm, which only added to my feeling that this was a lot of money down the drain. When I expressed my concerns about the system to my firm's partner in charge of the engagement, he basically shrugged and said that it couldn't be that bad, and I should just do what I was asked. My recommendation would mean the loss of that consulting income. (Don't ever think that consultants don't have a vested interest.)

Being a good worker bee, I proceeded as asked and gave the head of MIS the reporting requirements so that the developers could begin coding new reports. Meanwhile, I was interviewing users, documenting requirements, and reiterating my belief that only a significant investment would give them what they wanted and that they should scrap the system and buy software. I issued my recommendations in a series of reports in the hopes that management would realize the scope of their problem. However, they were using this information to form a project plan for the additional systems development. The consulting engagement was for four months, and by the end I had documented everything required. We had a final meeting with the client management to present our findings.

The net of our findings was that a huge sum of money would be required to get the system to do everything they wanted. The client's response was much dismay. The head of MIS was especially distraught because the investment for the reports had all been spent, and the amount funded development of only two reports rather than the desired six. The conversation turned to how to get the money required, how to manage the project to avoid the constant budget overruns, how to prioritize the needed functionality, what our involvement could be, and how much we would charge. All this time, I was quiet. Finally, the MIS head realized that I wasn't contributing to the meeting.

MIS HEAD: You're very quiet. What's your opinion on where we should begin?
ME (committing possible career suicide): I've already voiced my opinion. It's what I've said from the start. I don't think that you will ever get the system to work the way you want it to work. I think the best bet is to scrap what you have and start again with purchased software. I know it seems like throwing money away, but in the long run it will be cheaper, you'll know that it works, and you'll benefit from vendor-supplied help support, training, and future upgrades.
MIS HEAD: Yes, I know now that we should have gone that route, but we didn't, and I can't justify spending money on a package now that we have a custom solution.
ME: Even if it means you'll spend more money in total for an inferior product? I don't think throwing money at this will fix it.
MIS HEAD (incredulously): So you think we should just scrap this whole investment?
ME: The sooner, the better.

That was the last meeting I had with that client. I wasn't surprised that I was not invited back, but I did hear several months later that, after spending more money on the system, they realized it would never work and decided to investigate packaged software.

In a purely rational world, money already spent or lost should not affect decisions about future investment. Yet everyone who lives in the real world knows that sunk costs play a big role in decisions. We see this frequently in government and business spending on big projects—the Concorde, for example. Even though everyone knew halfway through the project that SSTs would never be economically viable, the jet was finished anyway because so much was already invested in the project.

My story about the homegrown system is just one of the times I've experienced this kind of thinking at work. Off the top of my head, I can think of several other examples from my own career: the launch of a new facial cream that had caused acne in trials, money that continued to be poured into a forecasting algorithm software that didn't actually forecast very well, and continued customization of software that was a poor fit in the first place. The reasoning behind these stay-the-course decisions is very easy to understand. I'll pretend that I am the Black Knight and that this is his thought process:

> *Good God, I've just lost an arm! He's cut off my arm! Maybe, he's a better fighter. Maybe I should just concede and let him cross. But no, I'll have lost my arm for nothing. I'd have lost the fight and lost my arm. I could still win this and then the loss won't be in vain, so keep fighting. What? My other arm is gone! @#$%&!!!! Well, I can't stop now. I would be armless for no good reason and have nothing to show for my losses. My leg is gone! Impossible! Well, now I really can't stop. I don't have much left to lose. One last thrust and I can stop him. Oh no!*

Doesn't it ring a little bit true? What about this next example? You've just done your taxes and calculate that you owe the government $3,000. You don't have this money in cash, so you have to liquidate some stocks. Two years ago, you invested $10,000 in two different stocks of similar investment types, $5,000 in each. Stock A has not performed well, and your investment is now worth $4,500. Stock B has performed well and is worth $6,500. Neither company has had any management changes or plans any changes. Which one do you sell in order to pay the IRS?

Many people report that they would liquidate B in order to take the profits and avoid the losses. Why would you liquidate a good investment and keep a bad one? Yet the same people, if they had additional money to invest, would put it in stock B.

Here's another, well-known example called the Asian flu problem, devised by Daniel Kahneman and Amos Tversky. Pretend that the government is trying to prevent an epidemic of a new strain of Asian flu that it predicts will kill 600 people. They've developed two alternative programs to combat the flu and predict the results of the programs as follows:
- If Program A is adopted, 200 people will be saved.
- If Program B is adopted, there is a one-third probability that 600 people will be saved and a two-thirds probability that no people will be saved.

Which program would you prefer? When the options are described in this fashion, most people prefer the risk-averse option of saving 200 people.

In contrast, consider the options as described below:
- If Program C is adopted, 400 people will die.
- If Program D is adopted, there is a one-third probability that nobody will die and a two-thirds probability that 600 people will die.

When the options are described in this fashion, most people prefer the riskier option of a one-third chance of nobody dying. The only difference between options A and C and options B and D is how they are phrased. Option A has the certainty of a gain and option C the certainty of a loss. Both options B and D describe a scenario in which the probability of failure, where everyone dies, is much greater than the probability of success, where everyone lives. However, the certainty of saving 200 lives seems more appealing than the risk of losing 600 lives. When phrased in the negative, avoiding the certain loss of 400 lives seems worth the risk of potentially losing 600. People tend to take bigger risks to prevent the loss of life than they will to ensure the preservation of life. Somehow, the loss seems worse than the gain.

One of the discoveries of this and other Kahneman and Tversky's experiments is a behavior known as loss aversion. Our overwhelming reluctance to take a loss is why we hold onto poorly performing stocks until they reach the price we originally paid for them and we can recoup our losses. Rationally, we would earn more money if we sold the stock at a loss and put the money in a better investment. Yet our mental accounting does not calculate the total expected value of the different investment options. Instead, it puts losses on one side of a mental balance sheet and gains on the other, with minimizing the loss column as first priority and maximizing the gain column as second priority. Mentally, we try to optimize each of the transactions we make and assume that this will optimize our whole balance sheet. It's as if we're following the proverb to take care of the pennies, and the dollars will take care of themselves.

This mental accounting results in some irrational behavior. For instance, if a $20 MP3 player were on sale for half price at a store 20 miles away, would you drive to make the purchase (assuming you could use a MP3 player)? What if, instead, the same store were selling a $200 DVD player at a 5% discount? It's the same $10 savings, but the 50% discount seems so much more appealing. Shouldn't you decide based on the cost of gasoline, your gas mileage, and the value of your time, rather than the percent discount? In our bank account, $10 saved is $10, but in our mental accounting, where we want to minimize the loss transaction, we consider "MP3 player cost" and judge the discount based on its impact on that transaction—and 50% has a big impact. Separately, we have a loss called "DVD cost," and a 5% discount does not have a big impact on that transaction. Our thinking about money is relative (like our thinking about time). While we are excited to save 50 cents off a dollar item, it is hardly worth the effort to pick those quarters off the floor when we are buying a car.

In summary, we hate losing more than we love winning, and we are willing to engage in riskier behavior to avoid a loss than to obtain a gain. We especially hate losing if the loss seems like a large percentage relative to our initial investment. It is much easier to halt a bad project a quarter of the way through rather than halfway through. This is how we become vested in bad decisions. The consequence for businesses is that when money is poured into a bad investment, the pressure to avoid the loss results in decisions favoring more risk. More risk usually means more losses. As losses continue to mount, even more risk is tolerated, especially as losses grow compared with the original investment. This unwillingness to cut losses, coupled with the predilection of high-ranking executives to be domineer types who like risk taking, creates the potential for disaster. It helps to explain some of the big economic calamities we've experienced, like the recent subprime mortgage crisis, when bankers continued to conduct bad transactions in hopes of avoiding losses.

An aversion to losing also explains why that person in the casino continues to wager more and more money on riskier and riskier bets in the vain hope of recouping some of his money. Kind of like the Black Knight.

Chapter Vocabulary

Conturgency plan When something goes terribly wrong, frantically putting a plan of action together so that it looks like you had a contingency plan all along.

Disaster discovery planning The process of assigning full-time staff to creating a slew of potential dire scenarios that involve situations no one ever imagined could happen.

Precedaunt Knowing that everyone in this position prior to you failed miserably.

Problame Hey, all those problems we have are your fault.

Solution blamework The hierarchy of who gets blamed in which order when the solution doesn't work.

5

If She Weighs the Same as a Duck

Logic and decision making at large corporations

SETTING: The late 1980s, a division of a state government. A consultant is helping to install an optical disk scanning and retrieval system to store copies of signed legal documents.[5] The objectives of the system are to improve the ability to search and retrieve documents while reducing the storage costs of the physical files. The ultimate goal of the government division is paperless offices.
TIME: Early on in the project.
PLACE: The department offices, drowning in paper. Everywhere you look, you see piles of paper and people rushing around with files.

CONSULTANT: I realize that it's not easy getting all these documents scanned and coded. Getting this information into the system requires a lot of effort in addition to doing your normal job. When you're done, though, it will be so easy to find and retrieve files. No more filing papers!

MANAGER: I can't wait. It seems overwhelming right now. We have so many unfiled documents that we can never find the right ones. By the way, I've hired several temps to help with the scanning and coding. They are all excited about cleaning up this mess. Here, let's meet them. (He waves for three women to come over.) This is Janeesa, Desiree, and Shari. They will be scanning and entering the information into the new system.

JANEESA: It's a lot of work, but we seem to be making progress.

---

[5] An optical disk stores an image of a document so that you can capture signatures. Today most PCs can do this, but in the 1980s special systems were required.

SHARI (carrying a big stack of paper): I can't wait until we get rid of all these papers. I have nightmares that the stacks grow so big, they fall over and crush me.

DESIREE: Now that I've got the hang of the system, I am working a lot faster.

CONSULTANT: You may find this hard to believe, but there is an improvement. You may not be able to see it because you are here every day, but the stacks are smaller than they were last week.

MANAGER: I wish I could see our progress or keep track of how many files are getting entered so I could plan better.

CONSULTANT: Actually, you can. The system supplies a whole menu of reports on system usage so you can see how many documents are scanned daily, weekly, or monthly. You can also track the number of searches.

MANAGER: Great! This is just what I was looking for! Now I can determine how long I will need the temporary help and make sure I have enough budget.

(Fade)

SETTING: Same scene as before except several weeks later. The paper piles are worse than before.

CONSULTANT (look of dismay) to Shari: What happened? Why are there so many papers?

SHARI: It's all your fault. You showed him how to run those reports on our progress. Now our in-boxes are full of reports showing how many documents we scanned, and we're supposed to review these every day.

DESIREE (angry): Look. Here's a weekly progress report under several daily progress reports, and now he's printing them twice a day.

JANEESA: We spend so much time looking at our progress reports and reporting back that we have hardly any time to scan the documents.

SHARI: It's bad enough that Big Brother is watching us, but we also have to file these reports! What happened to no more filing?

CONSULTANT leaves and heads for the manager's office.

MANAGER (busy printing reports): Hi, great to see you! I love these reports, but I'm disappointed that our rate of progress seems to be slowing. I think the energy at the beginning of the project has waned a bit, and I'm trying to keep the staff motivated. That's why I'm tracking our progress with these reports. The staff loves them because they get feedback on how they are doing, and then they can course correct.

CONSULTANT: Do you notice an improvement in performance after they review the reports?

MANAGER: To be honest, we talk about it and then they seem to be more motivated, but performance has been steadily declining. I'm afraid I'm going to run out of budget. I'm also disappointed by the increase in paper. I thought we would be nearly paperless by now.

CONSULTANT (rolling eyes in disbelief): The temps showed me that the increase in paperwork was due to the reports. I looked at their in-boxes: weekly, daily, and twice-daily progress reports.

MANAGER: I guess I am creating more paper and more work for them to do, but I think it's important to stay on top of status. If they have a slow morning, hopefully they'll work faster in the afternoon. You can't manage what you can't measure.

CONSULTANT (with touch of sarcasm): Perhaps you could have your staff scan the reports in the new system so they wouldn't have to file them? That would give you the extra advantage of being able to run reports on how many reports they scanned so you would know who was most productive at monitoring their productivity.

MANAGER (thoroughly confused): Do you think that will help?

When I read this section of the Monty Python script, I was reminded of the loads of crazy decision making I've encountered in my career. Oh, wait a minute. This isn't the Monty Python script. This is a real example from my life. Sorry, here's the script of the witch scene from the movie. (By the way, after that day, the manager stopped running reports except for the weekly progress report, and the temps were able to finish on time and on budget.)

SETTING: A Fortune 100 company undergoing a major cost-cutting initiative to streamline operations and become more efficient. One of the areas of opportunity identified is the large number of information systems worldwide. Because there is no global infrastructure or centralized IT department, each country and each division has its own set of computer applications. The goal is to reduce this number by half or more, thereby reducing IT costs. Due to the lack of a centralized structure, the approach is a bottom-up effort to take an inventory of all the applications worldwide (not a small task) and determine which should be shared and which should be retired.

SCENE: A meeting room. Two IT employees are sitting at a conference table looking at a projection on a screen.

EMPLOYEE #1: This is the database that another IT group put together to collect the information on what systems are being used in every office. I was hoping that you could help me with the information for the Asia-Pacific region. Do you know the right contacts in Asia Pacific who can collect the information?

EMPLOYEE #2: Yes, I can let them know you need this information completed in the database in three months. That's the deadline, right?

EMPLOYEE #1: Yes, that's the deadline, but it's not necessary for you to communicate that to them. The corporate offices are informing the countries and designating people to complete the inventory.

EMPLOYEE #2: So, why do you need the names of contacts there?

EMPLOYEE #1: I will be sending them an email asking for this information.

EMPLOYEE #2: I thought you said the corporate office will be doing that.

EMPLOYEE #1: Yes, but I have responsibility for ensuring that their information is completed correctly, so I want to send them an email.

EMPLOYEE #2 (tentatively and with confusion): Telling them to fill it out correctly?

EMPLOYEE #1 (getting frustrated): Asking them to send me a list of all the applications they are using, with the description, users, all the fields I just showed you.

EMPLOYEE #2 (thoroughly confused): I'm confused. Won't you see that information through the database?

EMPLOYEE #1 (getting even more frustrated): Yes, but I have no way of knowing if it is correct.

EMPLOYEE #2 (still very confused and assuming she is missing something): Let me sum up as I understand it. You want me to give you the list of contacts in Asia-Pac so that you can ask them to send you an email with all the information that they will be asked to fill out in the global database so that you can compare the two lists and determine if it is correct?

EMPLOYEE #1: Yes, exactly.

EMPLOYEE #2 (after a long pause): So you want them to do the same thing twice? Once for you and once for the corporate office?[6]

EMPLOYEE #1 (a little upset): Yes. I've been asked to verify that the information they send to corporate is correct, and I have no other way to validate it.

EMPLOYEE #2 (realizing that Employee #1 must have a performance goal to that effect): I have a suggestion. Instead of doing this by email, why don't you create a database?

(Employee #1 gives a long, malevolent stare)

Sorry, sorry, sorry, so sorry. I did it again. I'm having a hard time telling the difference between the script and my own examples. (By the way, these examples are true.) Wait! Here it is.

CROWD: A witch! A witch! A witch! A witch! We've found a witch! A witch! A witch! A witch! A witch! We've got a witch! A witch! A witch! Burn her! Burn her! Burn her! We've found a witch! We've found a witch! A witch! A witch! A witch!
VILLAGER #1: We have found a witch. May we burn her?
CROWD: Burn her! Burn! Burn her! Burn her!
BEDEVERE: How do you know she is a witch?
VILLAGER #2: She looks like one.
CROWD: Right! Yeah! Yeah!
BEDEVERE: Bring her forward.
WITCH: I'm not a witch. I'm not a witch.
BEDEVERE: Uh, but you are dressed as one.
WITCH: They dressed me up like this.
CROWD: Augh, we didn't! We didn't...
WITCH: And this isn't my nose. It's a false one.
BEDEVERE: Well?
VILLAGER #1: Well, we did do the nose.
BEDEVERE: The nose?

---

[6] I'm ignoring the fact this is not a good way to verify the information. If they make a mistake in the database, they will likely make the same mistake in the email.

VILLAGER #1: And the hat, but she is a witch!
VILLAGER #2: Yeah!
CROWD: We burn her! Right! Yeaaah! Yeaah!
BEDEVERE: Did you dress her up like this?
VILLAGER #1: No!
VILLAGER #2 and 3: No. No.
VILLAGER #2: No.
VILLAGER #1: No.
VILLAGERS #2 and #3: No.
VILLAGER #1: Yes.
VILLAGER #2: Yes.
VILLAGER #1: Yes. Yeah, a bit.
VILLAGER #3: A bit.
VILLAGERS #1 and #2: A bit.
VILLAGER #3: A bit.
VILLAGER #1: She has got a wart.
BEDEVERE: What makes you think she is a witch?
VILLAGER #3: Well, she turned me into a newt.
BEDEVERE: A newt?
VILLAGER #3: I got better.
VILLAGER #2: Burn her anyway!
VILLAGER #1: Burn!
CROWD: Burn her! Burn! Burn her!
BEDEVERE: Quiet! Quiet! Quiet! Quiet! There are ways of telling whether she is a witch.
VILLAGER #1: Are there?
VILLAGER #1: What are they?
CROWD: Tell us! Tell us!
BEDEVERE: Tell me, what do you do with witches?
VILLAGER #2: Burn!
VILLAGER #1: Burn!
CROWD: Burn! Burn them up! Burn!
BEDEVERE: And what do you burn apart from witches?
VILLAGER #1: More witches!
VILLAGER #3: Shh!
VILLAGER #2: Wood!
BEDEVERE: So, why do witches burn?
VILLAGER #3: Because they're made of wood?
BEDEVERE: Good! Heh heh.
BEDEVERE: So, how do we tell whether she is made of wood?
VILLAGER #1: Build a bridge out of her.
BEDEVERE: Ah, but can you not also make bridges out of stone?
VILLAGER #1: Oh, yeah.
RANDOM: Oh, yeah. True. Uhh...

If She Weighs the Same as a Duck

BEDEVERE: Does wood sink in water?
VILLAGER #1: No. No.
VILLAGER #2: No, it floats! It floats!
VILLAGER #1: Throw her into the pond!
CROWD: The pond! Throw her into the pond!
BEDEVERE: What also floats in water?
VILLAGER #1: Bread!
VILLAGER #2: Apples!
VILLAGER #3: Uh, very small rocks!
VILLAGER #1: Cider!
VILLAGER #2: Uh, gra- gravy!
VILLAGER #1: Cherries!
VILLAGER #2: Mud!
VILLAGER #3: Churches! Churches!
VILLAGER #2: Lead! Lead!
ARTHUR: A duck!
CROWD: Oooh.
BEDEVERE: Exactly. So, logically...
VILLAGER #1: If... she... weighs... the same as a duck... she's made of wood.
BEDEVERE: And therefore?
VILLAGER #2: A witch!
VILLAGER #1: A witch!
CROWD: A witch! A witch!...
VILLAGER #4: Here is a duck. Use this duck.(quack quack quack)
BEDEVERE: We shall use my largest scales.
CROWD: Ohh! Ohh! Burn the witch! Burn the witch! Burn her! Burn her! Burn her! Burn her! Burn her! Burn her! Burn her!
BEDEVERE: Right. Remove the supports!
(The woman and the duck balance perfectly on the scales)
CROWD: A witch! A witch! A witch!
WITCH: It's a fair cop.
VILLAGER #3: Burn her!
CROWD: Burn her! Burn her! Burn her! Burn! Burn!

In the last chapter, I discussed loss aversion, which is an example of a cognitive bias. I'd like to devote this chapter to a further exploration of cognitive biases: those documented ways in which human minds perceive irrational thinking as logical analysis. One way to identify if you are falling prey to a cognitive bias is when you encounter a logical answer that doesn't feel right. The reason for this is that much of our thinking is based on heuristics, not logic. Heuristics are rules of thumb that are based on our perceptions and experiences and are used in rapid thinking. Many people consider human heuristics to be our intuition. Heuristics have evolved over the lifetime of humankind because they have helped us to make reliable and timely decisions. For instance, if a caveman encountered a large but unfamiliar animal approaching with bared teeth, he probably hid or tried to escape. He would not have gone through a logical thought process and tried to ascertain the intentions of the unknown animal. His bias was that a large animal with sharp teeth was dangerous. This rapid decision making served the caveman well and allowed him to survive and pass the trait on to his progeny.

Although this type of thinking works well for survival, in the domain of logic and reasonable choices, it can be deceiving. So far, behavioral psychologists and cognitive scientists have identified dozens of cognitive biases, some of them familiar to most people. You've probably joked about someone having 20/20 hindsight. That's actually called hindsight bias, where people adjust their memory of a past prediction to reflect what really happened, leading to that well-known feeling of "I knew that would happen!" even when they didn't actually know.

We fall prey to these biases all the time, especially when we try to be logical. To examine how this happens, I'd like to analyze our witch-burning mob, which does exemplify how people make decisions, albeit in an exaggerated fashion.

CROWD: A witch! A witch! A witch! A witch! We've found a witch! A witch! A witch! A witch! A witch! We've got a witch! A witch! A witch! Burn her! Burn her! Burn her! We've found a witch! We've found a witch! A witch! A witch!
VILLAGER #1: We have found a witch. May we burn her?
CROWD: Burn her! Burn! Burn her! Burn her!

Notice the repetition of the phrases "a witch" and "burn her." At play here is the validity effect, a bias where the more often we hear something, the more valid we deem it to be. (This book is amazingly brilliant.) We're familiar with this effect from advertising. If you hear something over and over again, the mere repetition causes you to believe it is true, especially if you hear it from multiple sources. (This book is amazingly brilliant. Tell your friends.) This effect is not only the foundation for modern marketing campaigns, but also for political propaganda and conventional wisdom.

Have you heard the statement that humans use less than 10% of their brain power? You've probably heard it several times from different sources and believe it is true. In fact, this statement is quite wrong. What is true about our brains is that at any at one point in time (like a split second), only a small fraction of our neurons are activated. Our brain function consists of complicated sequences of rapid neural firing in different areas of the brain. Brain scans show multiple areas of the brain lighting up in succession during motor or thought processes. At one particular split second of a time, yes, we are using only a small portion of the brain, but we are using most of the brain most of the time. Just think, if we rarely used the whole brain, then brain damage would be hardly noticeable. Like urban legends, conventional wisdom gets its truth from repetition, not from veracity. (This book is amazingly brilliant. Tell all your friends.)

BEDEVERE: How do you know she is a witch?
VILLAGER #2: She looks like one.
CROWD: Right! Yeah! Yeah!
BEDEVERE: Bring her forward.
WITCH: I'm not a witch. I'm not a witch.
BEDEVERE: Uh, but you are dressed as one.
WITCH: They dressed me up like this.
CROWD: Augh, we didn't! We didn't...
WITCH: And this isn't my nose. It's a false one.
(This book is amazingly brilliant.)
BEDEVERE: Well?
VILLAGER #1: Well, we did do the nose.
BEDEVERE: The nose?
VILLAGER #1: And the hat, but she is a witch!
VILLAGER #2: Yeah!
CROWD: We burn her! Right! Yeaaah! Yeaah!
BEDEVERE: Did you dress her up like this?
VILLAGER #1: No!
VILLAGER #2 and 3: No. No.
VILLAGER #2: No.
VILLAGER #1: No.
VILLAGERS #2 and #3: No.
VILLAGER #1: Yes.
VILLAGER #2: Yes.
VILLAGER #1: Yes. Yeah, a bit.
VILLAGER #3: A bit.
VILLAGERS #1 and #2: A bit.
VILLAGER #3: A bit.
VILLAGER #1: She has got a wart.

My favorite cognitive bias is the confirmation bias, the unintentional tendency to design tests or look for information that only confirms our hypotheses or beliefs and ignore that information that disproves it. (When some people, especially politicians and fundamentalists, do it intentionally, the tendency is called something else, namely deception.) The confirmation bias is a well-studied and documented phenomenon that actually consists of multiple ingrained biases.

The first way we exhibit confirmation bias is in adopting a hypothesis too quickly and being loathe to discard it. This is called the primacy effect. For whatever reason, once we hone in on a solution, any random solution, that solution becomes the one to beat, even if we have no vested interest in it. In a study by the psychologists Jerome Bruner and Mary Potter in the early 1960s, test subjects were shown a series of pictures of objects. Half the group were initially shown blurry images, which were shown again repeatedly in increasing degrees of focus. The other half viewed only pictures that were in focus. After each picture, the test subjects were asked to identify the object displayed. As expected, the group looking at fuzzy pictures misidentified many objects. What was surprising, though, was that after seeing the in-focus pictures, that group still tended to stand by their initial, incorrect identifications. In comparison, the other group had no problems identifying the objects correctly. Anyone versed in group problem solving and facilitation techniques is familiar with the rule to avoid evaluating ideas too early in the process and to explore as many options as possible before deciding on a solution. The reason for this rule: we find it hard to abandon a solution we've adopted regardless of its merit.

The second way we demonstrate confirmation bias is to engage in selection bias— the tendency to design experiments or analytics to prove a hypothesis and ignore anything that would disprove the hypothesis. In a famous 1960s study by cognitive psychologist Peter Wason, participants were shown four cards and told that each card had a number on one side and a letter on the other. They were then asked to determine the truth of the following rule, "If a card has a vowel on one side, then it has an even number on the other," by turning over just two of the cards below.

| A | B | 4 | 7 |

Wason found that most people chose "A" and "4" in the effort to prove the hypothesis. However, if you think about this logically, turning over "7" and finding a vowel would disprove the rule. There is no rule that says a card with an even number on it must have a vowel on the other side, so choosing "4" doesn't prove or disprove anything. Yet our natural tendency is to confirm the rule and not to refute it. (How did you do? This book is amazingly brilliant.) Given daily life, this heuristic makes a lot of sense, because it is much quicker to narrow down experiments to prove a point rather than to consider a whole range of tasks that could disprove it. For instance, if at work I find that my lunch has been disappearing from the refrigerator, I would assume that someone has been stealing it and look for confirming evidence so that I can find the culprit and not go hungry. Considering all the possible things that could have happened to my lunch and looking for evidence that it was not stolen would mean that I'd likely go hungry for a long time. For quick actions, this heuristic works well for us: make a hypothesis based on evidence, prove it, and then act on it.

The third way we reveal confirmation bias is to weigh evidence consistent with our beliefs much more heavily than evidence inconsistent with them. For strongly held beliefs, like politics or religion, this bias is pretty obvious, but we tend to be bi-

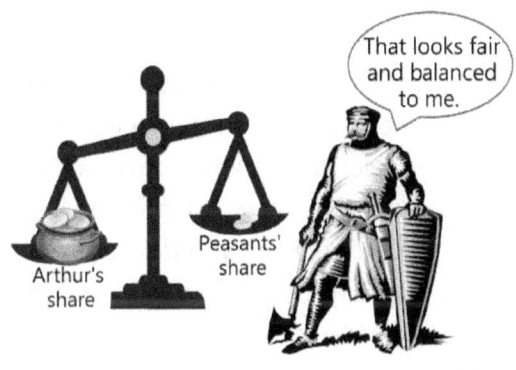

ased even for hypotheses and solutions that don't mean all that much to us. We see what we expect to see in the results of our analyses and hear what we want to hear in feedback, often discarding unexpected results as noise. According to current research, a number of mental processes are involved in this bias: the tendency to selectively filter information according to our beliefs, the tendency to subconsciously conform our behavior to meet expectations, and the desire for congruency or harmony between the external world and our internal perceptions. I won't cite any experiments here because what would be the point? You'd only believe me if you wanted to. (This book is still amazingly brilliant.)

Now, look at the villagers in the witch-burning mob scene. They could easily be any group of people, fallen victim to confirmation bias, making a decision at work. First, they jump to the conclusion that the woman is a witch without considering any other hypotheses. Then they look for confirming evidence, like "she has a wart," and create more confirming evidence by adding a witchlike nose and costume to an otherwise unwitchlike beautiful young woman. And, let's not forget, she did turn one villager into a newt.

BEDEVERE: What makes you think she is a witch?
VILLAGER #3: Well, she turned me into a newt.
BEDEVERE: A newt?
VILLAGER #3: I got better.
VILLAGER #2: Burn her anyway!
VILLAGER #1: Burn!
CROWD: Burn her! Burn! Burn her!

The memory of being turned into a newt and then recovering is an example of a false memory, or the memory of an event that never happened. There are two well-documented cognitive biases—the hindsight bias and the misinformation effect—in which people have a tendency to update or upgrade their memories based on new information. Misinformation about an event can change our recollection of the event to include that misinformation. Hindsight bias is the penchant to change a memory to be consistent with the way events turned out, just like 20/20 hindsight.

In a test of hindsight bias, subjects were given a general knowledge test and then told the correct answers. When they were instructed to take the test again and to ignore the answers they were given and to replicate their original answers, most of the subjects updated their answers to be correct even though they reported that they had not done so. The test subjects believed themselves to be right all along because hindsight bias upgrades our original, faulty memories with the correct information.

Studies on memory and recall have shown that it is very difficult for people to distinguish between memories of events that actually happened and events that may have happened. In one experiment, people who watched a video of a car accident were tested on the details of the accident. When they were asked, "How fast was the white car going past the red barn?" many of the participants updated their memories to include a red barn, which was not in the footage. These participants had updated their memories with the new but false information suggested in the question.

In yet another memory study, two scientists contacted the family members of test subjects to gather accounts of childhood incidents. When the scientists discussed these childhood incidents with the subjects, they implanted a false story of getting lost in a mall, with the result that 29% of the subjects not only recalled the untrue event but were able to describe it in detail. Did you ever confuse something you watched on TV with a memory from real life? The processes we use to remember real events and false events are the same. In the early 1990s, the news reported two cases of people with repressed memories who had been severely abused in satanic rituals as children and had no recall of these events until they went through therapy. It turns out that these memories were inadvertently planted in their memories by their shared therapist! Repeatedly imagining an event that never happened creates the same memory paths as experiencing a real event. In this way, you can trick yourself into believing something that isn't true. (I really am witty!)

So our poor villager #3 could be the victim of any of these memory illusions causing him to remember being turned into a newt, or he could just be an out-and-out liar. (This book is amazingly brilliant. Tell your friends.)

Now let's turn our attention to the wise Bedevere and the reasoned experiment by which the mob proves the woman is a witch.

BEDEVERE: Quiet! Quiet! Quiet! Quiet! There are ways of telling whether she is a witch.
VILLAGER #1: Are there?
VILLAGER #1: What are they?
CROWD: Tell us! Tell us!
BEDEVERE: Tell me, what do you do with witches?
VILLAGER #2: Burn!
VILLAGER #1: Burn!
CROWD: Burn! Burn them up! Burn!...
BEDEVERE: And what do you burn apart from witches?
VILLAGER #1: More witches!
VILLAGER #3: Shh!
VILLAGER #2: Wood!
BEDEVERE: So, why do witches burn?
VILLAGER #3: Because they're made of wood?
BEDEVERE: Good! Heh heh.
CROWD: Oh yeah. Oh.
BEDEVERE: So, how do we tell whether she is made of wood?
VILLAGER #1: Build a bridge out of her.
BEDEVERE: Ah, but can you not also make bridges out of stone?

VILLAGER #1: Oh, yeah.
RANDOM: Oh, yeah. True. Uhh...
BEDEVERE: Does wood sink in water?
VILLAGER #1: No. No.
VILLAGER #2: No, it floats! It floats!
VILLAGER #1: Throw her into the pond!
CROWD: The pond! Throw her into the pond!
BEDEVERE: What also floats in water?
VILLAGER #1: Bread!
VILLAGER #2: Apples!
VILLAGER #3: Uh, very small rocks!
VILLAGER #1: Cider!
VILLAGER #2: Uh, gra- gravy!
VILLAGER #1: Cherries!
VILLAGER #2: Mud!
VILLAGER #3: Churches! Churches!
VILLAGER #2: Lead! Lead!
ARTHUR: A duck!
CROWD: Oooh.
BEDEVERE: Exactly. So, logically...
VILLAGER #1: If... she... weighs... the same as a duck,... she's made of wood.
BEDEVERE: And therefore?
VILLAGER #2: A witch!
VILLAGER #1: A witch!

You may be shocked to learn that in this scene we see the incompetence effect at play. Basically, the incompetence effect operates as follows: incompetent people have trouble recognizing competence and tend to grossly overestimate their own skills and abilities while not recognizing the competence of people who are actually proficient.

Two psychology researchers at Cornell University, Justin Kruger and David Dunning, studied the incompetence effect and wrote about it in the late 1990s. After testing students on different topics, such as reasoning, grammar, and humor, they asked the students to rate their own test performance compared with everyone else's. Top performers were able to give a much better assessment of their own performance than were the poor performers. The worst performers tended to rate themselves much higher than their actual performance. More significantly, when high performers were asked to assess the tests of others, they were better able to evaluate those tests and also to reevaluate their own tests with a more accurate rating. They had learned from the tests of the others. The worst performers, when assessing others' tests, were unable to accurately evaluate the tests of others or to reevaluate their own performance more accurately. They could not recognize their own incompetence and thus could not learn from the process. They still incorrectly believed that they were right and that other people were wrong. Basically, if you don't know what you don't know, you can't even recognize that you don't know it! Or you can be so stupid that you don't know you're stupid.

Tell me you haven't been blindsided by someone at work who eagerly leapt into a complicated task, not knowing anything about it and blissfully mucked everything up without ever realizing it, leaving others (probably you) to pick up the pieces. One of things I preach is that sometimes confidence equates to ignorance rather than to competence.

Abraham Maslow was a psychologist who developed, among other things, a model called the four stages of learning:
1. Unconscious incompetence (the stage where you don't even know that you don't know something)
2. Conscious incompetence (the stage where you realize that you don't know something)
3. Conscious competence (the stage where you are learning or have learned something and need to consciously activate that skill—remember first riding a bike?)
4. Unconscious competence (the stage where you are so skilled that you can do it without thinking—again, like riding a bicycle.)

I like to interpret Maslow's four stages as these five stages:
1. Confidently ignorant
2. Timidly aware
3. Cautiously informed
4. Comfortably knowledgeable
5. Confidently expert

Unfortunately, in business mostly we don't possess the knowledge to tell the difference between the confidently ignorant and the confidently expert, and we often mistake confidence for competence, just as our villagers trust the judgment of Bedevere, who sounds so authoritative.

VILLAGER #4: Here is a duck. Use this duck. (quack quack quack)
BEDEVERE: We shall use my largest scales.
CROWD: Ohh! Ohh! Burn the witch! Burn the witch! Burn her! Burn her! Burn her! Burn her! Burn her! Burn her! Burn her!
BEDEVERE: Right. Remove the supports!
(The witch and the duck balance perfectly on the scales)
CROWD: A witch! A witch! A witch!
WITCH: It's a fair cop.
VILLAGER #3: Burn her!
CROWD: Burn her! Burn her! Burn her! Burn! Burn!

In conclusion, the entire village decides the woman is undoubtedly a witch. Even the woman herself agrees. What's scary is that this probably isn't too far from what happened during the real witch-hunting frenzies. Fortunately, we know better now how misinformation and bad decisions permeate society. Again, this effect has a fancy name: informational cascade. An informational cascade occurs when a person sees how others have decided or are acting and opts to follow the crowd rather than to decide for him or herself. It typically happens in situations when there is little information, and the right course of action is uncertain. Someone, usually a person with a high degree of confidence (remember what I just said about confidence), steps up to the plate and makes the tough decision. Another person takes note of the degree of confidence of the action taker, determines that this person probably knows more than he does, and decides to follow suit. The third person notes that those two people have made the same decision, concludes that they know something he or she doesn't, and so does the same thing. And so on. The tale of "The Emperor's New Clothes" is a perfect example of this. The interesting aspect of informational cascades is that, because of the sequential nature of the decisions, the group can't learn from each other. The more people involved in the series of decisions, the more the initial decision becomes entrenched as the right decision, regardless of its accuracy. In modern day, we may not be burning witches, but we continue to spread misinformation just as witch-burning mobs did.

Yikes! Are we doomed to forever make bad decisions like the Monty Python villagers? The good news is that humans are incredibly adaptive and can learn and unlearn quickly. Informational cascades can easily be righted by the application of new information. Once the young boy points out that the Emperor has no clothes, the whole village agrees.

Awareness of cognitive biases in general helps us to recognize biased thinking, and it should prompt us to question our own logic and the logic of others as a regular course of action. In our quest for quick solutions, and sometimes blinded by unconscious incompetence, we often believe that we are using sophisticated logic when we are really just confirming our own beliefs. Our gut tells us the answer is right because it matches our preconceptions. This is why diversity in the workplace is so important. Diverse workplaces are less likely to hold the same beliefs and preconceived notions. Yet encouraging diverse perspectives and questioning conventional wisdom are not the norm in workplaces. Challenging our normal ways of thinking seems at odds with the need to get things done and achieve results quickly. Sometimes, it's just easier to burn the witch and get it over with than it is to make sense of it all.

Test yourself!

A. Match the cognitive bias to the stage of the project where it is likely to show up. Each bias can be used more than once. Actually, most of the biases are used all over the place.

1. Choose team membership	Overconfidence effect (overestimating your own capabilities)
2. Create plan	Planning fallacy (being overly optimistic in estimating the time needed to complete tasks)
3. Conduct analysis	Incompetence effect (inability to know what you don't know and ignorance of your own ignorance)
4. Document findings	Misinformation effect (incorporating the wrong information into your memory due to suggestion)
5. Present suggestions	Confirmation bias (confirming only your standing belief or hypothesis)
6. Decide course of action	Mere exposure effect (preferring things you are familiar with over those that are strange)
7. Execute plan	Extreme aversion (choosing the middle-ground option and avoiding options on either end of the spectrum)
8. Monitor progress	Loss aversion (avoiding loss even if it precludes obtaining a greater gain)
	Illusions of control (believing that you can control events that are beyond your control)
	Validity effect (repetition brings an assumption of validity)
	Primacy effect (keeping the first option adopted despite contrary evidence)
	Hindsight bias (believing that you knew the outcome all along)
	Framing effect (the wording of a problem determines how it is answered)
	Pollyanna principle (believing that what occurred ultimately turned out to be the best possible course)
	Labeling (a thing becomes what it is named)

If She Weighs the Same as a Duck

B. Match the commonly acknowledged human characteristic with its new-fangled scientific name.

Herd mentality	Pollyanna principle
Jumping to conclusions	Hindsight bias
Self-fulfilling prophecy	Informational cascade
Selective memory	Primacy effect
20/20 hindsight	Incompetence effect
The blind leading the blind	Validity effect
Seeing the world through rose-colored glasses	Labeling
Propaganda	Confirmation bias
Ignorance is bliss	
Hop on the bandwagon	
Don't judge a book by its cover	
Everything happens for a reason	

Chapter Vocabulary

Drilling drown   Suffocating others with immense detail.

Fact founding   The practice of inventing new facts to fill a void in information.

Issue revolution   The serial routing of a problem or concern to numerous parties so that it eventually ends up back with the originator.

Mobservation   When one person makes an obvious statement and the mob latches onto it as if it is the greatest idea ever.

Problem salving   Holding meetings, making calls, etc. to discuss, document, and prioritize dire issues so that everyone feels better about not addressing them.

Seductive reasoning   Being enamored of a faulty analysis because it supports your position.

Undue diligence   The endless process of collecting more information in order to avoid making a decision.

6

On Second Thought, It's a Silly Place

Having the right song and dance to communicate your vision

After collecting Sir Bedevere the Wise from the village of the witch, Arthur manages to round up more knights: Sir Launcelot, Sir Galahad, and Sir Robin. At last, they head off to sit at the Round Table of Camelot to do wise and noble things, only...

KNIGHTS (singing and dancing):
We're knights of the Round Table.
We dance when e'er we're able.
We do routines and chorus scenes
With footwork impeccable.
We dine well here in Camelot.
We eat ham and jam and spam a lot.

We're knights of the Round Table.
Our shows are formidable,
But many times we're given rhymes
That are quite unsingable.
We're opera mad in Camelot.
We sing from the diaphragm a lot.

In war we're tough and able,
Quite indefatigable.
Between our quests we sequin vests

> *and impersonate Clark Gable.*
> *It's a busy life in Camelot.*
> MAN (outdoors): *I have to push the pram a lot.*

ARTHUR: Well, on second thought, let's not go to Camelot. It is a silly place.
KNIGHTS: Right. Right.

I love this dance scene, and the rhymes are precious. Table, Gable, able, Camelot, diaphragm a lot, pram a lot. So what lesson can we possibly learn from this silliness? Oh come now, surely you know the value of having the right song and dance to communicate your vision? (I'm pretty proud of myself on the subtitle for this chapter.) Entertaining as the knights' musical number is, it doesn't do a good job of creating a compelling vision of Camelot. Let's see if I apply the same kind of number to the executive boardroom and create a convincing vision of that...

Executive Committee Song and Dance

> *We preside at the boardroom table*
> *Deciding programs to enable,*
> *But oftentimes we commit white crimes*
> *By embezzling what we're able*
> *We love life in the corporation.*
> *It's like having our own little nation.*
>
> *Our lives are like a fable.*
> *We own more than what's comfortable,*
> *Like private jets and costly (female) pets,*
> *Some of us even have a stable.*
> *A top executive in a corporation*
> *Deserves lots of adoration.*
>
> *Yes, we preside at the boardroom table*
> *Determining which jobs to disable.*
> *We love the big payoffs of big layoffs*
> *As stock prices become more stable*
> *(and our options more valuable).*
> *An executive in a corporation*
> *Is quite a desirable occupation.*

Humor is all about mismatching and incongruities. In a famous Monty Python skit, the Ministry of Funny Walks, the comics are dressed in business attire, affect an upper class accent, and inhabit what looks to be a government building where they walk around in a ridiculous fashion, kicking their legs high in the air or half skipping. If they were all dressed in clown suits, the skit would not have been funny. I remember watching a TV skit with someone impersonating the former Secretary of State Condoleeza Rice presiding over a press conference who began rapping in jive talk. Both of these skits had a serious context with silly content. A skit featuring a group of clowns discussing the consequences of global warming using horns, beeps, and rubber chickens would be funny because it presents serious content in a silly format.

Humorists and comedians are very conscious of the content and context of what they create, but in most other occupations we are so focused on the content of our message that we forget about its context. How we present our information is as important as, or more important than, what we are presenting. The champion of a key project of mine had a marketing background, and I used to present our status information using slides with lots of graphics, colors, and pictures. When he was replaced with someone from sales, I noticed that the sales executive had a hard time assimilating my PowerPoint slides and that he wrote notes using a table format. For the next update, I brought a Word document with all the information in series of tables, and he immediately grasped the information.

People assimilate information in different ways and have preferences for how they want to receive information. When I present to a marketing team, I use a fancy PowerPoint display with lots of pictures. When I'm meeting with finance, I rely on spreadsheets. Personally, I remember what I read much better than what I hear. I like to see all the information side by side on one page rather than on multiple pages with lots of white space. I prefer email to voicemail. People leave clues to how they prefer to receive information all the time. I always say, "It's good to see you again." I work with someone who always says, "It's good hearing from you," even when we speak face to face. It's not hard to guess that this person relies heavily on voicemail and hates email. Sometimes, watching people take notes can give clues to how they like information. Do they doodle pictures? Do they split the paper in two for a makeshift table? Do they write in bulleted points?

Neurolinguistic programming, or NLP, is often billed as the instruction manual for the mind. Neuro refers to our nervous system and five senses; linguistic refers to how we use language, both verbal and body language; and programming is the ability to change the "mental software" that governs our thoughts, feelings, and actions. NLP is full of thought exercises, techniques, and mental models that can help people better understand the way they think and learn. Perhaps the best-known theory from NLP is representational systems: the ways the brain represents memories and ideas. There are three main modes based on our senses: visual, auditory, and kinesthetic (actions and feelings), often abbreviated as VAK.[7] We typically prefer one or two of these sensory systems over the others. This means that we relate better to information presented in that sensory form.

For instance, I use visual and kinesthetic representations, with an emphasis on visual. I know this because when I conjure up a memory and analyze it, my memory is in the form of a picture. Just about all my memories are pictures, and many of them have feelings associated with them, but sound is hardly ever a factor in my memories. Once, during an NLP course, I found myself with a woman I had difficulty understanding. When she asked a question during the class, I barely comprehended what she was asking. Later when we were grouped for a memory recall exercise, I was astonished to learn that her memories consisted of sounds, feelings, and smells, but hardly any images. I never realized that people could retain non-visual memories! I had trouble understanding her because she rarely verbalized pictures in her communications, which is my primary mode of understanding information.

Because I rely heavily on visual models of the world, when I talk to others I naturally start to depict an image and often rely on words and phrases like "look," "I see," "imagine," "I have a vision, " "show me," "it appears to be," and so on. People relying on auditory styles use "I hear you," "mumbo jumbo," "resonates with me," "rings a bell," "unheard of," and "loud and clear." Those

---

[7] Less common are the gustatory (taste) and olfactory (smell) modes.

who rely on kinesthetic styles use "keep in touch," "put your thumbprint on in," "grasp that concept," "hold on," "get up and running," "warm and fuzzies," and "leaves me cold." Knowing someone's preferences can help you tailor your message in that individual's preferred style. Communicating by using words another person prefers is an effective means of establishing rapport. Remember, we like people like ourselves. We click with people who speak the same language as we do.

Knowing preferences can also help you determine the format of your communication. Visualizers want to see well-crafted slides or visual aids. Those with an auditory preference expect you to explain everything and do not want to have to read. People partial to kinesthetics want to be engaged in some kind of activity. When you need to communicate to people in their least preferred method, you can choose your words to simulate their style. For instance, when talking to a visualizer, paint a strong, colorful image with the words he or she prefers. In writing to someone with an auditory preference, use language to create a distinct tone of voice and mimic oral language through alliteration and rhythm. Use action words or feeling words to communicate to a kinesthetically inclined person.

Another way to gain rapport is to use that person's actual words. As part of a class exercise, I was asked to describe why I like skiing and do not like attending Broadway musicals. My partner for the class wrote down my description of skiing and used my words to convince me that going to a musical would be a fun experience. This was the exchange:

ME: I like skiing because it gets me outside during the winter. I enjoy breathing in the crisp, cold air and riding the chairlift to the top, where I see a scenic panorama of the mountains around me with snow-covered trees. I usually stand at the top and drink in the scenery for a few minutes before I take off. Then I swish down the mountain, enjoying the sensation of movement and being part of the snow-covered trail. Usually, my family is with me and we can enjoy this activity together.

HER: The great thing about Broadway shows is that they get you out in the winter or any time of the year. As you walk up the theater stairs, you can drink in the atmosphere of the beautiful, old theater and breathe in all the aromas. Before you find your seat, you can stand at the top and admire the theater's décor and ornamentation. Then as the show begins, you can sense the excitement of the other people and enjoy being part of the audience. You can bring your family and enjoy this activity together.

Her description did make Broadway shows seem more appealing to me.

Besides matching others' words, another technique to gain rapport is to match body language and manner of speaking. We tend to do this naturally, like speaking faster around fast talkers. Consciously, we can use these techniques to change the dynamics of an interaction. For instance, when I was interviewing candidates for an open job position, I found that many of the candidates were quite nervous. As they sat very upright and on the edge of the seat, I pulled my chair around to face them and took on the same posture, matching their arms and legs, too. As they described their work experiences, I would start to lean back in my chair, and they would follow suit. Gradually, I would lead them into a more relaxed posture, and this helped them overcome their nerves and resulted in a much better interview. (If your interviewer tries to keep you on edge during an interview, imagine what he or she would be like as a boss.)

Another useful model from NLP is called metaprograms: filters or patterns that we habitually rely on to guide our actions and reactions. They reflect some of the fundamental beliefs we hold about the world, like being an optimist or a pessimist. Here are some key metaprograms that you can use to understand and motivate those around you.

Proactive/reactive A proactive person initiates actions, whereas a reactive person waits until others initiate them before joining in. Reactive people like to gather more information before acting, while proactive people like to learn by doing. Proactives tend to make decisions more quickly than reactives—which has advantages and disadvantages. Proactives tend to use the active voice and action verbs ("I aced the presentation"),

while reactives prefer the passive voice ("The presentation went well"). Reactive people tend to get the opinions of others before they offer their own. They want to know what the situation is before they respond to it. Proactive people tend to offer their opinions first in order to try to shape the situation. When you are in meetings, notice how some people wait until everyone else has spoken before they chime in. Some meeting facilitators can get very frustrated trying to get reactives to speak first and trying to get proactives to wait their turn.

Toward/away from motivation Some people are motivated by achieving a particular goal in the future and are "toward" focused. They know what they want and like to set goals to get it. They are often visionaries and work toward achieving their visions. Others are more motivated by avoiding problems or punishments. They are "away from" focused and know what they don't want. They are good at finding problems and errors and at learning from their experiences. Toward-motivated people tend to overlook past problems in order to focus on future goals, while away-from-motivated people tend to miss opportunities because they are too focused on all the potential problems. Consider the old adage of using a carrot or stick approach to motivate others. Sticks won't work on people who want to achieve a goal and will likely de-motivate them. Similarly, carrots won't work on people who need sticks, as future rewards are not as meaningful as avoiding potential problems now. Being aware of this metaprogram is helpful because people naturally use the method that motivates them, thinking that it works for everybody. If the carrot isn't working, try the stick.

Internal/external standards   If you ask me to determine if I've done a good job, I have an internal barometer that decides this despite what others may say. If others praise a job I've done but I'm not keen on it, then it wasn't a good job. Other people use external standards like the opinions of others to determine the quality of their work. If other people say it's good, then it's good. They use feedback to guide their actions, while internally guided people are more likely to ignore feedback if it doesn't align with their own perceptions. In extreme, internally guided people can be aloof and arrogant, ignoring those around them and doing what they want. In extreme, externally guided people can be too concerned with what others might think or say and flip-flop based on opinion. Benchmarking others and performance feedback play important roles for those who hold external standards. Internally guided people are less likely to change their behavior based on performance reviews. However, internally guided people are less likely to be swayed by a crowd or caught up in fads.

Options/procedures To determine a course of action, some people require a set of options or scenarios to choose from. These people do not believe in a right way to accomplish something, but in multiple right ways depending on the situation. Others believe that there is one right way to accomplish something; they are interested in developing the proper procedures to achieve the task at hand and are distracted by multiple options. Often, procedure-driven people grow impatient with explanations and say, "Just give me the answer." Options-driven people want plan A, plan B, etc., and find it hard to follow a methodology exactly—but they tend to be good innovators because they have a hard time adhering to rules and strive to find a better, or sometimes just a different, way to do things. They can be infuriating because they have to change the rules. People who need procedures are good at finding and disseminating best practices and working toward the most efficient processes. They are good at standardizing and creating fair and consistent practices. However, they are uncomfortable with thinking outside the box because they like to create the boxes.

General/specific General people think about the big picture and may gloss over the details. Often the dreamers, they like to take a top-down approach to a problem and understand the broad scope before they act on a specific issue. Specific people like to bite off smaller chunks of the world and put them in sequence. They prefer to work bottom up and are often the realists. I am a general/big picture thinker and need to understand the whole before I can relate to the part. For instance, when writing performance reviews for my staff, I do a first pass at all of them. In subsequent revisions, I become more detailed until all the reviews are done. I need to understand the big picture of relative performance before I can get specific about the individual. Other people prefer to write one review at a time. These same people like to master a particular piece of information before moving to the next piece. General thinkers can get into trouble by thinking too big and by constantly expanding the scope of what they want to tackle. Specific thinkers can get bogged down in details unrelated to the problem they need to solve, or they can miss the broader impact of their actions.

Match/mismatch   When comparing items, some people will naturally see what is similar. In learning something new, they will often use an analogy that this is much the same as that. Other people will naturally see what is dissimilar in a comparison. When learning something new, they will point out all the ways in which it is different from something known. Most people are capable of seeing both similarities and differences but have a preference for the order—first similarities, then differences, or vice versa. When talking to people who like to match, you'll notice that they tend to agree with you before they start to disagree. Mismatchers automatically play devil's advocate before they begin to see your perspective. Matchers may find mismatchers obstinate and contrary. Similarly, mismatchers may find matchers spineless and pliable. However, it is usually a matter of letting people process information in the manner most comfortable to them, agreeing or disagreeing, before they render their final opinion.

Keep in mind that these metaprograms are behavior patterns and not personality traits, meaning that people aren't just one way or the other and that they can change from one to the other. We have a preference for one pattern over the other in specific situations, like a habit. With conscious effort, we can identify and change our habits and also identify patterns in others. Being aware of our own preferences and those of our colleagues can help us tailor our message so that others can relate to it and act on it. Otherwise, much of what we say is just words with little meaning falling on deaf ears.

Even when we take care to craft both the context and the content of our message, sometimes we still have a hard time being heard. To be honest, I am only infrequently successful at getting people to take my advice. To be even more honest, I rarely heed advice given to me, even though I realize that some advice I've gotten has been incredibly prescient. Still I listen, and I nod my head, and I understand, sort of, but I rarely assimilate and act on the imparted wisdom. Some of this has to do with being internally directed, but some has to do with how we learn. My intellect gets the concept, but my subconscious mind, which really controls actions, is left out of the loop.

Think about it. The majority of the actions you take are controlled by your subconscious mind. You don't think about how you chew, how you walk, how you focus your eyes, yet you do all these things. Some actions, like those above, can easily become conscious and can be changed with some thinking.

Others are not readily controlled, like your blood pressure or heart rate, though biofeedback scientists and some swamis claim success with those. So why do we think that an intellectual understanding of a concept will change our behavior? Knowing that I need to exercise more and eat more vegetables doesn't make me do it. Knowing that I shouldn't get angry at my kids doesn't stop the emotion from welling up inside me when I see the mess they created in the living room. These habits are not controlled by my intellect, but by my subconscious. Does that mean we are doomed to never change? Of course not.

Serendipitously, my years in training and development coincided with when my children were little. I would experiment with my kids and then bring those insights to work, where I could experiment on adults. Teaching my kids that the street was dangerous was not about finding the right explanation. I created an experience for them. We stood on the shoulder of a busy road during rush hour, where we could feel the cars speeding by us, and it was frightening. Never once afterward did they venture into a street without me until they were old enough. Anytime I needed to teach them something important, I created the experience for them, and they learned. If I had explained it to them, all they would have heard is "blah, blah, blah." (Now that they are teenagers, all they hear is "blah, blah, blah.")

As you read this, you may be reminded of a training course that created a safe learning environment where you could try out new experiences and get feedback. For both adults and children, this is the most effective method of training. Primarily, we learn from our mistakes. When we err in a big way, our entire mind is engaged. We feel stupid, embarrassed, or ashamed, and we become more aware of our situation as the realization of how we negatively impacted the world sets in. Our normal thinking surrenders to an intensity of feeling. Our subconscious gets the message. We see to it that we never make that mistake again. We learn.

This is why so much self-help is ineffectual. It provides concepts and steps and advice and all sorts of "blah, blah, blah" that you already know. "I know that already! What I really need is something to make me do it!" you think in frustration as you hear the same advice over and over again. What you need to do is experience the consequences of your actions in a negative, emotional way.

I've tested this out in my classes. I structured two sessions, which were part of a weeklong training course, to embarrass and deceive the students. Essentially, the instructor would trick the class into doing the opposite of what they learned earlier in the week and then berate them for fouling up. These sessions always got very ugly when the instructor revealed the deception and told them it was all a setup to foment their learning. In the after-class evaluation forms, these classes got the lowest scores and lots of nasty comments. However, in the retention survey sent months later, they consistently ranked it the highest. The students remembered more of what they learned in those classes than in any of the others. By creating a stressful, humiliating experience, I triggered their subconscious learning. This is why boot camps, much more than typical training programs, are able to effect transformative change.

In another example, many years ago one of the people reporting directly to me had a habit of getting lost in details during presentations. Because giving presentations was an important part of his job, this was a big problem. Although I and others coached him, he had strong internal standards and just couldn't change. We would resort to finding others to present his material, which was impacting his career. Finally, I realized that he couldn't internalize the advice we were giving him, and I had to create an experience for him. I arranged for a number of senior management to attend his next presentation and filled them in on why they were there and asked them to be vocal when they were getting too much detail. My direct report was unaware of all this. At the meeting, he got lost in the details and received some feedback from his audience. He refocused, excelled for a while, and then got lost again. He received some stronger feedback. After the third time, when the comments got loud and derisive, he became emotional and then I saw a lightbulb go on in his head. His problem with excessive detail ended right there and then.

What this means is that if you have something to teach another person, and advice is just not working, stop telling that person and instead show him or her. It's not that the person won't listen, he or she can't listen. So if want to create a compelling vision of Camelot in order to motivate your knights, you need to think about how you want to say it, as well as what you want to say. Otherwise, you'll just end up with the same old song and dance that everyone tunes out.

> **Top 10 Reasons Why Singing, Rapping, or Dancing Business Presentations Should Be Banned**
>
> 1. I feel like I'm in kindergarten. When do I get a gold star?
> 2. Do I really have to sing in front of all these people?
> 3. How come I don't see upper management dance the quarterly earnings?
> 4. Hmm, what rhymes with transaction processing? No action progressing?
> 5. I think "cost improvement initiatives" lends itself to an iambic pentameter kind of beat.
> 6. I'll illustrate the new employee benefits portal with a pirouette followed by a running leap à la Twyla Tharp to demonstrate the freedom it provides.
> 7. That last song was about my dad, who was always there for me. This next song is about how we can lower our inventory levels.
> 8. Which would enhance my ideas for a new marketing campaign more—the bongos or timbales?
> 9. Everybody now, sing with me "low cost strat-e-gy, strat-e-gy, strat-e-gy now"
> 10. The new release of SAP really inspires me creatively.

Chapter Vocabulary

Emotivate   Using utopian visions of the future, dramatic pleas, and dire consequences to inspire an organization to change. *Related*: hamplify

Megaphor   When one metaphor just isn't enough.

Multi-tedia presentation   Using many ways to present boring information.

Resolutionary   1. A revolutionary new change program that just amounts to a catchy slogan and an expensive PR campaign. 2. Expecting a change to happen by declaring it so.

Verbi-age   1. The effect in which listening to certain people talk causes premature aging. 2. Others' use of jargon and slang causing a person to feel really old.

7
Oh, Don't Grovel

The proper way of sucking up

What are Arthur and his men supposed to do now that they've realized Camelot is a silly place? Fortunately, God arrives on the scene (He certainly has good timing) to give the men a mission and some purpose in their lives. Only, Arthur keeps groveling. It's really hard to talk to someone who keeps averting his eyes, toadying, and apologizing for his general unworthiness in the presence of the Lord. What's a God to do? He tells Arthur to knock off the prostration and assigns him the task of obtaining the Holy Grail. The men rejoice at their new assignment.

You can't really blame Arthur for groveling. The God of the Old Testament is quite a scary character, annihilating entire towns, turning people to pillars of salt, and having men swallowed whole by whales. I think I would suck up plenty to someone who had that much power over me. In modern corporations, the upper management does exercise quite a bit of control over the lives of their employees. They decide who gets promoted, who gets more money, who gets a sane lifestyle, and who keeps his or her job. So how do you deal with gods of the workplace?

The first lesson everyone who wants to stay employed needs to learn is that there is a right way to suck up, and a wrong way. The right way maintains your dignity and fosters better communication. The wrong way reverts you to being a child trying to butter up your teacher—though, sometimes, depending on your upper management, you have no choice but to act like a child.

In Chapter 3, I talked about how we tend to promote egomaniacs, but there are some good leaders out there, and fortunately I've worked for a few. Good leaders hate suck-ups. To get the best information available to them, good leaders encourage everyone to contribute as equals. They want to know all the opinions of their followers in order to make informed decisions. Leaders who surround themselves with sycophants usually do so because they need reassurance that they actually do possess the skills and intelligence needed for their jobs. They are also under the impression that, instead of relying on a good team, they need to be the heroes who have all the answers.

In the last chapter, I discussed the differences in how people perceive information. In this chapter, I explore roles that people play in workplace interactions, especially between superiors and subordinates, and how to suck up in a way that maintains both dignity and integrity. I'd like to illustrate with a story from my career.

When I was pregnant with my first child, I suffered terrible morning sickness and became very finicky about food. Usually, I eat anything put in front of me, but I found then that many foods, especially junk foods, turned my stomach. At the time, I was working on a very stressful consulting engagement, and my client was the chief information officer (CIO) of a fortune 100 company. He loved nothing better than to give consultants a really hard time. Presenting to him was always an exercise in self-preservation as he asked for details and more information and challenged every recommendation. He seemed to pride himself on being difficult, and we all dreaded our monthly updates. One morning, as I was preparing to present my findings to him, I suddenly became nauseated. After barfing in the women's room, I freshened my breath and, still feeling ill, headed toward his office, where several members of my team joined me. A very unhealthy spread of Danishes and donuts, the sight of which made me queasy, was available for breakfast.

I had already shown my recommendations to this CIO's direct reports and obtained their support as well as researched what other companies were doing in this area. I also knew, through his direct reports, that he agreed with the recommendations. After I presented my findings and recommendations, he began to grill me: "How many people did you talk to in each of the companies?" "What were their positions?" "How many companies did not answer your survey?" Not being in the best of dispositions, I gave a long sigh and put my hand up in a stop gesture.

"Look, I don't mean to be rude, but I'm seven months pregnant, and right now I'm experiencing a bout of morning sickness. If there is a particular recommendation you have issues with, I will be happy to do more analysis to address your concerns. But I'd rather not be raked over the coals this morning just for amusement's sake."

My colleagues were stunned and a sudden silence filled the room like an oppressive fog. The CIO looked surprised for an instant and then broke out in a smile. "Okay. I won't give you a hard time. I agree with almost everything you presented here today." He then asked me to investigate one recommendation further. After the meeting, I received lots of feedback, good and bad, on my boldness. The jury was out on whether it had been a good move. That was answered at the next early-morning status meeting. This time, the same breakfast spread was available with some additions. At one end of the table were small bowls of granola and dried fruits and nuts. He pointed to this when I entered and made special mention that he had asked his secretary to order healthy food, just for me. By standing up to him, not by being rude but by being candid, I had earned his respect. He never gave me a hard time again, and he supplied healthy snacks at all our meetings.

A similar scenario took place when I was a manager in a big corporation. One of the senior vice presidents was notoriously bad about keeping appointments. I had an office near his and often saw him in the hallway. As part of a major project I was leading, I asked him to take part in a 10-minute phone interview with a consulting company to determine his objectives and expectations. No one wanted to proceed on the project without getting his input first. I coordinated a time with his assistant and then informed him personally about the call's objectives and agenda. Every time I saw him in the hall, I reminded him about the telephone call in a joking way. The scheduled appointment came and went without him dialing in and without any prior cancellation, inconveniencing several people. The next time I saw him in the hallway, I gave him "the evil eye" and exclaimed, "You bum!" The others in the hallway looked quite shocked, and he was startled at first but then began laughing. When we met later on, he told me that no one else had ever complained to him about his unreliability, so he never addressed it. Afterward, he informed me whenever he couldn't make an appointment and always had someone reschedule, a courtesy he did not extend to everyone.

What worked in both of these situations is that I spoke up for myself in a tone of an equal talking to an equal. If I had taken the tone of a whiny child ("I'm pregnant, so stop picking on me"), I would have appeared weak and incompetent. Likewise, if I had adopted an accusatory stance ("Three people in Asia woke up during the night to accommodate your schedule and you didn't bother to show up"), I would have ended my career by treating a senior leader like a naughty boy. Yet the whiny child and scolding parent are natural reactions in these situations.

I believe certain roles are ingrained in our behavior. Take the typical family gathering at holidays, for instance. As adults, why do we still act like children around our parents, and as parents, why do we treat our adult children like kids? The CIO in the first example acted like a strict and scolding parent, with the subtext "you'll never be good enough." A natural reaction to this role is to behave like a child. In the second example, the senior VP behaved like a naughty child, not taking responsibility for his appointments. A natural reaction would be to scold him for that.

Transactional analysis (TA), developed by Eric Berne, author of *Games People Play*, is a simple model for understanding "transactions," or conversations between people. According to TA, we use three modes—adult, parent, and child—for communicating or dealing with others. In other words, in a conversation both parties can behave like adults or equals, or one party can play the role of parent to another's child. Adult/adult interactions are typically rational exchanges between perceived peers and are generally the most productive. Parent/child interactions entail one party assuming superiority over the other. These tend to be more emotional. When someone assumes a role, he or she dictates the type of response desired. Someone who assumes a parent role wants a child's response and vice versa, while adults usually want to deal with other adults. There are two modes of parenting—nurturing and controlling—and two modes of childishness—cooperative and rebellious.

Here's some background to the theory. I'm not sure if I believe all of it, but it is interesting. The parent part of us records events and experiences without analysis, in much the same way we listened to our parents when we were very young. Our parents taught us many useful things, like looking both ways before crossing the street and brushing our teeth before bedtime. We assimilated these concepts without actually testing them for ourselves. The child in us records our emotions and feelings, usually in response to something else. The child records the joy of splashing in puddles and the disappointment of having to go to bed. As a child grows up, he or she develops a new kind of mental processing, one that evaluates both events and feelings. This is the adult. The adult filters information and works with both the parent and child parts to determine beliefs and knowledge.

Parent—taught concept
Child—felt concept
Adult—learned concept

The parent mode demands unquestioning agreement from others on pronouncements that are based more on belief than reason. The parent decides what is good and bad and determines what is good for you. Depending on the situation, this role can be either very supportive (my child can do no wrong!) or critical (you can't do anything right!). Often a person's self-talk consists of a critical parent. In contrast, the child mode is fully spontaneous and emotional. The child in us is creative, imaginative, emotional, powerful, impulsive, self-centered, and fearful. Motivated by fear or shame or the need for approval and acceptance, our cooperative child obeys the parents. The rebellious child is obstinate and argumentative because of imposed parental control. Neither the parent nor the child is very reasonable. That role is left to the adult. The adult uses reason to weigh the emotions of the child and the beliefs of the parent in order to determine what is true. The adult is able to disassociate from a situation and take on other perspectives.

When we are very young, we learn certain patterns of behavior that work well for us as children. These patterns may no longer serve us well as adults, but often we use them anyway because we are habituated to them, just as at holiday family gatherings. Even though we're grown, we still feel like children reliving childhood angst! Worse yet, these patterns can carry over to the workplace. Have you ever found yourself feeling and acting like a child at work without wanting to and not knowing why? This is likely because someone is using the parent role as a management style.

Often, I've found that when certain personalities attain positions of leadership, they emulate role models of authority from childhood and resort to the role of parent. This is how they think they are supposed to act. You can recognize the role because these leaders typically turn every conversation into a lecture. They are also masters at using your words against you. If you voice a concern, they will ask you what you've done to address it. In this role, they effectively stymie adult communications from their direct reports (and even peers!) and force them into the child role. This has two net effects: first, the child's opinions are given less weight than the parent's, and, second, direct reports don't communicate candidly because they're afraid of getting in trouble or they want to be "good." Personally, I've always had difficulty assuming the child role, even as a child. (I went to parochial school and have the scars to prove it.) Whenever I'm forced into a child role, I either disengage from the conversation or become rebellious because it seems pointless to me to have an opinion, let alone express it.

How to tell if someone is using the "parent" on you:
- Physically, this person is trying to put him or herself above you, by sitting behind a desk while you are in front of it, or sometimes by sitting on your desk or standing above you. The person may also sit very upright or take up as much space as possible.
- The facial expression is usually a very calm, patient smile.
- The voice takes on a sing-song quality, like an actor in a performance, with a full, rich tone.
- Concerns and problems are turned around on you. So what have *you* done to address this?

- A two-way conversation quickly turns into a lecture on how it is (you are) or how it should be (you should be).

WARNING! *If your interviewer exhibits any of this behavior while you are on a job interview, run, don't walk, to the nearest exit.*

Being forced into a child role is completely unempowering. The only way to avoid becoming immobilized is to change the transaction from parent/child to adult/adult. Responding as an adult, rather than a child, helps to bring the conversation to the proper level. However, this is difficult if the other person wants to avoid adult interactions. Although confronting the situation may be uncomfortable, it will change the nature of the interaction. Here are some retorts you can use:
- "My purpose was to discuss the issues with you in a candid manner and get your opinion, not to jump to answers or to blame."
- "I feel you are not really interested in my opinion."
- "I'd be a lot happier if we could change the nature of the conversation from a lecture to a discussion."

Using "I feel…" statements may not be natural, especially to men, but they can be a very useful way to turn a conversation. People can't argue that your feelings are wrong.

Changing a parent/child interaction to an adult/adult interaction is the best way to suck up to your senior leaders. If you insist on acting like a responsible adult, you will gain newfound respect from both your superiors and your peers, and it may lead to an environment of dialogue over dictums. Tolerating patronizing interactions can have a devastating effect on an organization. Candid feedback, dissenting opinions, challenging debate, and bad news can get lost in an environment of "violent agreement" with the senior leadership. Worse yet, the intelligence of many minds can become subjugated to the dictates of the one, all-knowing Father, who may send you off to find the Holy Grail unchallenged.

> ## Suck-up Phrases
>
> Although most leaders who use the parental tone are doing it unconsciously, some can't tolerate adult conversations and will insist on your playing a subordinate role. When dealing with these leaders, be careful to suck up in the cooperative child mode. Personally I've had a hard time with this role, but I've picked out some of the best suck-up phrases to keep handy.
>
> | Childhood suck-up phrase | Workplace equivalent |
> | --- | --- |
> | You're the best teacher ever! | I really want to learn from you. |
> | Is there extra credit? | Tell me how I can do more. |
> | I can stay after school. | I don't mind putting in long hours. |
> | Will that be on the test? | What performance measures are you monitoring? |
> | That test was easy. | I'd like to add some stretch goals. |
> | This is my favorite class. | I love working on your projects. |

Chapter Vocabulary

A tension deficit disorder   The inability of a manager to recognize that you are overworked and stressed and so continues to pile on more work.

Employee emcowerment   Initiatives and training rolled out under the guise of managing change but are really meant to get employees to toe the line.

Idealation   Praising someone sycophantically for his or her superior creativity.

Intellectual carpital   That small clique who fancy themselves smarter than everyone else and snarkily deprecate management decisions.

Sod-off Phrases

It is also very useful to know the proper way to tell your peers that you don't want to do anything for them, and they should sod off. I mean, if you did everything you were asked to do, your day would be filled with work and not surfing the Internet and playing Sudoku online. However, done improperly, it could result in nasty comments on your 360-degree feedback review. Here's the right way to say "sod off" and the suggested order of use.

Sod-off phrase	Understood subtext
1. I'd love to help you, but my schedule is so jam-packed that I don't even have the time to do my own work.	I'm more important than you. Try some other time.
2. Unfortunately, I can't help you right now. I'm involved in a super-secret project for our next big breakthrough that is already consuming 120% of my time.	I'm so way more important than you. You could try again, but what's the point?
3. My manager has told me that my biggest development opportunity this year is to learn how to say "no."	Bugger off already!

8
Now We Leap Out of the Rabbit

The perils of poor planning

Once again, Arthur and his men arrive at a strange castle, which turns out to be French, and question one of the guards about the master of the castle, hoping to enlist him in their quest. This tactic hasn't worked out well for Arthur in the past, and it doesn't work out well for him now. The guard tells Arthur that they already have a grail. (You'd think Arthur would try something different, like sending a messenger or inviting everyone to a giant feast at Camelot or setting up a Facebook page called "Where's the Grail?" but, no, there he is, going door to door, like a Jehovah's witness or vacuum salesman expecting to be greeted with open arms. I mean, how do *you* deal with strangers knocking on *your* door?)

So Arthur is not well received at the doors of the French castle, and he and his men are summarily taunted and insulted by John Cleese affecting a ridiculous French accent. Some of the more memorable taunts are "Go boil your bottoms," "I sneeze at you," and "I fart in your general direction." Still, Arthur tries to reason with the uncooperative French guard, asking to speak to his master, until the French get physical and launch a cow over the wall and squash one of the pages (the red shirts [8] of this movie). An incensed Arthur issues the order to charge the castle, but more farm animals (along with farm animal by-products) rain down on them, and the grail seekers must run away. Is all hope lost for Arthur and his men?

---

[8] A red shirt is a character who dies soon after being introduced. It originated with Star Trek fans who noticed that expendable crew members always wore red jerseys on away missions.

Fortunately, Sir Bedevere, ever the clever one, has a plan to penetrate the French castle. He organizes the men to build a giant wooden bunny rabbit. After much collective sawing and hammering, the men wheel the rabbit to the doors of the castle, knock, and watch as the French guards take the bunny inside. "Now comes the surprise," Bedevere explains to the others, "where we all jump out of the bunny and take the French off guard." Only, the men have forgotten to get inside the rabbit. Epic failure! Perhaps, a giant wooden badger? While the men ponder their predicament, the French launch the wooden rabbit at them. Run away! Run away!

Who hasn't seen this type of absence of planning at work? Over the last two decades, I've seen less and less time spent on planning as people become more pressed for time. Recently, I participated in several projects where the prevailing attitude was "We don't have the luxury of doing the proper planning because we need to execute quickly." Needless to say, the time "saved" by not planning was then required three times over in rework.

What fascinates me is that we all know the benefits of project planning—which is why we have jobs titled "project manager," why we list "project management" as a requisite skill in job descriptions, and why we often seek project management certification (PMP)—yet we often abandon this practice and still believe that our project will run smoothly anyway. I'm going to assume that most of you are already acquainted with project management methods and won't belabor their benefits in this chapter. The only thing more boring than reading about project management is writing about it. Instead, I'd like to discuss two lesser known aspects of project planning that you won't find in your typical PMP course but are underscored in our Monty Python scene: planning fallacy and unintended consequences.

Planning Fallacy

Forgetting to get into the rabbit before wheeling it into the castle is probably less an example of bad planning than sheer stupidity. Yet we in business regularly act stupidly when it comes to planning, and much of that is due to planning fallacy. That's a fancy term for confidently believing that our own project will run on schedule, even while knowing that the vast majority of similar projects have run late. This occurs on the small scale, such as it should take me only three hours to clean out the garage even though it took me two days last time, and the large scale, such as major construction projects. The Boston

Big Dig was projected to cost $4 billion and finish in 1998 but actually finished in 2007 at a cost of nearly $15 billion. The Sydney Opera House was planned at a cost of $7 million and a completion date in 1963, but a scaled-down version was actually finished in 1973 for $102 million.

In study after study, psychologists have documented the tendency of people to underestimate how long it will take to complete a task, even given a history of their performance in the past. Thus, telling people to use better planning techniques and to err on the conservative side has little effect. People will still create an overly optimistic forecast despite having a history of the contrary. Psychologists have some theories about why this happens.

Typically, when we plan a task, we start to internalize all the steps required and how long the steps will take. Again typically, we assume a best-case scenario: all the resources will be available, I'll be mentally sharp that day, the equipment will work, I won't get distracted by other things, and so on. With this rosy picture of how everything is going to work out well, we plan our timelines, resource requirements, and costs. Sometimes, we add a fudge factor to account for one or two steps going wrong. The end result is a forecast of how the project should work, given a few mishaps. In actuality, more things will go wrong with a project than will go right. This is why we often cite Murphy's Law. Unfortunately, we usually think of Murphy in hindsight, after the project and not while we are planning it.

When presented with evidence of how past examples took longer, we find exceptions in the history that shouldn't apply to the future. For instance, it should only take me three to four hours to clean out the garage this weekend even though it took me two days the last time I did it. The reasons it took me longer last time was because I found a box of albums from my college days and reminisced over those for a while, and then I found a box of the kids' old toys, and again I reminisced. After that, I found some of the neighbor's tools and returned those to him, and we started chatting, and he ended up showing me his new home theater, and I stayed and watched a movie. I'm sure nothing like that will happen this weekend when I clean out the garage.

In addition to adopting the best-case scenario as our baseline, we also tend to think that our project or situation is unique. Somehow we possess the knowledge, skills, or luck that everyone else lacks. Here's an example from my experience.

*WARNING! *Techno-speak ahead.*

ME: I see in your plan that the ERP [enterprise resource planning software] implementation for Europe will take 18 months. Didn't it take you three years to implement it in South America?

PEER: Yes, yes, but that was our first implementation, and now we know so much more.

ME: Didn't we choose South America to implement first because that was the least complicated business and should have been the easiest implementation?

PEER: Yes, that's true, but now we have all the information and reporting structures set up so we can use them in Europe.

ME: But doesn't Europe have vastly different and more complicated requirements? Did you already build their requirements into the South American system?

PEER: No, no, we don't have the European requirements done yet, but we can use what we built already and just modify as needed. We know so much more now than we did when we began that it shouldn't take as long.

As an outsider to the project, I could easily see the folly of thinking it would take 18 months to complete the complicated ERP implementation, especially when the easy project took three years. Yet, those on the project, even with the knowledge that most implementations take two to three years, still believed their timeline was viable. Psychological studies show that people do a much better job predicting how long it will take others to perform a task than they do predicting their own performance. The difference in the thinking is that when we judge others' performance, we use external information, such as past performance and how long similar tasks took. When we judge our own performance, we use internal narratives that discount our histories by chalking them up to exceptional situations (otherwise known as making excuses) and build an optimistic step-by-step picture of how we think things *should* go. Finally, we are felled by the "better than average" bias into thinking that we can do a much better job than those other people in their projects, because we are smarter or more knowledgeable or better managers. This is the same thinking behind the phrase "It won't happen to me."

The simple way to eliminate the planning fallacy is to look at how similar projects fared in the past and use that as the starting point instead of using the internal step-by-step of how the project *should* proceed. Also, keep Murphy's Law in mind and calculate timelines on the worst-case scenario rather than thinking that everything except for one or two activities will go well.

Unintended Consequences

Now that we've got a plan that accounts for the planning fallacy, we need to think about all the consequences of our plan, like how the wooden rabbit turned into catapult fodder. Obviously, our knights did not consider this when they built it, but what else would you do with a wooden rabbit? Systems thinking, or systems dynamics, is a way of thinking that considers multiple variables and consequences as a complex system that reacts with itself. Linear, or straight line, thinking relies on looking at one variable at a time in a step-by-step process, such as doing A results in B, which then impacts C. In a linear relationship, it is assumed that A has no impact on C, and C has no impact on A or B. It is also assumed that impacts are proportional. Small changes result in small effects. We are taught to think this way throughout elementary school and high school, using sequential steps to solve math and science problems. However, most of the problems we encounter in life are non-linear. Changing B affects A as well as C, while changing C affects A and B, which also has an effect on C, and so on with all sorts of feedback loops.

Most of the relationships found in nature are non-linear. We've often learned this the hard way when introducing non-native species into an environment in order to eradicate another non-native species. Instead, the introduced species wreaked havoc on the entire ecosystem. Now, through an awareness of systems dynamics, we are discovering that most of the relationships in life are non-linear, and short-sighted policies that act linearly often have unintended consequences to the opposite effect. Here are two examples where legislation had exactly the opposite effect of what it intended.

The first is the Endangered Species Act of 1973, which was put in place to protect plants and animals that may potentially become extinct. This act protects the habitats of endangered species, meaning that no development or changes can occur to the land where the species live. Unfortunately, after a species is given endangered status, it can take years before its habitat is designated as protected land. In the meantime, there's nothing to stop owners of property that may be up for protection from making that land uninviting to the endangered species but inviting to developers, putting the species at even greater risk.

In a second example, the Waxman-Hatch Act of 1984 was intended to lower prescription prices and break the monopoly of big pharmaceutical companies with their patented drugs by making it easier for generic products to gain approval and reach the marketplace. This would usher in cheaper alternatives once the patents expired. As a result, the pharmaceutical companies have only a limited amount of time in which to reap profits on their patents, and they substantially increase the margins on their drugs while the patents are still in effect. Unable to compete with generics, they need to recoup all their investments in the short period before expiry, hence the unreasonably high prices of non-generic, prescription drugs (in the United States.)

Similarly, many corporate policies often seem to have the opposite effect of what was originally intended. Management by objectives is my favorite example. Although on the surface it seems like a good way to ensure employees are focused on achieving a common set of corporate objectives, I think it may have the opposite effect in practice. Here goes:

Behind-the-Times Corporation (BTC) decides to implement management by objectives (and pay for performance) in order to give employees an incentive to work hard on corporate goals and not on tasks that won't contribute to strategic objectives. This new compensation plan includes salary plus a performance-based bonus of some combination of cash, raise, stock, and stock options. For instance, a manager performing at a satisfactory level would get a 10% bonus, 2% raise, 100 stock options, and no stock. After a talent search, BTC hires a new HR director, Sheila, who starts in February and will work full time to implement the policy before the end of the year.

Sheila is a certified project manager so she starts by putting together a plan. The corporate goals are already well defined, so she doesn't have to worry about those. She starts to outline the steps needed:

1. Determine bonus pool
2. Determine stock options and stock grant pool
3. Determine performance rewards by job level (e.g., associate, professional, manager, director, etc.)
4. Determine performance rewards by performance level (e.g., unsatisfactory, satisfactory, exceptional, etc.)
5. Develop process and form for performance evaluation
6. Communicate new process
7. Conduct training
8. Implement new process

As Sheila enumerates these tasks, she realizes that each is a major project in itself. Plus, Sheila has assumed that the performance ratings and job levels are standard across the company. After a few weeks, she discovers that R&D and marketing use a rating scale of 1 to 6 while other departments use a scale of 1 to 5. Worse yet, job titles and levels vary widely. Sheila reports her findings to the CEO, and they decide to put together some project teams to address these issues and work on the various tasks. The CFO takes ownership of determining the size and scope of the cash and stock bonus pools, and he hires a compensation consultancy to manage these efforts. Sheila hires an HR consulting firm to lead the effort to standardize performance levels and job levels across the company. This second initiative ends up involving numerous employees across many departments, and, because of the contentious nature of the results, this initiative ends up taking eight months. At the end of the project, many employees are disgruntled because their job titles as well as their performance ranking scale were "flattened" as a result of layers of hierarchy being eliminated. Sheila extends the consultants' contract to conduct change management sessions to deal with these issues, which seem to be the center of everyone's attention.

Now that she has standardized the performance rankings and job levels, Sheila puts together a model of how the process will work and the new evaluation forms. She sets up meetings with each of the department heads to get their input. Sheila receives some very helpful feedback and gets mostly positive reactions. Aiming to roll out the new system by the end of the year, Sheila realizes that she has only six weeks to communicate and train everyone. She also realizes that for the first go-round, it will have to be a paper-based process.

Sheila explains her predicament to the internal communications and training departments, pleading with them to help her get the information out to the organization as quickly as possible. The internal communications and training groups jump through hoops and pull together some excellent communications and training materials. However, this is at the cost of postponing new product training for the sales force, and now they will have to be pulled in from the field during the new year. Sheila knows she will get complaints because normally sales training occurs during the end-of-year slow period and not when the salespeople want to be out at their customers.

Sheila spends the next six weeks training everyone so that the new process will be in place for the year-end evaluations. The process and the forms are fairly easy to understand, so Sheila doesn't get many questions or requests for help. However, the various departments are using a word document and altering the form as they wish, resulting in multiple versions. Worse, collating the information is time intensive and error prone. Because Sheila can't possibly collect and verify the data on her own, she solicits everyone else in HR to help her, delaying the new benefits rollout, and also hires temporary help. Many people become upset that these temps have access to very sensitive information, so Sheila promises not to do it this way next year.

After an arduous few weeks, Sheila audits some of the information and realizes that many of the evaluations were completely arbitrary, as the goals were not written in a SMART (Specific, Measurable, Actionable, Realistic, and Time-bound) format. It was also apparent that some departments were hard graders while others were easy, meaning that bonuses were not fairly distributed across the departments. Thankfully, that information is not shared beyond HR and the CEO and CFO. Sheila determines that the first priority for the next go-round is to improve fairness. Her goals for the new year are:

1. Implement an automated process to ensure oversight of the entire process
2. Train the organization on SMART goals
3. Develop standardized evaluation criteria to improve fairness

Sheila meets with a manager from the company's IT department to find out what it will take to develop a system. The manager informs her that IT does not have a budget to work on this system and asks how much she has in her budget. Sheila realizes that she will have to ask the CFO for money. Meanwhile, the IT manager is to put together a cost estimate.

A week later, the IT manager sends Sheila an email with a spreadsheet detailing 525 project tasks. Sheila scrolls down the page to look at the bottom-line cost and nearly has a heart attack. The estimate is $350K, which includes the cost of a full-time project manager, a part-time analyst, and programming consultants. The IT manager explains that because she did not include this project in the annual budgeting and planning process, she will have to pay for consultants to do work normally done by internal staff. What he doesn't explain is that IT has an unwritten policy of doubling the estimates for HR projects because of some prior bad experiences. Sheila brings the cost estimate to the CFO meeting, and they agree that all this work is not needed for a simple performance evaluation system. The CFO sets aside $150K, but the two agree that they will tell IT that they only have $100K.

Let me now skip ahead and summarize what happens over the next year. After the initial pilot of a simple and inexpensive system, they realize that they need a better system to collate data, get the reports needed for slicing and dicing information, and integrate with the current HR and financial systems. They spend $350K to get the system up and running. IT also hires a full-time person to support the system and a part-time person to staff the help desk. The procedures Sheila puts in place to ensure fairness across departments become quite complicated, and an HR person is needed to facilitate the meetings. A permanent employee is added to the HR department.

After year two of the new process, HR becomes inundated with complaints because goals evolved over the year and could not be modified in the system and were thus rated as unmet. Another complaint was that reviewing the performance objectives at the end of the year did not improve performance as it was too late to impact the results for that year. Sheila realizes that the company should review goals more often in order to be effective and decides that a midyear review is required, but those changes require new procedures as well as new functionality in the system.

In year three, the organization now conducts periodic reviews that consist of revising goals, ensuring SMART compliance, approving revised goals, summarizing performance to date, reviewing performance with managers, and documenting this activity in the computer system. This typically takes about four days per review. Managers spend less "face" time with their direct reports in order to complete and approve paperwork and attend calibration and evaluation sessions. All other work grinds to halt during the review cycles.

In year four, the organization begins to layer itself so that, in order to limit the paperwork burden on each individual, no one has more than three or four direct reports. Job levels are adjusted to reflect the new layers, causing HR to revisit the standard job levels, causing a ripple effect in every system and process that uses job levels, including the pay-for-performance system. Eventually, someone will ask why the company has so many middle managers, and an initiative will ensue to de-layer the organization, likely run by a consulting company.

Wow!!! That's a lot of work and expense just to focus on corporate goals. I hope that implementing pay for performance is actually one of the corporate goals, because Behind-the-Times Corporation has added permanent employees, processes, and systems dedicated to this goal. How was Sheila to know what the ultimate consequences of her job were going to be? Sheila acts as any manager in a large corporation would act. She has a goal and she achieves it. She encounters a problem and she addresses it. She encounters another problem and she solves that one, too, and so on in a linear fashion. Yet, the consequences of implementing one simple performance improvement system end up having a huge impact on the organization.

Earlier I mentioned the terms "systems thinking" and "systems dynamics" that refer to looking at the world as a complicated system in which many factors affect many others. The beauty of systems thinking is that it is a different model that shows non-linear relationships. Our brains adapt to models and use them to govern our thinking. Unfortunately, most models are linear, providing simple step-by-step, one-cause-with-one-effect relationships. Look at the steps I outlined for the pay-for-performance implementation. This is very typical of how we look at the world and is the format we use for plans and standard operating procedures. Step 1 leads to step 2, which leads to step 3, and so on in a linear fashion. Sometimes we include a feedback loop or two that says "return to step x."

We approach project plans with the same thinking. A Gantt chart lays out all of our steps with beginning and end dates in a sequential fashion, and, to make the chart more useful, some of us will include dependencies and critical paths. Although this thinking is helpful and would have been useful to determine that you need to get inside the rabbit *before* you wheel it into the castle, it, too, is a linear model of the world. A flowchart is a definite improvement, yet it operates under the assumption that most of the steps are linear with just some branches and feedback loops. A flowchart with lots of branches and loops is incomprehensible. This leaves us with the problem of how to depict a messy, complicated world in which everything affects everything else?

I'm not sure who first developed the following technique for modeling complex systems, but John Sterman and Nelson Repenning at the MIT Sloan School of Management teach a course and have written numerous articles and a textbook on how to model complex problems using it. Basically, the model starts with identifying a simple feedback loop and determining if it is a reinforcing loop or a balancing loop.

Positive or Reinforcing Feedback Loop	**Negative or Balancing Feedback Loop**
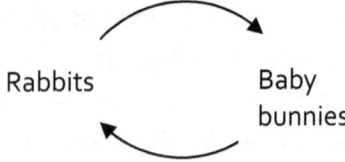	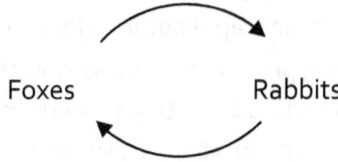
A population explosion is a well-known example of a reinforcing loop. Two pro-creating rabbits can easily turn into a nightmare, as the number of babies increases the number of eventual adults, which increases the number of babies. The result is exponential growth of the rabbits over time. The loop also works in reverse, with a decrease in babies resulting in a decrease in adult rabbits, ending with an exponential decline of the population.	The predator/prey relationship is a familiar example of a balancing loop. As the number of rabbits increases, more rabbits are killed by foxes, allowing more foxes to reproduce. As more foxes reproduce and kill rabbits, the less the rabbits reproduce. Hence, the lack of rabbits for food has a negative impact on the fox population, allowing more rabbits to multiply. Balancing loops move toward a steady-state condition.

A more complicated set of loops showing the effect of stretch goals (extending yourself to the limit) on employee performance looks like this:

Adding Stretch Goals Causal Loop

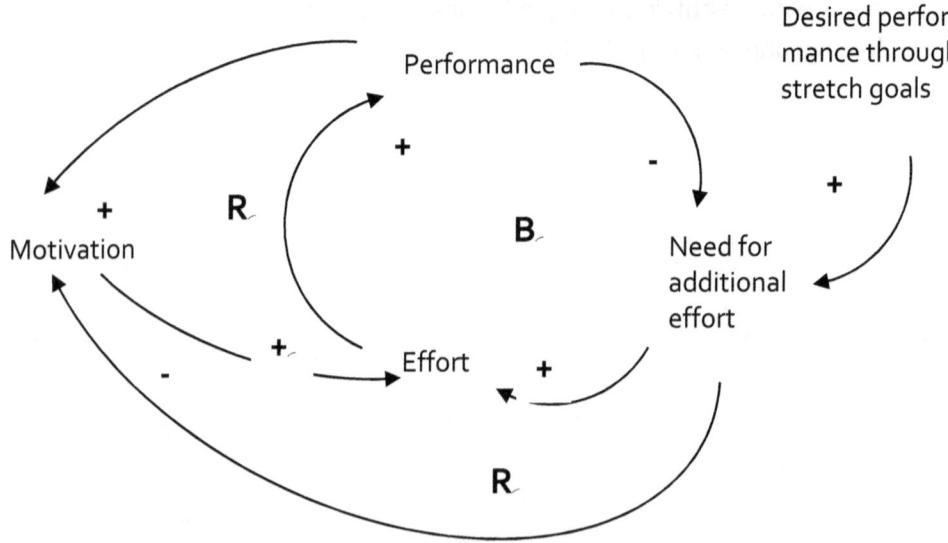

(Repenning, *Theory Building with Causal Loops*, 2006)

Starting in the upper right of this diagram, the desired performance through the use of stretch goals leads to a need for additional effort, which leads to more effort and greater performance. Greater performance offsets the need for more effort. This is a balancing loop, as noted by a "B," and tends toward a steady state. All balancing loops, like prey and predator relationships, tend toward equilibrium. If the predator eats too much prey, there will be less prey to support the predator population, which will then decrease from starvation, allowing more prey to survive, and so on.

The loop on the left shows the relationship between performance and motivation. The loops marked with an "R" are reinforcing loops. Reinforcing loops are also known as vicious cycles. Increasing performance leads to higher motivation, which leads to more effort and better performance (our reinforcing loop), but which, as a result, requires less effort and less of a need for effort, and a happy steady state returns. However, as the bottom loop depicts, continually stretching the goals and applying more need for additional effort lowers motivation, decreases effort, and decreases performance, which then increases the need for more effort, which decreases motivation, and so on. At some point, the system reaches a tipping point, where the happy steady state changes into a downward spiral of ever poorer performance. I have seen this particular dynamic play out in businesses when management continually asks for more and more performance from fewer and fewer resources. At first, this mechanism works, but eventually employees burn out or become disillusioned, and the whole cycle breaks down. Ultimately, you can't do more with less. You do less with less—perhaps with less waste—but definitely less.

Of course, you don't need a fancy diagram to tell you this. Using some common sense to ask "What happens next?" "And after that, what happens?" is probably more useful than any model. What will happen if we continually overwork and stress our employees? How much time and effort have other companies put into implementing pay for performance? What happens when we increase the administrative burden of our employees? Why can't we trust our managers and employees to work toward our mission without a monitoring system? Bedevere, what do you think the Frenchmen, who just lobbed live animals at you and Arthur, will do with a large wooden rabbit?

Arthur Decides to Decentralize

DIRECTOR: Action!

HISTORIAN: Defeat at the castle seems to have utterly disheartened King Arthur. The ferocity of the French taunting took him completely by surprise, and Arthur became convinced that a new strategy was required if the quest for the Holy Grail were to be brought to a successful conclusion. Arthur, having consulted his closest knights, decided that they should separate and search for the grail individually.

(Unfortunately, after this narration, the historian gets killed by a knight while his wife watches.)

And so Arthur spaketh to his minions, er, men:

> *My knights, together we are slow and unwieldy. We are unable to be nimble and respond quickly to our competition. Our slowest performers have become a weight around the necks of our fastest knights, who must bear their burden. Let us separate into different divisions, where we can each concentrate on our strengths unencumbered by the needs of the other operating units. Separately, we can be quick and flexible and react quickly to our environment. We will cover more ground as individual units, and we will induce friendly competition amongst each other that will improve our performance.*
>
> *Let us separate and each use our strengths to discover the goal, er, grail.*

The French Guard's Guide to Planning

Before you develop your plan, here is a helpful checklist to make sure you take into consideration both the planning fallacy and the law of unintended consequences.

- ☐ You stupid sod, did you even think to find other people who have done the same project? It's not like in this information age, with all the interwebby connections upon which you waste half your day, you can do some research or find other people with experience.

- ☐ No, you are not smarter in any way, shape, or form than the other people who have led similar projects. Frankly, I see your lips moving as you read this, you slow, useless excuse for a peon. Add more time to your plan because the rest of world operates in fast forward compared to you.

- ☐ So you think your project has a higher priority than all the others and will get the most attention from your team? You stupid, sodding pimple on the face of the earth, the mere fact that you are leading it means it has the lowest priority, you son of a mouse herder.

- ☐ Your mother was a gooseberry and your father smelled of skunk farts, and your team does not like you and will not work doubly hard to meet the deadlines. They make raspberries in your general direction. Tthhhp, tthhhp.

- ☐ Of course, Murphy does like you, and his law will prevail over everything you do, you silly corporate, sit-in-a-cube-like-a-caged-gerbil, expendable-as-a-pet-goldfish staff member.

- ☐ Did you really think there would be no negative impacts from your project? Ever hear of yin and yang? Ever hear of everything's connected? Ever hear of using your dim-witted, once-in-a-while-a-light-goes-on, cobweb-filled brain? There are no unintended consequences, just consequences you, marshmallow-minded walking fount of feebleness, didn't think of.

- ☐ Of course, your human resources are 100% efficient and don't need any maintenance or down time. Just like your machine resources. Always up and running, like the diarrhea that has replaced your brain tissue, you silly, smug project mangler.

- ☐ Did you think through how the other departments, customers, etc. would react? Did you think they would just roll over and do what you want, like Arthur commanding the Frenchmen? No passive aggression? Do you think you are king? Do you think you are God? Your being is as insignificant as a dust speck on a hair on a paramecium crawling on an ant. Go soak your pituitary in a pot of boiling antelope urine.

Chapter Vocabulary

360-degree needback   Obligatory surveys of your coworkers to assure your management that you are not Hitler reincarnated.

Annual abjective setting   The process of developing annual goals that you know are completely unachievable.

Deventralizaton   Cutting out the belly of the organization, usually a vital function, in an attempt to be more competitive.

Implamentation   The lengthy and remorseful explanation of how extenuating factors and external influences prevented successful execution, usually accompanied by chest beating, finger pointing, and whimpering.

Implementation phrase   The handover from the conceptual team to the execution team with the instruction "just do it."

Implementation faze   Realizing that the conceptual design cannot be executed without major rework.

Inventivize   An attempt at devising creative incentives for employees that don't involve money.

Performance praisal   The act of writing about your yearly accomplishments in the most glowing terms possible.

Project mangler   That person whose ineptitude at managing the simplest tasks prevents everyone from moving forward.

Speed-to-make-it   The consequence of wasting time at the beginning of project, resulting in a shortened production timeline.

9
Cut Your Own Head Off

The dangers of corporate infighting

Now that King Arthur and his knights have split up, each proceeds on his own adventure. This tale is of Sir Robin the Not-So-Brave and his minstrels.

Robin passes through a forest with danger signs warning of a certain death to all who trespass. As Robin and his minstrels continue on, they pass knights impaled on spears and others with axes through their heads. Suddenly, standing before them is a huge, ominous three-headed knight. The knight (Or is it knights? Does a body with three heads qualify as an individual or as three?) demands to know who wants to proceed, and Sir Robin quiveringly tells them that he is a knight of the Round Table. At this, the first head declares his intent to kill Sir Robin, but the second head isn't so sure. The third head thinks definitely not this time. Now the three heads are bickering among themselves—"You talk too much," "Your breath stinks," "You don't brush my teeth"—until they finally agree to kill Sir Robin and then go have some tea. However, Robin has escaped with his minstrels while the heads were distracted by their internal power struggle.

When Jack Welch was the CEO of General Electric, he was considered the leader to emulate and certain practices at GE became industry standards, like Six Sigma and their leadership development program. One of their very visible practices was succession planning. To determine his successor, Welch set up a very public three-way competition between Robert Nardelli, Jeffrey R. Immelt, and James McNerny, all heads of separate business divisions. Eventually, Immelt got the job and both Nardelli and McNerny left immediately to become CEOs of other companies. In theory, "friendly" competitions between business heads seems like a good idea. The competition pushes people to perform better, stretch out of their comfort zones, and strive to continually improve. However, this approach can have some fatal flaws. First, your losers aren't going to stay with company, and, second, sometimes the competition isn't so friendly.

Ode to a Corporate Three-Headed Knight
(based on a true story)

There once was a CEO, we'll call him Frank,
Whom, for this chapter, I would much like to thank
Because he created a three-headed knight
Amongst whom the heads did mortally fight.

To pick his successor, Frank started a race
And appointed three vice chairs to quicken the pace.
The first, a well-known woman, was the most favored heir;
She ran the main business for many a year.

Sales and production all answered to her.
The throne would go to Head 1, for sure.
Until one met Head 2, the old CFO
In charge of most corporate functions, you know.

He had finance, IT, facilities, and such.
And to wrangle the top job, oh, he did much
Like blaming Head 1 for declining sales
In the hopes that he would somehow prevail.

While Head 1 tried hard to just wait him out,
Collecting key allies to maintain her clout,
And preparing for Head 2's speedy demise
Once she had won the coveted prize.

The remaining vice chair was quite a dark horse,
Plan C, if Frank needed such recourse.
Surprisingly, chief counsel was the option three
With little experience, but a big law degree.

Then one day in August met the whole corporate board.
Tired of the stock price, they in unison roared,
"Get rid of the chairman. We need someone new.
For Head 1 and 2's strife, let's give them their due.

Chief Counsel will get the top spot. He's untried, that's true,
But better him than the squabbling two.
Thus, Frank will retire with millions in hand,
And hopefully, prosperity will reign once he's canned."

Even if a company is prepared for the resignation of the losers, is it prepared for the infighting and, in the worst case, the sabotage that accompanies these "friendly" competitions? Does anyone really believe that the competitors will put the good of the company before their personal gain? How did they get where they are in the first place?

Competitions can be useful to spur innovation, improve performance, and have some fun, but they need to be temporary and with defined limits. Contests and awards can be great motivators, but competition as a lifestyle can be very damaging, especially when careers are at stake. You can never collaborate, learn from anyone else, or negotiate a win/win if your incentive is to beat others, not to mention the temptation to undermine the other contestants. Competitions always result in losers, many more than winners, and is that really the best way to motivate and develop an organization over the long term?

The moral of the story: Three competing heads are no better than one.

The Tale of Sir Matrix the Not-So-Decisive

10
Let Me Have Some Peril

Sometimes good opportunities aren't in the plan

After the knights separate to pursue the grail, each embarks on his own adventure. Next up is Sir Galahad, who, traveling on a dark and stormy night, sees the shape of a grail flashing over a castle like a beacon. Rushing toward the castle, Galahad falls and injures himself. He bangs on the door of the gloomy castle, which is opened by a beautiful young woman named Zoot. In fact, the Castle Anthrax (not a very good name, now is it?) is inhabited solely by beautiful women between the ages of 16 and 19½ with nothing to do but undress, bathe, cavort, and dress. All these women want is to tend to Galahad's wounds, give him a nice comfy bed, and bathe him, but Sir Galahad the Pure fights off the enticement of these evil temptresses and insists on being shown the grail.

As two "doctors" try to examine (or probe is more like it) his wounds (or really his naughty bits), Galahad breaks away and discovers more half-naked women in the castle who want to tend to his needs. He finds that the grail he saw is a fake, a flashing light that Zoot uses to attract knights. The girls persuade him that a good spanking would punish Zoot, and that really they all could use a good spanking. As Galahad starts to succumb to these girls, Launcelot breaks in to rescue him. But Galahad wants to stay and face the peril! The scene ends as Launcelot drags Galahad away from the foul, evil temptresses while Galahad protests.

For poor Galahad the Pure, the Castle Anthrax is proving a challenge to his very identity as a chaste and noble knight. It doesn't take that much convincing for him to abandon this whole celibacy business and recognize that a short romp at the castle is a good opportunity even if it doesn't lead to the grail. Drat that Launcelot! He ruined the occasion by insisting they continue their quest. Galahad is not alone in his frustration. Many an employee who found a great business opportunity has been thwarted because that opportunity wasn't part of the corporate strategy.

Conventional business wisdom states that if it's not in the strategic plan, don't do it. Business success depends on executing the strategy—that's the mantra of management literature. However, I posit that sometimes great opportunities aren't in the plan, and all too often a strategic plan can inhibit a company's growth. Oh, I hear some of you saying, "The strategy is supposed to be a living document, not a hard and fast rule." To you I say, "Have you worked anywhere where the strategic plan was revisited and updated on a regular basis?" In my career, I've seen two companies— Gemini Consulting and Pfizer—ruin themselves by getting stuck in a strategy. Gemini no longer exists. Its remnants were swallowed up by Cap Gemini Ernst and Young. Of course, Pfizer is still around, but it is not the admired company it used to be and is using acquisitions to achieve growth. There are many similarities in the two cases, but I'd like to start with what happened at Gemini Consulting when it embarked on a new strategy.

The Gemini Consulting story started when two consulting companies merged in 1990 and exploited the recession to market downsizing and cost-cutting services. For a few short years, Gemini became the go-to consultants to drastically reduce the number of permanent employees and increase efficiencies under the banner "business process reengineering." Unlike other consulting companies, we actually implemented the recommended changes and promised specific results in the form of cost savings. Every consulting engagement had a benefits case that detailed the savings we promised to deliver. The company became very successful at this and grew rapidly. Our engagements also became larger and larger, and in some cases we reengineered entire divisions and even entire companies at one time.

The leadership team, like all good corporate leadership, decided that Gemini needed a strategy to take us to the next level. Until that time, we were operating like most consulting companies—selling whatever work presented itself as an opportunity. A small team of leaders decided that the next iteration of process reengineering was "business transformation," and Gemini would offer its services under this brand. This approach would tackle business strategy, business processes, information technology, and organizational design all in one fell swoop, completely remaking a company. The vision of Gemini

Consulting as the business transformation company was communicated to all the employees and also published in a book. Managers were told to turn down work that did not fit into the transformation tenets. Although we had some huge reengineering engagements at the time, our bread and butter—as is the case generally for consultants—was a steady stream of small projects. We started to turn down work that did not meet a certain revenue size.

Unfortunately for us, but fortunately for the rest of the world, the economy picked up and companies were no longer desperate to downsize. No one was interested in buying business transformation because essentially it is a disruptive, costly, and painful process. Although our leadership eventually realized this folly, we had already pissed off some of our best clients with our dollar threshold and were losing a steady stream of talented people who did not enjoy lopping off heads for a living. Plus, our company name was strongly associated with downsizing. No one wanted downsizing. This new thing called the Internet and the associated e-commerce, about which we had no experience, was all the rage. The company started cutting its own heads and embarked on the death spiral of "cost cutting your way to growth." Gemini dissipated within a few short years and became a small organizational development group within the Cap Gemini Company, later acquired by Ernst and Young.

A decade later, I lived through a similar experience with Pfizer. When I joined Pfizer, the company had just gobbled up Warner-Lambert in order to acquire Lipitor. Two years later, a massive sales force had turned Lipitor into the best-selling drug in history. Pfizer had also turned Viagra into a juggernaut, and it was buying Pharmacia, which had Celebrex, in order to do the same thing. Under Hank McKinnell, Pfizer's strategy was to use its massive sales force (at least twice as large as the nearest competitor's) to create blockbuster drugs. In the early '00s, Pfizer had an impressive array of blockbuster drugs and more in the pipeline. In fact, at the time Pfizer wouldn't even consider developing a drug that didn't have a potential market value of $1 billion.

In this time frame, Pfizer started to shed its non-pharmaceutical businesses because they were diluting its earnings per share. When I heard someone explain this strategy to me, I was speechless. Didn't pharmaceutical companies traditionally diversify in order to mitigate the risks in developing drugs? Wasn't this "let's focus only on developing blockbuster drugs" strategy perhaps the riskiest one a pharmaceutical company could undertake? Needless to say, its pipeline of potential blockbusters went bust. Cox-2 inhibitors like Celebrex, Vioxx (a Merck drug) and Bextra turned out to have harmful side effects. The other potential blockbuster drugs in its pipeline, including torcetrapib, Exubera, Chantix, and Rezulin, had problems and suffered a similar fate. The Pfizer stock price went from $42 to $17 during this time (before the market crash of 2008.) A friend who still works there told me that the threshold for new drug development is now a potential market of $100 million.

Of course, arrogance bred from success was a factor in the ill-conceived strategies of both Gemini and Pfizer. But if you look at these cases from a strategy textbook perspective, both companies did many things right. They conceived an innovative strategy based on core competencies that would result in unbridled growth (transformation and blockbusters). They focused on the one area in which they had a competitive advantage (process reengineering and sales). They communicated the strategy down through the ranks with real measures that could be implemented. Their strategies were based on past successes in the marketplace. For Gemini, transformation may have been a great business if the economy hadn't picked up. For Pfizer, who could predict that there would be all these problems with their pipeline? Only in hindsight can we say for sure that these were bad strategies. However, putting all your eggs in one basket is always a risky plan of action.

Quite simply, even the best laid plans often go awry. In fact, as I discussed in Chapter 8, it is quite certain that things won't turn out as planned. This is why strategies often fail. We get everyone in the organization aligned around achieving one goal, and they accomplish that goal. Only sometimes that goal is just a flashing neon light and not the real grail. Am I saying that companies should abandon strategies and strategic plans? Not exactly. What I'm saying is that we've abandoned common sense in order to adopt the latest management mantra without questioning that mantra's downside.

To explain how I think strategies should work, I would like to get personal. In my career and in my personal life, I've had the good fortune on multiple occasions to be led through a self-discovery process. I'm not big on self-help books, nor do I believe that if you wish hard enough your dreams will come true, but I've found that these exercises help me identify what is important in my life and where I want to expend my energy. I tend to be a reflective person, and I find that thinking through problems and plans is a good use of my time.

The following exercises are part of a self-discovery process. Doing them is completely optional, but if you feel the need for some self-reflection, I recommend that you do them in this order.

1. *Write your epitaph.* Think about what you would like on your tombstone when you die. What one sentence best sums up what you'd like to be remembered for? Rodney Dangerfield's epitaph is "There goes the neighborhood." The one I've written for myself is "Loving wife and mother, known for infinite generosity and wisdom." Your epitaph provides insight into the one or two values that are most important to you. Obviously, for Rodney Dangerfield comedy trumped family.
2. *Know your guiding values.* Choose three to five values that are most important to you in your life. In other words, you don't want to live without these things. Some examples are having a close family, pursuing meaningful work, having a satisfying career, learning new things, using your talents and skills, having good friendships, going on adventures, traveling, meeting new people, sharing your life with a partner, taking care of pets, making a difference, having financial security, and finding inner peace. It is important that you choose no more than five. You really can't have 10 priorities in life, and this choice will help you realize if your career is more important than your friends.
3. *Choose people you admire.* Who are your heroes, and what qualities do you most admire about them? Albert Einstein? Mother Teresa? Martin Luther King? Choose four or so people whom you admire and would like to emulate in your life, and the two or three qualities that make them role models. How does your answer match with your values and epitaph? Revisit those earlier items if you need to do so.
4. *Know your strengths.* Make a list of what you enjoy doing and are good at. Be sure to include hidden talents like being a good listener, writing concisely, parenting well, and other things you may do every day. Are any of these strengths unique? How do your strengths currently match your occupation? What could you do that would better leverage your strengths, especially unique ones?
5. *Create your bucket list.* What things do you want to do before you die (kick the bucket)? Write a book? (That was one of mine. Done). Take a safari? Learn to scuba dive? Have children? Build the house of your dreams? Start your own company? Learn French? Pick out some items

that you could do now and in the near future, and create a plan to do them. If you have a big ticket item, like starting your own company, pick a time frame and start planning now.

6. *Now ask yourself, what would you do with your life if you won the lottery?* Although you may consider moving to a tropical island, what would you do when you tired of the beach? Compare your answer with your values.

7. *What would you do if you found out you had only 12 months to live?* What, if any thing, would you do differently? Would you quit your job? Again, compare your answers with your values. And consider why you aren't doing any of those things now instead of waiting until you know you're dying.

Many people, me included, are not really sure what they want to be when they grow up. Going through these exercises is a way to determine how much satisfaction we are getting from our lives and course correcting if we are unhappy. It also helps us determine our priorities in life. It was quite an eye-opener for me when my career didn't make my top five guiding values.

Now look at the table below and see if you can find some similarities between this self-discovery process and what we do in corporations.

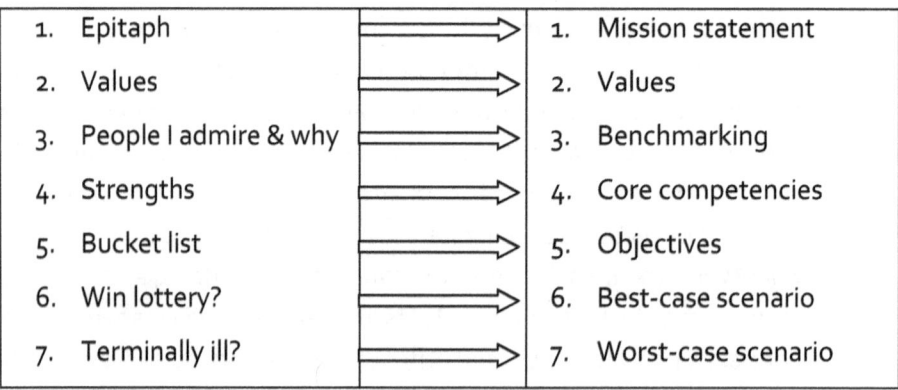

1. Epitaph	→	1. Mission statement
2. Values	→	2. Values
3. People I admire & why	→	3. Benchmarking
4. Strengths	→	4. Core competencies
5. Bucket list	→	5. Objectives
6. Win lottery?	→	6. Best-case scenario
7. Terminally ill?	→	7. Worst-case scenario

These are the steps involved in developing a corporate strategy. The thought process is really no different from that of determining what you want to do in life. The big difference lies in the way the insights are implemented and used.

Let's pretend for a minute that I am 24 years old, not long out of college, and trying to figure out what I want to do in life. I plan to spend the next three years in consulting and afterward attend a top business school for two years. My plans include marriage and children sometime in the future, but I want to develop my career first. In my mind, I imagine that I will be ready to marry around age 32 and start having children at age 35. What happens if I meet the man of my dreams at age 25, and he doesn't want to wait seven years to get married? Would I turn him down? What happens if I get offered a great job that precludes my going to business school full-time? Would I turn that down? In life, we know that good opportunities don't come often, so we take them when they do.

A life plan provides a guideline for what's importance to us, but we don't really expect to execute it as designed. Who knows what life will bring? Yet in business we go through the same process and expect to execute the strategy as written. Unfortunately, sometimes this means turning down good opportunities. Am I saying that we shouldn't bother implementing the strategy? No, I am saying that the planning process is more valuable than the actual plan. No matter how wonderful the developers of the plan are or how thorough the process, no plan can anticipate what the real world will bring.

With that in mind, I would like to turn again to our self-discovery analogy and dissect corporate strategy development through that lens. Typically, strategic planning is an event that occurs every few years. A few people create the future vision of the company, which is then communicated to everyone else in the organization for execution. Carrying this analogy over to our personal lives, we usually take stock every New Year or during a crisis. When we are finished, we don't put our plan on a fancy piece of paper and tell ourselves that we are done for the next two to five years. If we are true to ourselves, we revisit the plan in our heads almost every day of our lives. We live it and make adjustments all the time. Then, when New Year's Day comes again or a new crisis arises, we go through the process anew. Hence, real strategic planning is not an event, but a way of living. Can you imagine if every January you created your household budget for the entire year and expected to adhere to it? Yet in business we like to have firm plans and budgets. We commit to budget and sales numbers at the beginning of the year, and then try to meet those goals throughout the year. If we don't, we are dinged on our reviews or worse, and we spend profligately every December to use up our unspent budget. We do this because we treat planning as an event and not an ongoing process. Strategies, plans, budgets, and targets are all dependent on external factors and should be reexamined all the time, not annually or semi-annually.

Now let's examine the "few people" aspect of corporate planning. Typically, a select team is created, led by the CEO or other senior leader, and augmented by consultants who do lots of analyses and actually create the strategy recommendations. This is a lot like your mom and Uncle Harold getting together with some career coaches to decide what you should do with your life. Besides the obvious fact that you should be involved in decisions regarding your own life, you don't get any of the value of learning from the career coaches. Similarly, only a few people get exposed to the strategy development process. Worse, all the information on competitors, trends, regulatory issues, core competencies, and organizational values walks out the door when the consultants leave.

A second point about the select few revisits a theme I discussed in Chapter 3, that the strategy and plan should take into consideration the values, competencies, and desires of the organization. When this happens, the plan is easy both to implement and to manage. If the strategy is truly based on the wisdom of the organization, then the organization can regulate itself when executing the strategy. If an opportunity arises that is not a good fit for the company, most people will recognize that and won't pursue it. Only when the strategy is based on a few people's ideas of what should take place does the organization have to follow a checklist of items to determine if the opportunity is a good fit. When the organization is living the strategy, no checklists or committees are required to determine a strategic fit.

Now let's discuss "create the future vision." In the persona of my 24-year-old with ambitious plans for career, marriage, and family, I would like to create the future vision of my family. My husband will look like…? He'll do what for a living? My children will be like…? Is there any value at all to this exercise? As Yogi Berra said, "It's tough to make predictions, especially about the future." But if you know your values and priorities, you have a better chance of finding a suitable life partner. In contrast, in business we expect our leadership team to create a vision of the future, the action plan to get there, and the measures to make sure the organization will do it. Is it any wonder that the plans often end up useless? This is because strategy development is a self-discovery process, not a creation process. It is the learning, not the result, that has value. This is what Dwight D. Eisenhower meant when he said, "In preparing for battle I have always found that plans are useless, but planning is indispensable."

In writing about his Civil War battles, Ulysses S. Grant devoted many pages to describing the lay of the land and to meticulous maps of the areas. He studied the land to determine where to position his men and how to choreograph the battle. As the battle took place, often he had to abandon his original plan, but knowing the lay of the land was essential in developing a new course of action. This is how Grant won the Civil War. It's what you learn about the industry, the competitors, the emerging technologies, and the organization itself that is the value of strategic planning. Future actions and decisions can be shaped by the wisdom gained in strategic thinking and don't need to be dictated by the particular steps outlined in the plan. This is the secret of success.

Successful people are able to recognize and then exploit the opportunities that present themselves. Bill Gates never had a personal career goal to found a software company. However, he did love computer programming and was able to exploit the opportunity to buy MS-DOS and then continue to exploit the resulting opportunities. He knew enough about computers to know that software would be at least as important as, if not more important than, hardware. IBM at the time was set on its strategy of selling mainframes and blind to the PC revolution, allowing Microsoft to dominate software unchallenged. Successful companies exploit the opportunities that present themselves, and they know which ones they are able to exploit because they've been through a self-discovery process.

My eyes were first opened to the downside of having a strategy when I was at Deloitte Haskins & Sells (DH&S) in the late 1980s. When I joined, each office had its own local consulting practice and sold whatever work they were able to—pretty much anything. After I had been there about a year, the consulting leadership decided to develop a more prestigious consulting practice on a national level. It started with a strategic vision, and we organized around industrial expertise, like banking or manufacturing, and developed service offerings. At the time, this seemed like a good idea to me. I'd rather be part of a well-organized consulting practice than an ad hoc one. Although in hindsight, I was spending less time with clients and more time developing the service offerings. However, when we merged with Touche Ross, they took over the consulting division because company leadership deemed that they had the better consulting practice. I was shocked when I discovered that they were still using the local office, ad hoc model. Yet, they had more clients and more revenue. While we were focusing internally to pursue bigger clients, our actual sales were dropping. Touche Ross was still bringing in a steady stream of client engagements using the old model. Our strategic focus had caused us to be on the losing side of that deal, and many of the DH&S consultants were let go. To be fair, all the accounting firm consulting practices did eventually develop into more organized practices with particular service offerings, but I learned that pursuing a strategy does actually have a downside, that of lost opportunities. Opportunity costs are rarely factored into the quest to become a strategically aligned company.

The Amazing Vision-o-matic!

It slices! It dices! It cuts and pastes the most common phrases from vision statements to make one for your company! Save thousands of dollars of consulting fees with the Vision-o-matic!

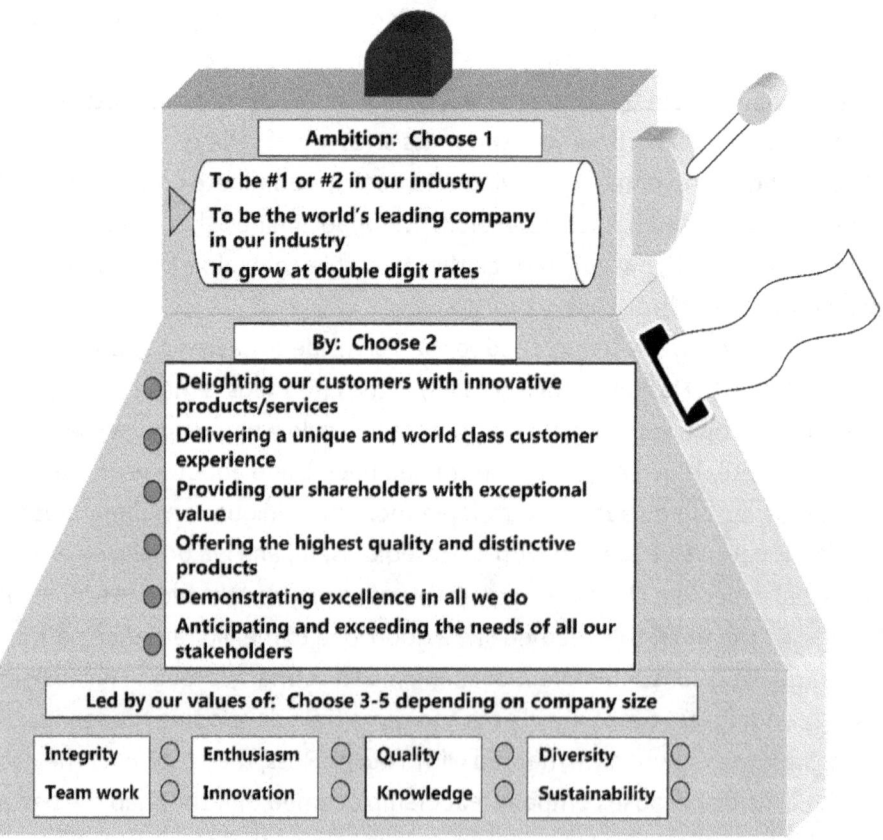

The other aspect that I rarely see factored into the strategy development process is to analyze how much of the strategy is within the company's control. Business literature is full of Cinderella stories where poorly performing companies focused all their efforts on improving quality, becoming innovative, or meeting customer needs and accomplished some amazing results. Notice how all these efforts are internal changes that a company can control. A company can become more innovative by hiring experts, offering training, launching initiatives, and setting goals, and, if all goes well, the result will be innovative products that customers purchase. However, how does a company enact "outgrow the competition by 2%"? Even if you implement all sorts of improvement programs, how can you guarantee that your competition won't grow faster? Sabotage? What steps can you take to make sure your drugs are blockbusters? Short of bribing doctors and the FDA, it's really just an exercise in wishful thinking. It's like having "win the lottery" as a life goal.

Four times now, I've been part of company that embarked on developing and achieving a strategic vision. In pursuit of the strategic vision, we neglected other opportunities, sold off businesses, laid off employees, and generally had a miserable time. None of those companies succeeded in achieving its goals. Each was acquired, went bankrupt, or abandoned its vision in order to survive. Poor Galahad has a great opportunity at the Castle Anthrax, but it won't help him in his quest. Not only does he lose out on this once-in-a-lifetime opportunity, but (as you probably realize) he will never find the Holy Grail—just like so many corporations that fail in their quests for their own Holy Grails.

Chapter Vocabulary

Blight space   That marketplace opportunity that no one else has gone after, usually for good reason.

Corporate version statement   A grand business strategy that takes into account only the company's perspective of the industry.

Corporate wishin' statement   Because you know you'll never get there.

Glean business practices   In the attempt to adopt more environmentally friendly practices, learning that they all have different but just as harmful impacts.

Mess customization   An ill-conceived initiative whereby a manufacturer of standardized products decides to embark on a strategy of customization using its existing facilities.

Misdisintermediatization   Getting rid of the wrong middleman.

11

We Are Now the Knights Who Go "Neow Wum Ping"

Keeping up with the latest corporate initiatives

HEAD KNIGHT OF NI: Ni!
KNIGHTS OF NI: Ni! Ni! Ni! Ni! Ni!
ARTHUR: Who are you?
HEAD KNIGHT: We are the Knights Who Say... 'Ni'!
RANDOM: Ni!
ARTHUR: No! Not the Knights Who Say 'Ni'!
HEAD KNIGHT: The same!
BEDEVERE: Who are they?
HEAD KNIGHT: We are the keepers of the sacred words: Ni, Peng, and Neee-wom!
RANDOM: Neee-wom!
ARTHUR: Those who hear them seldom live to tell the tale!
HEAD KNIGHT: The Knights Who Say 'Ni' demand a sacrifice!
ARTHUR: Knights of Ni, we are but simple travelers who seek the enchanter who lives beyond these woods.
HEAD KNIGHT: Ni!
KNIGHTS OF NI: Ni! Ni! Ni! Ni! Ni!...
ARTHUR: Ow! Ow! Ow! Agh!
HEAD KNIGHT: We shall say 'Ni' again to you if you do not appease us.
ARTHUR: Well, what is it you want?
HEAD KNIGHT: We want... a shrubbery!
 (dramatic chord)
ARTHUR: A what?
KNIGHTS OF NI (shouting aggressively): Ni! Ni! Ni! Ni!
ARTHUR and PARTY: Ow! Oh!

ARTHUR: Please, please! No more! We will find you a shrubbery.

HEAD KNIGHT: You must return here with a shrubbery or else you will never pass through this wood alive!

ARTHUR: O Knights of Ni, you are just and fair, and we will return with a shrubbery.

HEAD KNIGHT: One that looks nice.

ARTHUR: Of course.

HEAD KNIGHT: And not too expensive.

ARTHUR: Yes.

HEAD KNIGHT: Now... go!

(Later ......)

ARTHUR: O Knights of Ni, we have brought you your shrubbery. May we go now?

HEAD KNIGHT: It is a good shrubbery. I like the laurels particularly. But there is one small problem.

ARTHUR: What is that?

HEAD KNIGHT: We are now... no longer the Knights Who Say 'Ni.'

KNIGHTS OF NI: Ni! Shh!

HEAD KNIGHT: Shh! We are now the Knights Who Say 'Ecky-ecky-ecky-ecky-pikang-zoop-boing-goodem-zoo-owli-zhiv.'

RANDOM: Ni!

HEAD KNIGHT: Therefore, we must give you a test.

ARTHUR: What is this test, O Knights of– Knights Who 'Til Recently Said 'Ni'?

HEAD KNIGHT: Firstly, you must find... another shrubbery!

(dramatic chord)

ARTHUR: Not another shrubbery!

RANDOM: Ni!

HEAD KNIGHT: Then, when you have found the shrubbery, you must place it here beside this shrubbery, only slightly higher so you get the two-level effect with a little path running down the middle.

KNIGHTS OF NI: A path! A path! A path! Ni! Shh! Ni! Ni! Ni! Shh! Shh!...

HEAD KNIGHT: Then, when you have found the shrubbery, you must cut down the mightiest tree in the forest... with... a herring!

(dramatic chord)

ARTHUR: We shall do no such thing!

HEAD KNIGHT: Oh, please!

ARTHUR: Cut down a tree with a herring? It can't be done.

KNIGHTS OF NI: Aaaaugh! Aaaugh!

HEAD KNIGHT: Augh! Ohh! Don't say that word.

ARTHUR: What word?

HEAD KNIGHT: I cannot tell, suffice to say is one of the words the Knights of Ni cannot hear.

ARTHUR: How can we not say the word if you don't tell us what it is?

KNIGHTS OF NI: Aaaaugh!

HEAD KNIGHT: You said it again!
ARTHUR: What, 'is'?
KNIGHTS OF NI: Agh! No, not 'is'.
HEAD KNIGHT: No, not 'is'. You wouldn't get very far in life not saying 'is.'
BEDEVERE: My liege, it's Sir Robin!
MINSTREL (singing): Packing it in and packing it up,
 And sneaking away and buggering up,
 And chickening out and pissing off home,
 Yes, bravely he is throwing in the sponge.
ARTHUR: Sir Robin!
ROBIN: My liege! It's good to see you.
HEAD KNIGHT: Now he's said the word!
ARTHUR: Surely you've not given up your quest for the Holy Grail?
MINSTREL (singing): He is sneaking away and buggering up—
ROBIN: Shut up! No, no. No. Far from it.
HEAD KNIGHT: He said the word again!
KNIGHTS OF NI: Aaaaugh!
ROBIN: I was looking for it.
KNIGHTS OF NI: Aaaaugh!
ROBIN: Uh, here— here in this forest.
ARTHUR: No, it is far from this place.
KNIGHTS OF NI: Aaaaugh!
HEAD KNIGHT: Aaaaugh! Stop saying the word! The word...
ARTHUR: Oh, stop it!
KNIGHTS OF NI: ...we cannot hear!
HEAD KNIGHT: Ow! He said it again!
HEAD KNIGHT: Wait! I said it! I said it!
 Ooh! I said it again! And there again! That's three 'it's! Ohh!
KNIGHTS OF NI: Aaaaugh!
(Arthur and the knights pass through the forest and ride away.)

Take 1: "Ni, Ni, Ni, Ni, Ni, Ni, Ni, Ecky-Ecky-Ecky-Ecky-Pikang-Zoop-Boing-Goodem-Zoo-Owli-Zhiv"

We are the management consultants who say "Rightsizing." Bring us lots of money and your best resources, and you will be able to pass through the forest of inefficiency.

Now we are the management consultants who say "Outsourcing." Bring us even more money and we will let you let pass.

No wait, now we are the management consultants who say:

"Balanced Scorecard, Management by Objectives, Pay for Performance, Learning Organization, Continuous Improvement,

Business Process Reengineering, Six Sigma, Statistical Process Control, Zero Percent Defects, Demings Cycle, High Performance Technology, Intellectual Capital Management, Business Intelligence...

...and then when you have finished phase 1 of the project, you must embark on phase 2, which requires even more money and resources and..."

Enough, enough, you say, stop, be quiet.

"Change Management, Disruptive Innovations, Total Quality, Demand Driven Supply Network, Global Supply Chain, Innovation, Customer Relationship Management, Customer Relationship Marketing, Strategic Intent Core Competences, Competitive Advantage, Vision Engineering, ISO xooo, Innovation Engineering, Blue Ocean Strategy, Strategic Selling, Cascading KPIs, Human Capital Management, MRP, ERP, BRP, Cloud Computing, Business Process Monitoring, Web 2.0, e-business, e-commerce, e-learning, Design for Engineering, Design for Manufacturing, Product Lifecycle Management...

...all your competitors are doing it, so you must do it, too..."

Stop, stop, stop. Don't say anymore. I can't bear it.

"Outsourcing, Insourcing, Rightsizing, Downsizing, Benchmarking, Accordian Management, Decentralization, De-layering, Shared Services, Centralization, Lean Organization, Lean Manufacturing, Just-in-Time, Kaizen, Systems Dynamics, Empowerment, Core Competencies, Participative Management, Emotional Intelligence, Time-based Competition, Engagement, Community 2.0, The Wisdom of Teams, The Wisdom of Crowds, Crowd Sourcing, Virtual Corporations, Virtual Collaboration, Virtual Teams, Gamification, Big Data..."

Enough! Enough!

And just when you get versed in one of these management methods, another one has taken its place that is suddenly *the* answer to your organization's woes. After you become learned in enough of these concepts, a great gestalt moment arises when you realize that what you have been doing all along is buying shrubberies.

Take 2: **Not Really a Fable**

This is a tale based on the true story of an innovation initiative. Any resemblance to actual people and events is purely intentional.

The Idiot Village

A long time ago, in a company far, far away, there was a king...ooops, president, and one day he looked at the future sales growth and determined that in order to meet strategic goals, his land needed innovation. He realized that although his people were good and wise, they would not survive using the old ways. The king knew that he needed help, and he searched high and low for a prince, knowledgeable in the ways of innovation. A prince was found and with great fanfare and a town parade, innovation was declared across the land. The prince set about creating innovation capabilities in the townspeople, and a select cadre of townspeople and projects were chosen for the new innovation ways. The new ways were going to solve all the problems and create a better life for everyone.

News of the innovation projects was broadcast throughout the land, and the farmers and villagers longed to be included in the new ways. A nine-step process was declared by the prince, and this was transcribed and sent by courier to all the villages and farms far and wide with the specific edict that everyone in the land must know and use the nine-step process. When the process and edict came to one village, the village elders assembled and proclaimed that they would use the process to solve all their problems. So the villagers gathered up all their problems to bring to the village square on innovation day. On that happy day, everyone in the village assembled with great fanfare and excitement to apply the new ways to their problems.

At first the villagers were confused. Their problems were diffuse and numerous, and they had various opinions on what exactly their problems were. One villager, recently back from a sojourn to the Land of Six Sigma, suggested using root cause analysis techniques. Some other villagers objected. Surely, that was an old way, not a new way. They looked to the town elders for guidance. The elders did not know any more about the new ways than anyone else but advised the village to "trust the process." After struggling through the new ways, the villagers developed many, many, action items to address their problems. They were tired and overwhelmed by the amount of work required but excited by the prospect of living a better life. One villager suggested that perhaps they should address only a portion of the actions at one time, but the rest of the villagers objected. Everyone wanted to be part of the new ways. They did not want an exclusive team to be the only ones using innovation. So the villagers embarked on innovation initiatives, and everyone was excited and happy using the new ways.

Until, at the regular meeting of the town elders, the eldest elder stood: "We have serious problems. Our fields are lying fallow, our crops are rotting on their stalks, our horses are unshod, and our shops are empty. We have abandoned all our old ways, and now we have no working farms or village shops. Let us go back to the old ways, for the new ways do not work."

Other elders objected, "But we cannot abandon the new ways. The villagers are happy, and the king will be disappointed. They will say that we are old and do not understand innovation."

Another elder persisted, "Yet many of the villagers are complaining that there is no food. They, too, have noticed that the old ways are needed."

Listening earnestly to the discussion, the eldest elder, being wise in the way of politics, had an answer. "We do not want to lose our village and yet we do not want to appear to *stifle the new ways. We will appoint a council called the Ways Council to govern the use of the new ways and the old ways in the village."*

Thus the Ways Council was commissioned, but those on the council soon realized that they did not know enough about every old way and every new way to judge which to use. So, they commissioned two councils, the New Ways Council and the Old Ways Council to determine which ways to use. From then on, every villager wanting to embark on work presented his concept first to the New Ways Council to determine its fit with the new ways and then to the Old Ways Council to get recommendations on its fit with the old ways before submitting his work to the Ways Council for the final decision. Yet those on the Ways Council were often afraid that they would accidentally anger the town elders by making a wrong decision, so they determined that all decisions would have to pass before the town elders before any action could be taken. Everyone was happy with this new process, which seemed fair and enabled most of the villagers to be on important new committees.

So the fields lay fallow, the crops rotted, the shops were empty, and the towns problems went unaddressed while the villagers spent their days discussing the best ways to run the village. Meanwhile, the prince went on to find a new land to innovate, and the king went off to war to defend the land against conquerors. The villagers lived happily ever after for about three weeks until they starved (actually they were taken over by another country).

The End

The moral of the story is that relying on the initiative du jour to improve an organization is a lot like using "Ni" as your entire vocabulary.

Take 3: It's Still the Same Damn Thing

In 2005, I was asked to participate in a large-scale restructuring initiative with the goal of eliminating $4 billion in costs. The company had grown through mergers and acquisitions and, in many cases, added on the new company's operations to the acquiring one's. The result was a morass of processes and procedures, and even though some lay-offs would be involved, most employees welcomed the opportunity to streamline operations. In a surprise, upper management decided not to hire a consultancy to help, but instead organized internal teams to identify cost-saving opportunities. One of the key tools was a web-enabled suggestion box, where all employees could enter ideas on how to improve operations or cut costs.

During the ensuing weeks, employees were encouraged to meet as teams to discuss ideas for improvement and submit these ideas through the website. Employees also received numerous email solicitations reminding them to submit suggestions. As a result, thousands of ideas were submitted, overwhelming the initial idea selection team so each department created its own team to evaluate the ideas pertaining to that department. At first glance, this seems like a reasonable construct, but let's deconstruct what actually occurred.

Most departments already had numerous ways to put forward ideas including special meetings, suggestion boxes, websites, and surveys, which were regularly reviewed by their management. If nothing resulted from the idea, it was usually due to one of several reasons: it wasn't a good idea, no one had responsibility for making it happen, it wasn't politically viable, no one understood it, or we lacked the capability to implement it. Now employees were submitting their same ideas to the corporate suggestion box where they got reviewed by a centralized team, catalogued, categorized, and distributed right back to the management team in the same department. This management team reviewed the ideas, many of which they have seen before, and then determined that it wasn't a good idea, or not politically viable, or... You get the picture: the same people reviewed the same ideas with the same outcome.

My observation on many of these improvement programs is that companies would benefit more if they spent that time and effort building a capability within a company rather than executing a one-off initiative. If we had implemented a process in which good ideas were funneled to a multi-departmental team on an ongoing basis and given some people responsibility for implementing these ideas, we could have saved a lot of time and turmoil. Plus, we would have implemented a capability and culture of continuous improvement, rather than a one-time project that bore an amazing similarity to trying to cut down a tree with a herring.

Take 4: Spinning Wheels Got to Go Round

I'd like to return to the concept of systems dynamics and share one of my favorite quotes from "Nobody Ever Gets Credit for Fixing Problems that Never Happened," by Nelson Repenning and John Sterman:

> *Techniques touted as today's "core competencies" all too often become tomorrow's failed programs. Once an effort has failed, there is an almost irresistible temptation to label it as a fad or "flavor of the month." However, digging a little deeper shows that many such techniques have useful content. It should come as little surprise then that many currently popular innovations are little more than old ideas with new acronyms. The core disciplines associated with statistical process control and variance reduction become six sigma; what was once called a quality circle is now a high-performance work team.*

The problem with many initiatives is that they rarely get implemented correctly with proper resources, adequate time, and necessary training. The mindset companies have toward these programs is similar to how many people approach weight loss: go on an extreme diet for a short period. This short-term focus on a fad diet is no more effective than a short-term focus on a fad program (as in our tale of the idiot village). The only method that sustains weight loss is a change in lifestyle that incorporates sensible eating and exercise. Similarly, the only way to corporate health is to adopt sustainable processes and behaviors with a long-term focus.

Borrowing heavily from Sterman and Repenning's work on systems dynamics, I've identified two common scenarios that occur when a company embarks on an improvement program. I have lived through both of these more than once, and perhaps you have, too. Continuing with the eating analogy, I call them "the best thing since sliced bread" mania and the "have your cake and eat it, too" syndrome.

"The best thing since sliced bread" mania

In this scenario, Company C hires an expert in "the best darn improvement program ever" to improve efficiency in department D. The expert, "E," works with the department head to develop a charter, plan, and objectives for "the best darn improvement program ever." The department head and a few of his direct reports attend an intensive four-week training program. These few employees are then dedicated to implementing the program in their department with the help of the expert. The expert offers advice and helps customize the program to meet their particular objectives. Under the supervision of "E," the team implements a very rigorous improvement plan and also become mini-"experts" themselves, benefiting from direct coaching by "E." Most of this work is kept hush-hush because the department head wants to get results before he promotes his program.

Once the department has real results, both the expert and the department head embark on a self-promotional spree and earn the attention of the CEO, who thinks other departments could benefit from "the best darn improvement program ever." However, not wanting to pay "E" for his time, the CEO assigns one or two of the "e"s to help the other departments with their programs. Not being strong advocates themselves, none of those other department heads send their resources for the intensive training but instead opt for the "e"s to give them mini-sessions and advice. Of course, the "e"s are still responsible for their own departmental jobs and don't devote as much time as they should. Still, the program is implemented, not quite as rigorously as before, and some benefits are achieved, but they're not quite as dramatic as those in department D. Word of these successes spreads through intercompany PR articles, presentations, and emails, and now everyone wants the program, or at least the CEO wants everyone to want the program (same difference).

The "e"s are asked to develop mini-training programs because the company cannot afford to send everyone to the four-week training program. Besides, the main messages can easily be boiled down to one day. They conduct these one-day training sessions for a number of their colleagues, and those trainees are sent out to implement the program in their areas. Although these other departments have very different issues than department D, the same approach is used because no one is aware of any other approaches, but the method is simplified to implement quickly without the bother of all that rigor.

The departments then pick and choose what they feel like implementing without understanding how each step contributes to the overall success. Those responsible for implementing the program in their areas still have their full-time jobs and are not using "E" to help because he costs too much. In other words, they don't devote much time or effort to learning about or implementing the program. In this iteration of "the best darn improvement program ever," few benefits are realized, and everyone looks back on the program as a lot of hype and a big waste of time. In essence, it's a lot like dieting on Thursdays.

The "have your cake and eat it, too" syndrome

In this second scenario, some event or crisis provokes the corporate leadership to see a need to change, and they decide to embark on a capability-building program. They bring in some consultants du jour and, with great fanfare, announce the rollout of the new corporate initiative. The halls of the company are plastered with the initiative's mantra (zero percent defects, #1 in customer satisfaction, lean manufacturing, etc.) and the entire organization is mobilized to reach the stated goal. Everyone knows that the consequences of not succeeding are dire. During this time, employees attend training sessions and participate in focus groups. A new idea-collection system is implemented, and Friday afternoons are dedicated to ideation sessions. Each department sets up its own team to implement the suggestions and monitor their progress. The entire organization is mobilized to achieve the specific objective, and energy and morale begin to build.

Three months after the initial rollout, there is no discernible impact on quarterly earnings. "It's too soon to tell," everyone says, and they continue their capability efforts. After the second quarter, the earnings report shows a sharp drop in profits! The leadership team now hires back the consultants to find out how this could be. After a quick analysis and a hefty fee, the consultants report that, because everyone is working hard on the improvement initiative, no one is working hard on his or her actual job, hence the slip in performance. With meeting quarterly earnings targets the number one priority in most companies, the leadership decides that the organization has gone way off track. Although they understand the need to build the capability, it can't be at the expense of quarterly earnings, so the employees are told to concentrate on their jobs and give the initiative their second priority. As a result, the focus groups, ideation sessions, and implementation teams are radically scaled back *before* having implemented their changes. They do have some great documentation, though.

The new mantra is now "regain parity," and the organization focuses on trying to match its pre-initiative performance. Some hardy souls continue the improvement initiative, as well, and they end up working 60 to 80 hour weeks and eventually burn out and become disillusioned. After about two quarters, the company has regained its former performance, and the capability initiative is reintroduced. It takes much longer to remobilize the organization, and it doesn't quite meet the initial levels of enthusiasm and energy. Here's where one of two possible paths occur.

One: Leadership is certain to ensure that the job priorities come first, and so the initiative never really takes off and/or the employees become overworked and don't perform either their job duties or their initiative tasks very well. The company never realizes any improvements and just hobbles along much the same as before.

Two: After a much longer start, the initiative takes root and employees are working diligently on building the improvement capability. At first, the initiative doesn't affect earnings, but soon earnings drop because employees are not focusing on their job responsibilities! Once again, the CEO steps in and restarts the focus on "regain parity." This "have your cake and eat it, too" syndrome is a lot like halting an exercise program because your muscles hurt.

Just as the Knights Who Say "Ni" can't bear to hear "it," an unavoidable word, our corporate leadership can't bear to hear an unavoidable fact—namely, that making long-term improvements requires time, effort, money, and some amount of discomfort in the short term.

Take 5: Sir Matrix, Three-Headed Knight, Spurs an Initiative

Take 6: About Hiring Those Consultants...

NARRATOR: And so, Arthur and Bedevere and Sir Robin set out on their search to find the enchanter of whom the old man (in a previous scene) had spoken (who knew how to find the grail). Beyond the forest they met Launcelot and Galahad, and there was much rejoicing.

KNIGHTS: Yay! Yay!

And so Arthur spaketh once again to his men:

> *Knights, separately we are weak and uninformed. We waste much time reinventing the wagon. Let us band together and centralize our resources so that we may leverage our size and share our knowledge. Together we will realize efficiencies of scale and eliminate redundancies. Together we will be strong in the face of competition.*

Reunited, Arthur and his knights set off to find the powerful wizard who knows where the Holy Grail is hidden. They happen upon a man who is conjuring fire from the ground and making the surrounding trees and bushes burst into flame. It is Tim the Enchanter, the powerful wizard for whom they are looking. While they talk, Tim continues to magically appear and disappear all the while creating powerful fires. Without being told, Tim knows who they are and what they seek. Arthur and the knights are intimidated and can hardly summon the courage to ask for his help. (I'm not sure, but I think Robin wets himself again in this scene.) Arthur finally asks if perhaps Tim, even though he's obviously busy, could possibly point them in the direction of... Being an all-knowing enchanter, Tim already knows that they want his help.

TIM: To the north there lies a cave—the cave of Caerbannog—wherein, carved in mystic runes upon the very living rock, the last words of Olfin Bedwere of Rheged...
 (boom—a fire)
   ...make plain the last resting place of the most Holy Grail.
ARTHUR: Where could we find this cave, O Tim?
TIM: Follow. But! Follow only if ye be men of valor, for the entrance to this cave is guarded by a creature so foul, so cruel that no man yet has fought with it and lived! Bones of full fifty men lie strewn about its lair. So, brave knights, if you do doubt your courage or your strength, come no further, for death awaits you all with nasty, big, pointy teeth.
ARTHUR: What an eccentric performance.

And so the executive team met with the high-priced consultant, and he dazzled them with his multimedia slide presentation and knowledge of their industry. He used big fancy words and lots of jargon and acronyms and intimidated the men with his magic-speak, animated graphics, and tales of the difficult project ahead:

> *I can help you reach your mission, but only if you do exactly as I say. Your competition is lean and mean. You must restructure, de-layer, and achieve efficiency, leaving only the skeleton of the present fat and unempowered organization behind. You must have the resolve to make the tough choices if you are to survive these tough economic times. It will be hard, and we want only those committed to the project on the team. If you aren't committed, then expect to be devoured by your competitors.*

The team looked in awe at the high-priced consultant with the flashy presentation and imagined the tough journey that lay ahead. The CEO mused, befuddled at this response to his request for a benchmarking study. Hence, he spaketh, "I wonder if this pricey management consultant really is worth the fee."

Chapter Vocabulary

Client engougement   A consulting gig.

Corporate inertiatives   What they really should be called.

Expanse account   Unlimited budget for pet corporate growth initiatives.

Inunvate   To overload with innovation initiatives.

Idearation   During brainstorming, secretly counting how many ideas each person contributes to determine who is smartest.

Kraizen   A mad obsession with implementing improvement programs.

The yearning organization   An organization that constantly strives to become profitable by rolling out the latest management training programs.

12

And Make Sure He Doesn't Leave

The current, confusing state of corporate communications

Now comes the tale of Sir Launcelot, except that, being about Launcelot, the tale takes place over two scenes and has three subplots. This is the setup scene where we learn that the king of Swamp Castle is about to marry off his son, Prince Herbert, to a princess who has huge tracts of land. The prince isn't happy as he really doesn't like the girl and would rather sing about finding his true love (cue music). It turns out his father hates musical theater. It also turns out the prince may not like girls (wink, wink, nudge, nudge). The king will have none of this. Being the king of Swamp Castle, he could really use those tracts. But the real point of the scene is the dialogue between the king and the two guards. The king asks the guards to make sure the prince doesn't leave his room until he comes to get him. In a nod to Abbott and Costello's "Who's on first?" routine, the two inebriated guards misconstrue the instructions. The dialogue goes something like this: "Don't let the prince leave even if the king comes to get him?" "No, the king needs to convey the prince to the wedding." "Don't let the prince enter the room?" "No, the prince is already in the room. Don't let him *leave*." "But if he has to leave, can we go with him?" "If who has to leave? The guard? It doesn't make much sense guarding a guard." "No, it's the prince who has to leave. Should we let him?"

Who would have thought such simple instructions could be misinterpreted in so many ways?

Corporate Communications 101 Quiz[9]

Please read the following selections and answer the questions pertaining to the passage. In addition, please identify each instance of:

- Hidden agendas behind the purported purpose of the piece
- Self-serving objective, like promoting yourself or imposing your opinion rather than opening a dialogue
- Obfuscation with the use of jargon and clichés and reliance on passive voice
- Way too much spin and not enough candor

Because this is a timed test, you will only have enough time to *read each passage once*. Good luck.

Question 1: (10 points)

From: C---
Sent: Tuesday, June 13, 2006 10:35 AM
To: G---
Subject: Chart of Accounts
Importance: High

G---,
    I have discussed the chart of accounts question with Jack, Kurt, Rita, and Rob. The overall conclusion is that utilizing the EFSS/Pfast Chart of Accounts (COA) "as is" while doable would represent a less than optimal approach. However, a complete Greenfield approach is also recognized as inappropriate because of the time and effort involved. The main concern is that the EFSS/Pfast COA was designed for the corporate business which is viewed as being a significantly different organization than "spinco," resulting in a COA which underemphasizes some aspects necessary for a pure play, agile global consumer business while containing potentially many unnecessary account structures relating to the corporate business.
    The recommended approach to resolving this would be to identify the subject matter experts (SMEs) who with appropriate consulting support would finalize the COA. We can also identify where this activity will take place in our 30-60-90-120 day plans. The Team would have a hard-stop time limit to force decision making. The absolute worst case scenario would be to adopt the

---

[9] These are all real examples, with grammar unchanged, taken from my various jobs. However, I have shortened them, severely in some cases, to spare you tedium. Please note that all of these passages were more lengthy, confusing, and redundant in their original form.

EFSS/Pfast COA. Rather than engage in further analysis relating to the COA, I feel our efforts would be better spent in identifying and planning the priority activities to take place in the first 30-60-90-120 days and the recommended make-up of the teams who will be charged with addressing the issues. This will enable us to determine the staffing needed who I imagine will be in short supply in the event of a spin.
Your thoughts?

Regards,
C---

The central idea of the email above is:
   a. Using EFSS/Pfast COA for spinco is a 30-60-90-120 day activity.
   b. The writer can use lots of important-sounding buzzwords and catch phrases.
   c. Structuring everything in the passive voice is a good way to avoid accountability.
   d. The task you've assigned to me is a boneheaded idea, and I've asked other people, who think it's a boneheaded idea, too.

Question 2: (15 pts)

The following passages pertain to a laboratory system that is undergoing an audit to ensure it complies with corporate and good manufacturing policies required by the U.S. government.

-----Original Message-----
From: Allan
Sent: Wednesday, May 18, 2005 4:50 PM
To: Peter; Linda; Kara; Chandra
Cc: Gary; Wayne; Dan
Subject: WI-00414 and the 15 min screen saver requirement

Colleagues,
It has come to my attention that we may have a compliance issue with the work instruction (WI) that pertains to screen savers. WI-00414 Security of Computerized Validated Systems contains the following requirement:

4.4.3.3 The system will include an automatic inactivity lock to force re-verification of the user's identity if more than 15 minutes of inactivity has lapsed after user authentication was granted. (e.g., re-entry of user password)

Typically this is enforced by workstation screen saver policy. R&D Workstations, by policy, are set to activate the screen saver after 10 minutes. It is the Compliance dept's interpretation that validated laboratory systems are out of compliance with the work instruction (WI-00414) if their screen saver is set to 10 minutes. They read 4.4.3.3 as saying that the screen saver must be set to 15 minutes. My argument is that if the screen saver activates after 10 minutes it will have fulfilled the requirement of 4.4.3.3.
How do you read the requirement?
Allan

From: Peter
Sent: Wednesday, May 18, 2005 5:08 PM
To: Allan
Subject: RE: WI-00414 and the 15 min screen saver requirement

I read 'more than 15 minutes' as anything less being in compliance which would include 10 minutes. That said aren't the lab systems under group policy? If they are then they will be set to 15 minutes.

From: Dan
Sent: Thursday, May 19, 2005 11:04 AM
To: Allan; Peter; Linda; Kara; Chandra
Cc: Gary; Wayne; Dana; Preetha
Subject: RE: WI-00414 and the 15 min screen saver requirement

It clearly reads "if more than 15 minutes." 10 is less than 15, what's the problem? What am I missing?

From: Wayne
Sent: Thursday, May 19, 2005 11:12 AM
To: Dan; Allan; Peter; Linda; Kara; Chandra
Cc: Gary; Dana; Preetha
Subject: RE: WI-00414 and the 15 min screen saver requirement

I agree with Dan and Allan. If the screen saver or inactivity lock occurs at 15 minutes or less then it is in compliant.

From: Gary
Sent: Thursday, May 19, 2005 10:40 AM
To: Allan; Kara; Peter; Linda; Chandra
Cc: Wayne; Dan
Subject: RE: WI-00414 and the 15 min screen saver requirement

A setting of 10 minutes exceeds the requirement "force re-verification of the user's identity if more than 15 minutes of inactivity has lapsed after user authentication was granted". The operative words are "if more than 15 minutes". i.e. as long as reverification is required when the system has been idle for 15 minutes or longer, you're in compliance. Since this actually happens at 10 minutes for R&D instead of the standard 15 because of another R&D requirement/SOP, you're still in compliance. If it locked 30 seconds after inactivity started, you'd still be in compliance because you'd already be locked out by the time you hit 15 minutes. You should only have to go through all these other steps that are being discussed if someone had written the document as "exactly 15 minutes", or "if more than 15 minutes and no sooner or else", or something along those lines.

This seems like a non-event to me.

From: Dan
Sent: Friday, May 20, 2005 9:33 AM
To: Allan
Cc: Wayne; Linda; Peter; Preetha; Dana; Kara
Subject: Screen Saver Timeout
Importance: High

While you explained to me your position that the WI indicates not more than 15 minutes of inactivity would be allowed, that is unfortunately what you wrote in the WI. The statement (copied below) does not mean what you told me the intention was.

4.4.3.3 The system will include an automatic inactivity lock to force re-verification of the user's identity if more than 15 minutes of inactivity has lapsed after user authentication was granted. (e.g. re-entry of user password)

I suggest you re-write the WI to say "The system will include an automatic lock which allows no more than 15 minutes of inactivity. Once the system locks, the user's identity must be re-established (e.g., re-entry of the user password).

From: Dana
Sent: Friday, May 20, 2005 9:55 AM
To: Dan; Allan
Cc: Wayne; Linda; Peter; Preetha; Kara
Subject: RE: Screen Saver Timeout

I agree with Dan. This is the position we have stated from the beginning. It is just a matter of wording, but the wording in the WI does not give us any flexibility. I believe the wording Dan has suggested will fix the issue.

From this chain of emails, the reader can conclude that:
  a. 10 minutes is less than 15 minutes.
  b. 10 minutes is no more than 15 minutes.
  c. 15 minutes is not exactly 10 minutes.
  d. In compliant, in compliance, and incompliant all mean the same thing.
  e. No more than 10 people were involved in this email discussion.
  f. No fewer than 10 people were involved in this email discussion.
  g. A, B, D but not E
  h. A, C, D but not F
  i. All true except H
  j. What was the question again?

The most important point to learn from these emails is that:
  a. You should consider the ramifications of certain wording when writing work instructions.
  b. You should never read work instructions too closely.
  c. If you discovers such a discrepancy, you should keep it to yourself.
  d. This is the type of pointless activity most people in corporate America spend the majority of their time on.

Question 3: (25 points)

Question 3: (25 points)

Background to the following email:

A well-known pharmaceutical company was experiencing a downturn in business and a stock price decline of 40%. The anticipated drugs in its pipeline either failed to gain approval, had severe harmful side effects, or lacked the efficacy of other drugs in the class. Even the drugs that were acquired as part of expensive mergers failed to meet expectations. The failed launches had received considerable press coverage and the stock price reflected that.

To make matters worse, the plan to choose a successor for the CEO turned into a very public and nasty battle between the candidates, disrupting the business operations further. The company had been through several rounds of layoffs and more were expected.

At a meeting of the board, the CEO and Chairman was summarily fired and his successor named. The two losers in the contest soon resigned. All of this was covered extensively in the press, including the amount of the CEO's unprecedentedly large severance package at a time when employee compensation was being cut. The following is the first communication from the new CEO that was sent to the entire company.

Message from the new CEO

Dear Colleagues,

It is my privilege to write to you today. I assume my new responsibilities as Chief Executive Officer with respect and admiration for what our company represents—and with great confidence that we can accelerate our transformation to meet the challenges of the rapidly-changing environment in which we operate.

We move forward from a position of strength—with outstanding people, extraordinary operating and financial flexibility, the industry's best pipeline of new medicines, and unique opportunities to pioneer new directions in healthcare delivery and services. These unmatched assets are a testament to the leadership of our Chairman, to (the other contestants who didn't get the job) who have contributed so much to our growth and success; and to all members of our team around the world.

Just in the past few weeks, when I attended the U.S. launch meetings of our most-recently-introduced medicines, I was reminded of the unique spirit, dedication and enthusiasm that characterizes our colleagues. The excitement and professionalism of our world-class field force was really something to behold. I've also had the opportunity over the last year to spend a lot of time with our scientists, who demonstrate every day a powerful commitment to finding new cures and exploring the most-innovative approaches to medical research. These two groups—the scientists who discover and develop new medicines and the professionals who educate health professionals and patients about those medicines—are supported by thousands of experienced and highly-skilled people in all the critical functions of our company around the world.

My basic premise is that for us to be as successful in the future as we have been in the past, the company must do business in new ways. And to do that, we need to change—and change in ways that are fundamental and sustained. We need to look at everything we do with fresh eyes to make sure we're adapting to our changing environment as rapidly as that environment is changing, to make sure that we're operating nimbly and decisively, and, most of all, to make sure that we are meeting the needs of the patients we serve.

Our goal, working together, should be to focus on actions that deliver life-sustaining medicines to patients and create value for our shareholders—and to do that with a sense of urgency.

I look forward to working with you to put our knowledge of health and wellness to work so that all people live longer, healthier lives.

The new CEO's omission of mentioning the layoffs, decreased employee compensation, former CEO's severance package, and the bad publicity around his succession shows that:

    a. It is contrary to corporate culture to admit mistakes.
    b. Reality is a matter of perspective.
    c. The view from the top is much rosier than from elsewhere.
    d. The new CEO has been partaking of the free pharmaceuticals.

The probable impact of this communication on the employees is to:

    a. Place their trust in the straight-talking CEO.
    b. Motivate them to update their resumes.
    c. Remind them that the first step in the grieving process is denial.
    d. Get them psyched for more layoffs!

Question 4: Essays (50 points)

Please rewrite the passages above in the clearest possible manner, using the U-It-I (You, It, and I) model, below:

You: Instead of thinking of yourself all the time and trying to figure out how best to make yourself understood, start from a position of empathy. Imagine what the person on the receiving end will think of what you have to say. This is especially important when your audience is undergoing layoffs and receiving less-than-expected compensation due to poor company performance and record-low stock price while the just-fired CEO walked away with $60 million. Your audience's biggest issues need to be addressed first because everything else will just be ignored.

It: The "it" is a realistic and honest assessment of the situation. Please, no jargon, no clichés, and no sports analogies. Feel free to include the positive aspects of the situation, but glossing over the problems never does anyone any good. In many corporate cultures, sharing bad news is frowned upon because no one wants to look bad. However, without candid communication, small problems become big ones, and the right people cannot address them in a timely fashion.

I: The third element of "I" comes into play once you've addressed your audience and the situation in an open and honest manner. Now it's time to talk about what you want in an open and honest manner. No hidden agendas, please. Just say what you mean and mean what you say. Use of feeling words like "I fear" or "I hope" or "I want" can be very useful if you are unaccustomed to expressing yourself candidly.

In your rewrites, you will be awarded extra points for your creative use of the words "synergy," "strategic," and "innovative."

Teachers' Answer Key

1. Chart of Accounts

G---

I have investigated the use of the corporate chart of accounts for Spinco and am afraid that what I've found is not what you want to hear. I realize that you and the team are under great pressure to get Spinco up and running quickly and that all of our systems rely on the chart of accounts, but the structure of the corporate CoA will be too cumbersome for a much smaller and less heavily regulated consumer business.

I've talked with pretty much the whole finance team, and we all agree that, because everything else will be built off the CoA, it is critical that we get it right in order to avoid lots of hassle and rework downstream. In the big picture, taking longer to build the correct CoA will help us get up and running more quickly than having to retrofit and redo later on. I think the best thing to do is to put together a team and hire consultants to work on it now. I realize that we have resource constraints, but if we put it in the plan of the critical 30-60-90-120 day activities, we will see where it fits in *synergistically* with our priorities.

Your thoughts?

C---

Students should have determined that the original structure of the email was an attempt at disguising the fact that the author believed the idea of reusing the chart of accounts was a very bad one. Correct answers should address directly and non-confrontationally the concern that G wants a quick solution and probably won't like what C has found.

2. Screen saver email

I am sending this email out to all those in regulatory and compliance for your guidance. I know that we like to err on the conservative side of compliance issues, and I came across something that may violate the letter, though not the spirit, of the law as it is written. Our new computers in R&D have a screensaver that comes on after 10 minutes of inactivity and requires the user to login again with their ID and password. The work statement actually says [yada, yada, work statement].

In essence, the new PCs surpass the security requirement but don't meet the language of the work statement. In an effort to avoid the non-value adding work of rewriting the work statement and going through all the signature approvals, I am appealing to you for your *strategic* advice. Do you think we will have an issue in an audit?

Students should address overtly the key point of wanting to avoid having to rewrite and reapprove work instructions when the new PCs actually have tighter security than warranted. Students may also want to add how busy the author is and state that the author couldn't possibly rewrite the work instructions for at least several weeks (bonus points).

3. CEO's first message

It is a privilege for me to be contacting you as the new CEO. I want you to know that despite what you may have read in the press, I have great respect for the previous leadership and for the successes they helped bring about over the past few years. However, although we have a great legacy, presently we have many problems we have to address. Many of you have seen colleagues let go, have had reductions in your budgets, and felt the impact of our languishing stock price.
This is why we need to change. I believe our fundamentals are strong: outstanding people, extraordinary operating and financial flexibility, and unique opportunities to pioneer new *strategic* directions in health care delivery and services. We have an excellent foundation on which to build, *innovative* scientists committed to developing groundbreaking new drugs, knowledgeable and caring professionals who teach health care providers about our medicines, and all the dedicated and highly skilled colleagues who support these *synergistic* functions. So I am asking you, our creative and resourceful colleagues, to look at how we operate with fresh eyes and find ways that we can be more efficient, more effective, and more nimble……..
[Yada, yada, yada]
……..so that all people can live longer, healthier lives.

Students' revised emails should incorporate several reality checks:
- Acknowledging the wide-spread press coverage of the CEO's forced retirement, his huge retirement package, and the bad publicity surrounding the competition to choose the successor
- Acknowledging the tough situation of the employees and the record-low stock price
- Omitting references to the "great" pipeline and the new drug launches which were receiving lots of bad press

The revised email should be sure to gain the trust of the audience by directly addressing the problems of the company and its bad press and afterwards offering hope for a better future. Although a specific path forward to get out of the present mess would be appropriate to inspire confidence and optimism, it is probably too much to ask at this point. Award bonus points for using all three of the terms: "strategic," "innovative," and "synergistic" in one paragraph.

The revised email should be sure to gain the trust of the audience by directly addressing the problems of the company and its bad press and afterwards offering hope for a better future. Although a specific path forward to get out of the present mess would be appropriate to inspire confidence and optimism, it is probably too much to ask at this point. Award bonus points for using all three of the terms: "strategic," "innovative," and "synergistic" in one paragraph.

Good communications are not all that difficult. You just tell the truth—the plain, unspun, unadulterated truth. If you are holding the prince captive to make him marry against his wishes, and you want your guards to ensure he doesn't escape before the wedding, first, make sure your guards aren't inebriated. Second, make sure they understand the urgency and importance of the situation, and, third, just tell them in plain English what you want them to do.

> **Top 10 Management Communication Skills Rules**
>
> 1. Never, ever say what you mean.
> 2. Never, ever mean what you say.
> 3. Never communicate bad news. Emphasize the positive, no matter how bad the situation.
> 4. Readily admit to being wrong about trivial things to show how humble you are. Never admit to being wrong about matters of substance.
> 5. Use as much business jargon as possible. Make sure that no one outside the business world will understand a thing you say.
> 6. Invent acronyms for everything, including acronyms (e.g., AFLA: another four-letter acronym)
> 7. Use sports analogies liberally because the whole company really does act like a sports team.
> 8. Always use the passive voice in order to avoid responsibility. Besides, tasks complete themselves magically.
> 9. Always use five words in place of one pithy word. Similarly, use five sentences where one will do.
> 10. Above all, cover your ass at all times.

Chapter Vocabulary

An-acronym   An outdated abbreviation.

Cutting pledge practices   Claiming ordinary performance as "cutting edge." *Related:* best practice ordination

Irradical   When someone blathers endlessly about some trite concept being totally groundbreaking and innovative.

13

Let's Not Bicker Over Who Killed Whom

Stuck in a competitive paradigm

The tale of Sir Launcelot begins with Launcelot and his trusty page, Concorde, galloping through the countryside on their pretend horses. Alas, out of nowhere, an arrow with a message attached pierces Concorde's chest. The note is from the prince in Swamp Castle who is being forced to marry. Of course, Launcelot assumes that the note is from a damsel in distress, and, ever the opportunist, he seizes the chance to prove his mettle and launch a daring rescue. He bids a last farewell to the dying Concorde (actually, I feel fine, sire) and charges toward the castle wielding his sword, ready for battle. After he fights his way through the guards at the gate, Launcelot proceeds to slaughter the guests who've arrived for the betrothal of Prince Herbert to Princess Lucky (the one with the huge tracts of land). He annihilates everyone in his path to rescue the "damsel in distress." When Launcelot bursts into the tower, Prince Herbert is so overjoyed at being rescued that he starts to sing (cue music.) Launcelot is confused. Surely, there must be a mistake? Where's the beautiful princess?

Upon hearing the music, the king arrives, distressed that some of his guards and guests, including the princess's father, have been recklessly slaughtered. Launcelot explains himself to the king, while Herbert climbs out the window on a rope. Learning that Launcelot is from Camelot, fine pig country, the king starts to plot anew. He decides to give Launcelot a tour of the grounds and, as he passes the window, cuts the rope. He has other plans now.

Who Moved My Holy Hand Grenade?

The king and Launcelot return to the wedding reception where the guests start to riot against Launcelot. He just murdered their aunties! He reacts by reaching for his sword and battling again until the king stops him. Launcelot apologizes. He can't help himself. He just gets carried away with being a hero and all. But the king has bigger things on his mind than who killed whom, and he announces that because the bride's father is dead and his son has fallen to his death, how about a union of Princess Lucky and Sir Launcelot? Of course, having such affection for the bride, he, the king, would act as her legal guardian. Too bad neither the bride's father nor Prince Herbert is actually dead. As the prince starts to sing about how he survived his fall, Concorde arrives just in time to save his master from certain doom.

In Chapter 10, I talked about two of the downsides of implementing a business strategy: missed opportunities and the risk involved in putting all your eggs in one basket. The main purpose of the chapter was to challenge the assumption that you have to have a business strategy to be successful. This dogma is woven so intricately into the canvas of corporate conventional wisdom that I rarely hear or read anything that questions it. My other beef with business strategy is its focus on competitive strategy. Fortunately, this dogma is being challenged today, but not nearly as hard as it should be.

In 1980, Michael Porter, a Harvard professor, published a book called *Competitive Strategy: Techniques for Analyzing Industries and Competitors* and ushered in the age of business strategy consultants. When I was a consultant at Deloitte Haskins & Sells in the late 1980s, Porter's book was required reading. His main theme is a five forces model, which shows the external and internal factors facing businesses: competitors, potential entrants, potential substitutes, buyers, and suppliers. Once you analyze these forces, you can develop a business strategy that gives you a competitive advantage. He also outlined some successful generic strategies like the low-cost producer or the provider of a unique offering. Other strategy tools that were and still are a must for strategy development are the SWOT (Strengths, Weaknesses, Opportunities, Threats) analysis and the BCG (Boston Consulting Group) portfolio matrix. (Turn to Appendix B in this book for an overview of these models.) Back in the 1980s, armed with these models, we could call ourselves strategy consultants and charge a significant premium over operations consultants or information technology consultants. Unfortunately for us, it wasn't until the 1990s that strategy consultants really caught on, and by that time our unit had been taken over by Touche Ross. So our strategy of becoming strategy consultants was foiled by external influences. If only we had had a model to help us see that coming!

Since that time, corporate strategizing has become a big business, not just for consultants, but also for authors, publishers, periodicals, professors, and preachers. Yet if you keep up with the press, you'll notice that they all have their roots in competitive strategy. Listen to how the business world talks about strategy: "beating your competition," "finding a competitive advantage," "exploiting a gap," "marketing warfare," "price wars," "outmaneuvering," "defending your turf," "launching a marketing offensive," "competitive pricing," "zero-sum game," "first-mover advantage," "defending market share," and "attacking the opposition." These are all terms of warfare. Besides Porter's book, two other popular books for formulating strategy are *The Art of War* by Sun Tzu and *On War* by Carl von Clausewitz. Sun Tzu's book is over a thousand years old and von Clausewitz's over two hundred years. These were written in the time of city-states, not in the time of NAFTA and the European Union. Surely, there must be some new ideas since then?

Although I wholeheartedly endorse the process of analyzing your business and planning for the future, I find the war analogy both limiting and depressing. It assumes that businesses operate in a zero-sum battlefield, meaning any gain of growth or market share is done at the expense of the others in the industry, like everyone fighting over the same bits of land. You can find evidence of this mind-set in corporate mission statements. Many state as their goal to become number one in their industry or to grow at a pace faster than the competition. To achieve their strategies of beating everyone else, companies engage in marketing battles by launching imitative products or blitzkrieg-like advertising campaigns. Although many manufacturers have learned the cost of price wars, where competitors continually undercut each other's prices until there is little profit to be made, they still engage in costly advertising wars and retaliatory products. People complain about the stress of today's workplace, and I think that stress has its origin in companies warring with each other. Personally, I believe peace offers more prosperity than war. I'm waiting for someone to publish a book called *Collaborative Strategy: Techniques for Creating Innovative Opportunities and Wealth for Everyone*.

In the business press, the most common ailment mentioned by executive management is the lack of innovation. How can people be innovative when they are busy beating the crap out of each other? The number of lawyers in corporations increases to attack or defend product positions while non-essential R&D is cut. (How do you know which part is non-essential? How many great products were discovered by accident?) One of the most important components of building an innovative organization is creating the time to innovate. The modern workplace offers little time for employees to even think, let alone plan and execute something innovative. If our competitor does something, we are compelled to react. If a plan or campaign does not meet its targeted projections, it must be reworked immediately in order to make the numbers. All of these actions provoke reactions in our competitors, which in turn require our reactions. This is the never-ending cycle that is inherent in complex systems until one side decides to stop. Sun Tzu's ancient book has a section on when not to go to war, but I think his fans missed that part.

I'm a big believer in win/win solutions. Successful negotiators talk about deconstructing the paradigms of the two sides and finding creative solutions that meet both sides' conditions rather than compromises that meet only some their conditions. These are the win/win solutions. Although business people love to use the "win/win" phrase, they really don't operate in a win/win mode. When a company opens up a whole new business opportunity, competitors rush in and flood the market with me-too products, making that opportunity less attractive. If a company offers an innovative product, again there is a rush to play in the same space. In other words, the current marketplace is competitive. By its very definition, a competition has a winner and losers. It is not win/win. Although there are times when a friendly competition can motivate people, especially those with a domineer personality, businesses rely too heavily on competition when collaboration is needed more. The tale of the three-headed knight is one such example, as are many performance-based reward systems in which employees need to best each other to get more bonus dollars.

If we look back in time, cavemen struggling to survive had a few options when they encountered other caveman tribes. They could start a war and fight it out until one group won. This would, of course, result in serious casualties that could risk the survival of the group. They could hide out and periodically raid the other tribe and expect that they would be raided in return—not a way to live that fosters prosperity. They could run away and find somewhere else to live. Possibly they could try to live in the same area but hunt different prey and seek different food sources. Finally, they could try to collaborate and pool their resources with the other tribe, which might eventually give them the time and resources to pursue agriculture. Our caveman ancestors used all these strategies, but companies today engage primarily in the first two competitive strategies. Companies used to be content to sell in their niches, but today everyone wants to play everywhere. Luxury car makers have moderately priced models, and mass market car manufacturers have luxury brands. Toothpaste makers are expected to offer toothbrushes, flosses, mouthwash, and whiteners. Clothing designers create clothes, handbags, accessories, and perfume under multiple names to appeal to different price markets. No wonder companies are stuck trying to beat the crap out each other. There isn't much room to do anything else.

I realize that the argument for an intensely competitive environment is that the consumers win by getting low-priced goods, but I question if we have calculated the true costs of these goods. Many goods that used to be more durable, such as small appliances, furniture, and clothes, have become readily disposable. Who fixes a toaster or a TV these days? My mother owned one microwave and one toaster for most of her adult life. I seem to go through them like paper plates. Even expensive clothes are not particularly well made. I don't think my chairs from Ikea will be handed down as family heirlooms. A second cost is how much time and attention is lost to advertisements. There is no respite from advertisers. They are everywhere, creating an obstruction between us and what we want to do. The irony is that the only way to support these big marketing budgets is for us to buy more, and, to do that, these companies need even bigger marketing budgets to get our attention, and so on in a vicious circle. Third, many people now realize the cost to our environment of all these disposable goods. I laugh at all the advertisers who tout their "green" products and try to convince you that buying those products will help the environment. The best way to be green and help the environment is by not buying anything at all (although that doesn't help the economy). Finally, there is a human cost. The phrases "increasing efficiency" and "lowering the cost of production," which are bandied about so frequently, are euphemisms for layoffs, longer workdays, and lower pay.

What's the alternative? Pouring more money into R&D than marketing, investing in the development and well-being of employees, building partnerships with other companies, and understanding customers' needs are the building blocks of innovative companies. How much convincing do customers need to use Google or buy iPods and smart phones? A study conducted by the Human Capital Institute found a positive correlation between investment in employee learning and development and company stock price and revenues. Companies that have a reputation for great, innovative products also have a reputation for being great, innovative places to work. This is not news to anyone. The building blocks of great companies are not news, either. Yet, it is rare to find companies doing more than paying lip service to these tenets. They are struggling to meet earnings commitments and profit projections and to defend their market share. The company leaders tell themselves that one day the competition won't be so fierce or the economy will be better, and when that day comes they'll invest in employees, research, partnerships, and providing real value for their customers. Stuck in battle mode and fighting for survival, companies can't invest in the foundations for peace and prosperity.

Another famous book, *The Innovator's Dilemma*[10] by Clayton Christensen, describes how companies are unable to create disruptive innovations[11]

---

[10] Certain business books are able to articulate important ideas for their times, and their influence spreads throughout the business community. Both *The Innovator's Dilemma* and Michael Porter's *Competitive Strategy* are such books. However, I've realized that, although the terminology may have spread, most people using the jargon have never read the books. Imagine my surprise when my business unit was asked to come up with a disruptive innovation goal. I asked the CIO if he really wanted to put the unit out of business, and he just stared at me. My rule of thumb is that half the people using the jargon have actually seen the book. Of that half, only half have purchased or borrowed the book to read. Of that half, only half have opened the book. Of that half, only half have read it. Of that half, only half understood the concepts. Of that half, only half were able to assimilate and apply the concepts. This, of course, proves Zeno's paradox that businesses can never advance a new concept.

[11] A disruptive innovation is one that puts an existing product or industry out of business. For example, DVRs disrupted VCRs, and smart phones are disrupting cameras.

in their own industries because they are too focused on advancing their current position. As a product line becomes successful, manufacturers offer upscale, more expensive versions and begin to ignore the low-cost market in order to maximize profits. Small competitors gain entrance to the marketplace by exploiting the low-cost niche and offering a cheaper alternative. The established player is too entrenched in its current niche to pay attention to the new technologies that may disrupt its products because usually they enter the marketplace as cheap and/or unreliable. Eventually, the low-cost products evolve to more upscale versions and displace the established offering. This is Christensen's explanation for why large companies are unable to develop disruptive innovations. They are too preoccupied with dominating or defending their market to develop competing technologies or even to recognize the potential of competing technologies.

If companies truly want to innovate and create new opportunities, they need to put down their battle-axes and start plowing some fields and signing some peace treaties. However, like Launcelot, corporations have become habituated to this war paradigm and can't help themselves from going to battle, even when it involves slaughtering the dinner guests.

Uncover the Enemy Within

I have met the enemy, and he is us. While many companies think that their enemies lay externally in the form of new competitors, new entrants, regulations, or other forces, most business failures are due to problems within the organization. The enemy within is more fearsome than the enemy outside. To help an organization identify its internal enemies, I've adapted the aforementioned strategy tools to help organizations diagnose their internal problems.

Five Farces Model
Five farcical beliefs shared by many medieval kings and modern companies that lead to poor performance

Belief in the Power of Goals/Grails
Just like Arthur and his knights, all we have to do to obtain the Holy Grail is gather a group of noblemen and start a quest. Translated into corporate-speak, we can become creative, responsive, and innovative by instituting an initiative, putting together a team, and mandating the goals. Simply mandating from above is all you really need to do.

Belief in Knighted Loyalty
There really is no better way to inspire the loyalty of your men than enlisting them in a futile quest, sending them over bridges of death, and making them fight vicious, albeit small and furry, monsters. Similarly, you can get the most out your employees by treating them like any other capital asset that can bought, sold, and eliminated at will.

Disbelief of Competitor Catapults
How extraordinary that the French would use the wooden rabbit against us. Surely, our competitors won't take retaliatory actions if we go after their businesses (and they don't have the same goal to be number one as we do.)

Belief in Customer Campaigns
If the Black Knight and the Frenchmen aren't going to help us in our quest, we'll just have to fight them until they see things our way. If our customers don't want to buy our products, the best thing to do is bombard them with marketing messages and sales promotions. The quality and design of products and how well they meet customer needs are of lesser importance.

Belief in Sharecropper/holder Variable Interests
Our village peasants enjoy the thrill of war with our neighboring castles and the rollercoaster ride of glory and despair in battle. What fun is long-term growth and stability? Our corporate shareholders feel the same way and demand double-digit growth in the stock price at the expense of company stability and long-term growth.

BKG (Bunnies, Knights, Grails) Priority Portfolio Analysis
A model for determining the potential impact of your corporate activities

Time to completion ↑

Black Knights
Tasks that just won't die

Annual goal setting & updates
Interim & annual performance reviews
Development planning & tracking
Budget planning, tracking, revisions & approvals
Preparing for audits & audits
Documenting regulatory compliance
Keeping SOPs up to date
Systems maintenance & upgrades
Systems & regulatory training

Holy Grails
Tasks you'll just never get to

Spawning new businesses
Improving operations
Establishing a creative environment
Implementing new ideas
Creating great new products
Building new capabilities
Improving relationships
Helping the world
Having a life

Killer Bunnies
Those little things you just can't get past

Boss's urgent requests for information
Boss's boss's urgent requests for information
Email
Voicemail
Instant messaging
Expense reporting
Helping coworker with PC problems
Coworker's need for venting
Boss's need for venting
The internet

Trojan Rabbits
They seemed like good ideas at the time

Voicing a dissenting opinion
Outsourcing customer service & help desk functions
Replacing long-term experienced workers with cheaper, inexperienced part-timers
Winning a bidding war for an acquisition
Selling off non-core business assets
Centralizing all your functions
Then decentralizing all your functions

Potential impact →

SWEAT Analysis

These are the killer bunnies (see next chapter) in modern corporations that take vicious little bites out of efficiency, energy, effectiveness, and enthusiasm. In other words, they suck you dry, drip by drip.

Scheduling	Waiting	Email	Ass covering	Team meetings
The amount of time it takes to get a meeting on the calendar with all the required parties and the amount of time it takes to reschedule due to all the conflicts that arise once you have a meeting on the calendar.	The extent to which everyone must wait for everyone else to show up and be present at meetings and conference calls, including the time taken by early arrivers who get distracted by other tasks, like email, and end up being later than the late arrivers.	The extent to which employees rely on email as the sole source of communication. Symptoms include in-box backlogs of hundreds of emails, glancing through items without understanding them, responding with unintelligible replies, and copying everyone under the sun.	The amount of time and energy devoted to documenting all the ways in which you are blameless for the shit that is about to happen and copying everyone under the sun on the documented ways in which you are blameless for the shit that is happening.	The extent to which the day is full of meetings that don't accomplish anything and just rehash the prior meetings that didn't accomplish anything either because no one had time to prepare because their days are full of useless meetings where no one comes prepared.

> **Top 10 (Okay, 11) Signs Your Company Is Stuck in Battle**
>
> 1. You use survival training as team building.
> 2. Your employees must attend a boot camp at some point in their careers.
> 3. You start your company meetings with a battle cry (We're number 1!).
> 4. Your projects and initiatives go by secret code names.
> 5. Your employees have unofficial security clearances, and only a select few know what the company is really working on.
> 6. You have a team dedicated to enemy surveillance.
> 7. You regularly conduct readiness drills in the event of a crisis.
> 8. You have a special team of people you call in to rescue a faltering project.
> 9. You have a small team sequestered to work on a secret weapon.
> 10. *The Art of War* is required management reading.
> 11. This chapter has totally pissed you off.

Chapter Vocabulary

Best-in-crass Constantly touting how superior your department is to others.

Clobboration Achieving consensus through the use of force.

Cost confeignment Playing around with budget numbers so it looks like you are saving money.

Knowledge transblur Ensuring that the person you are supposed to train (usually to replace you) gets the wrong information.

Mushing the envelope 1. Setting your stretch goals to be easily achievable. 2. Pretending that ordinary operations are extraordinary.

Thought bleeder A person recognized for creativity who has stolen all the best ideas from coworkers.

World class ordination Proclaiming your approach, process, or methodology as being best in class when, in reality, it is equivalent to what everyone else in the world already has.

14

Behind the Bunny?

It's the little things that bite you

Tim the Enchanter leads the gang to the cave where the grail is supposedly hidden. Only the cave is guarded by the most fearsome and vicious monster. As the men wait in fear for the monster to show itself, out hops a bunny rabbit of the white, fluffy kind. Tim shouts something like "There it is, the beast!" but the men are confused. It's only a little bunny rabbit. Is there a beast behind it? Apparently, not. Arthur dispatches one of his men to slay the rabbit, but to his dismay the bunny grasps the knight by the throat and rips it apart. Total chaos ensues as all the knights attack the barbaric beast only to be bested by the bunny, which nimbly leaps to each man's throat. Dead knights lay strewn about the entrance to the cave, and Arthur realizes that a different tack is needed.

That's the story of the little killer bunny rabbit. This is my story of the little thing that bit me. It is the story of the worst night of my life.

During the winter of 1988, when I was a consultant with Deloitte Haskins & Sells, I was working on an engagement for Hills Pet Products, a division of Colgate-Palmolive. I was 25 years old and a typical type A personality: very stressed, no sense of humor or perspective, driven, and image conscious. I had a collection of designer suits to die for. With me on the project was Jay, a manager from the Atlanta office, while I was out of the Newark office. We were wrapping up a project to create an implementation plan for a Material Requirements Planning (MRP) manufacturing system at two sites, one in Topeka, Kansas, and the other in Richmond, Indiana. At the end of the planning phase, we were trying to sell more work by either helping with the implementation or finding a different opportunity at Colgate-Palmolive.

Every consulting engagement concluded with a final presentation that was both a summary of our accomplishments and an assessment of other opportunities that could benefit from our help. We had scheduled our final presentation for a Wednesday at 9 A.M. in Topeka with both Hills' upper management and some senior management from Colgate-Palmolive. This was our first opportunity to present in front of C-P, and we were very anxious to win some work from them. We had been working on the final presentation for a few weeks and had drafted most of the content. We just needed to turn it into slides. Remember that this is 1988, before email, before Kinkos on every corner, before LANs, and before LCDs. We would be using acetate overheads.

Taking no chances with the normal typing pool, I hired extra help to type and print the presentation. I also rented a Macintosh computer and a printer so that we wouldn't have to share equipment with the other staff. At that time, computers, printers, and support for computer-related tasks were still limited in most offices. Most of our staff were using Wang (word processor), and documents were usually handwritten and then typed by secretaries. Monday morning, I arrived at the office early to help set up the rented equipment. Fortunately, the temp had also arrived early, and together we unboxed and connected the Mac to the Epson printer. When we tested it, we learned that the Epson was not compatible with the Mac, so I placed a service call to the rental company.

Meanwhile, Jay had arrived from the Atlanta office and was anxious for us to sit down and pull together the final presentation. I left the temp with the instructions to make sure the printer issue was addressed. I wasn't too concerned because we didn't really need the printer until the next day. Jay and I began revising and drafting slides. The morning came and went without the arrival of the technical support, so I placed another call, this one testy, to the rental company. In the interim, we kept the temp busy typing our slides. The goal was to finish the complete flow of the presentation and the content, leaving Tuesday for revisions only. The Mac was new to us and enabled us to create charts and graphics that we hadn't planned on creating but that we thought would impress our clients. Even the temp was having fun with the graphics capabilities. During the afternoon, the technician for the printer finally arrived and ascertained that the proper drivers were not installed and that he had not brought the right ones with him. He would return in the morning to install them. Getting nervous, I made him guarantee that he would be there first thing. As evening came, the three of us elected to work late to ensure that Tuesday could be spent just on revisions and printing.

On Tuesday morning, I woke up early, packed, and dressed in a winter-white designer wool suit and a black, high-necked silk blouse. I also wore conservative black pumps, a pearl necklace, and pearl earrings. (My attire becomes important later. Remember that it is very businesslike clothing.) I like to travel light and decided not to bring a coat because I'd be indoors mostly, and I would be flying that night to Topeka, where it would be warmer. Arriving at the office early, I was heartened to see both the technician and the temp working on the printer. Forty minutes later, we successfully printed a test page in full color. Hurray! We were in business!

When Jay arrived, we asked the temp to print out the presentation in black and white, so that we could review it. It took a while to print, because it was about 90 pages long and full of charts and graphics. We expected that. Because we didn't have any spare ink cartridges, we didn't want to waste the color ink. We planned that it would take about an hour to print out the full color version, so we decided that we needed to wrap everything up around lunch time in order to make our 5 P.M. flight to Kansas. Jay and I worked feverishly, fixing typos, adjusting spacing, and wordsmithing, and decided to skip lunch in order to get this finished ASAP. We could grab some food at the airport later. A little before 2 P.M., we were happy with what we had and told the temp to print it all out. The temp sent the file to the printer, and we all waited to see our beautiful, color creation printed on acetate. We watched the green light on the printer flash, and we waited and we heard the printer purring, but nothing came out. After about 20 minutes, I called the rental company. They suggested that we had overloaded the printer's memory and asked us to print just one slide as a test. We printed one slide as suggested, which worked, but it took about 5 minutes. The solution was to create smaller files to send to the printer. The temp broke the file into several smaller files and sent those. Nothing. She kept doing this until we had a small enough file size. Only three slides! At five minutes per slide! It was already past 3 P.M., and we had only one slide printed! Jay and I began to manically eliminate slides from the presentation; we had too many, anyway. We deleted and printed in a frenzy, with the temp hand-feeding the acetates one at a time because static was causing them to stick together.

I started to panic when I realized we wouldn't make our flight. Jay retrieved his OAG (Official Airline Guide, remember those?) and made arrangements for us to fly to Kansas City at 7 P.M. The drive from Kansas City to Topeka is about an hour and a half, so no problem. All we had to do was wait for the slides to print. After about an hour and a half of watching the printer spit out 15 slides of 70, the acetates began to melt because the printer was overheating. We had to turn it off and let it cool. I called the rental company, but it was after 4 so they had no other equipment or any interest in helping us. I asked my secretary to find out if there was a production company we could use, but there was no one nearby who could work with a Macintosh file and print in color on short notice. We began calculating: it would take us another six and a half hours to print out the slides at the rate we were going. Manically and disappointedly, we began stripping our pretty graphics and colors from the slides and tried again. They printed but only moderately faster. At 6, we were only half done printing, and Jay decided to head for the airport (this was before 9/11, so it didn't take long to check in and go through security), taking the slides we had with him. I would wait for the rest to print and catch a later flight. I thought there was one at 9 P.M.

The temp and I alternated feeding the acetates by hand because they were sticking together, and I realized that we hadn't eaten lunch and now it was dinner time. I sent her off in search of food, but this being Newark in the '80s, nothing nearby was open, and she didn't want to go far by herself in the dark. Starving, I reassured myself that I would get a meal on the plane, albeit a bad one. Worrying about making the 9 o'clock flight, I made the call to print out the rest of the presentation in black and white. They printed only a little faster, and all the colors translated to black, resulting in undecipherable black-blob slides. (We had never heard of grayscale at the time.) I reversed my decision, and we printed in color again. I decided to confirm the 9 P.M. flight and called the business travel agent.

ME: I need to get to Topeka, Kansas, or to Kansas City tonight. Is the 9 P.M. flight to Kansas City the last flight tonight?
SHE: I don't have any flights to Topeka or Kansas City showing tonight. The last flight was at 7 and that was to Kansas City.
ME (starting to panic): Okay, what do you have that gets me to that area of the country tonight?
She: I don't have anything tonight. I can book you a flight for tomorrow morning, but you won't get in until noon.
ME: I really need to be there tomorrow morning.

SHE: There are no more flights tonight.
ME (trying to be calm): Okay. What's flying tonight going west?
SHE: There are still flights to Chicago's O'Hare. There is one at 9 and one at 11.
ME: Is there a way I can get from Chicago to Topeka by 9 A.M. tomorrow?
SHE: There's a 5:45 A.M. flight from Midway to Kansas City that will get you in around 9.
ME: Perfect. Can you make the reservation on the 9 to O'Hare? Is there space on both in case I have to change?
SHE: Both of the flights have plenty of seats.
ME: Okay, please make a reservation for the earlier flight and the flight from Midway to Kansas City.

In my mind, I began calculating: the flight is about two and a half hours long with a time difference of one hour, so I should be able to make it to a hotel before midnight. Hotel? I didn't make a reservation, but I'd often just shown up at an airport and stayed at whatever hotel was nearby. (Traveling in those days was very different from today. Business travelers frequently just showed up for flights and walked into hotels without any reservations.) Although I'd been to O'Hare a few times, I had no experience with Midway, but I was sure I could find my way around. I returned my attention to the printer, which just died from overheating. I felt relieved that I had an 11 o'clock flight as a backup.

At 9 P.M., I finally had a complete set of color slides. I grabbed my Coach briefcase and overnight bag and headed toward the train station to grab a cab to the airport. As I left the building, I was hit in the face by raindrops. "Of course, it's raining," I said to myself, "and of course I didn't bring a coat. Oh well. At least it's not snow." There were still taxis waiting at the station, and I got to the United terminal almost without incident. Exiting the cab, I got splashed by a car pulling away from the curb, and my white suit was sprayed with gray splotches. I checked in, purchased my tickets, and looked for food on my way down to the concourse. As it was 9:30, nothing was open. I was starving, but I'd taken the flight to Chicago before, and they served a sandwich and peanuts. I really needed a drink to calm myself, but because of renovations nothing was open in this terminal.

I found a quiet seat and reviewed the presentation while my stomach growled something fierce. I started feeling light-headed and the onset of a headache. "I really need to eat," I thought to myself. At about 10:30, we boarded and I realized that the flight was unusually full for this time of night. I overheard another passenger talking and learned that the 9 P.M. flight had been cancelled due to weather delays. The passenger was grateful that this flight was still scheduled. I sighed, happy that I didn't know this until now, and found my seat and settled in. The flight was completely full.

I took out a book to read, but my thoughts were on getting a drink and something to eat. I was impatient for the flight to take off so they could start the meal service. I checked my watch and saw that it was now past 11. Other passengers were starting to grumble, and we tried to get the attention of the flight attendants, but they were intentionally ignoring us. At about 11:30, the captain announced that Newark and Chicago were experiencing weather delays, and he hoped that we would depart by midnight. My head was hurting, and I felt a knot of frustration, fury, and hunger begin to well in my stomach. I pulled myself together and got the attention of a flight attendant and begged her for peanuts. "I've had a really rough day, and I haven't eaten since breakfast," I pleaded. She replied that she was not allowed to serve food until we were in the air. I wondered how they manage to get around this prohibition in first and business classes, but I didn't say anything because being nasty to the flight attendant could have a high price.

Finally, at 1 o'clock in the morning, we took off. A few minutes later, the cabin crew began the meal service. When it was my turn, I asked for a gin and tonic, but the flight attendant told me that there was no alcohol on this flight as she handed me two bags of peanuts. With a sudden realization and sense of dread, I asked what the meal would be.

FLIGHT ATTENDANT: This is it. Peanuts. We don't serve a meal on a flight at this time. We are usually pretty empty, but because of the weather, we've got a crowd tonight.
ME (putting on my best drowned-puppy face): Could you please give me some extra peanuts, then?
FLIGHT ATTENDANT: I'll see what I can do.

Forty minutes later, she returned with about a half dozen bags of peanuts. The passengers around me saw this and began exclaiming that they wanted more, too, and a ruckus ensued over who was going to get the extra peanuts. I ended up with one bag and a dirty look from the flight attendant.

I tried to lean back and sleep but was so stressed and frustrated that I couldn't stop my mind from calculating how long it would take to get to O'Hare and then Midway and Topeka. I'd never been to Midway Airport and had no idea how far it was from O'Hare. Prepared for the worst, I was surprised that we landed without a problem at 2:30 A.M. As I passed through the empty terminal, I looked for a hotel service board or desk to check out hotels at Midway. I wanted to have a destination. However, there was nothing open anywhere at this time, and I soon regretted this detour. When I exited the airport and made my way to the taxi stand, I got drenched with sleet and saw that there were no taxis waiting. On top of being hungry and tired, I was now cold and wet. The arrival area was completely deserted. I trudged back inside to find a pay phone and yellow pages and called for a cab using a calling card that required about 27 digits. I had to dial three times before I entered all the numbers correctly. About 20 minutes later, my cab showed up and a man ran out of nowhere and tried to get in it! Furious, I grabbed my briefcase like a bat in order to beat him with it. Luckily, I had specified my name, and the cabbie didn't let him in. I offered to share, but the man was not heading toward Midway and seemed a little frightened of me.

While we drove to Midway, the cab driver asked me where I was staying. I relayed my whole ordeal to him, and he was surprisingly sympathetic. He offered me a cup of coffee from a pot he had brewing on the front seat, and asked me if I was familiar with the Midway area. I told him no. He told me that it was not a nice area and was concerned about my finding a place to sleep. I didn't fully understand until we drove up and down the street, and I noticed that the motels advertised an hourly rate. Because it was sleeting, the normal contingent of call girls was not out on the street.

Finally, we found a motel that was somewhat suitable, and he waited while I checked it out. It looked clean. It would have to do, and I paid the cabbie a big tip. The man at the desk was very surprised to see me, and I recounted my tale of woe to him. Connected to the motel was a restaurant, closed at this hour, and I asked if he could possibly bring me something to eat—crackers, bread, peanut butter, mints, anything. He responded that he didn't have the keys, but there was an all-night diner a few blocks away. It was no longer sleeting, and he offered to drive me. I agreed and he fetched the motel shuttle to take me. I was half-afraid that he was going to kidnap me and half-elated at the thought of finally having a place to sleep and getting a meal. When we pulled into the parking lot of the diner, I stopped worrying and realized that I was coatless in the Chicago cold, my feet and hair were drenched, and my white suit was a mottled shade of gray. It was 4:30 A.M.

After I entered the diner, I was surprised to see that a few of the tables were full. The hostess seemed surprised to see me and asked if I wanted a table. "I just want a cheeseburger and fries to go," I said, keeping an eye on my ride, fearful that he would leave me stranded. She replied, "I'm not sure if the grill is still open. Let me check." I stopped her and said, "I'll have whatever the cook is able to make. A sandwich would be okay. Anything would be okay." She walked toward the kitchen and came back a few minutes later with the good news that I could have the burger. I think she must have taken pity on me, so I paid her in advance and again checked on my ride. I observed that the diner's other clientele left something to be desired and decided to occupy myself with the menu in order to avoid eye contact.

As I studied the menu, a man, about my size and obviously drunk, approached me. "Honey," he said, pointing to the parking lot and nodding his head toward a car, "I'll give you forty dollars." His expression was quite eager. Now, even though I've had a rough night, I was wearing a formerly winter-white designer business suit, matching pumps, a high-necked silk blouse, and a pearl necklace and earrings, so at first I didn't understand. When it dawned on me what he wanted, I became infuriated. All the frustration, stress, discomfort, and hunger of the last 18 hours rose within me in an overwhelming wave of wrath that would be unleashed upon this misfortunate man looking for a thrill.

I couldn't keep myself from screaming incredulously. "Forty dollars? Forty dollars!" I cried, "What do you think I am? " Even louder, I screamed again, the only words that would come out, "Forty dollars! Forty dollars?!! Forty dollars?"

The man stumbled backwards, quite taken aback, and then tried to gain some composure. Everyone in the diner was looking at us. He raised his arms and hands in a half-apologetic, half-questioning gesture and said, "Okay, okay, okay. Fifty."[12]

All my anger, stress, and frustration melted away in hysterical laughter. I started to cackle uncontrollably, and the woman at the counter rushed to get my food and usher me out. The motel shuttle was still waiting, thank God, and I ate, showered, changed, and rested for a few minutes before he drove me to my flight. My flight arrived in Kansas City early; I sped to Topeka in an hour, and arrived with the slides as Jay was showing his last one. I placed the rest on the overhead projector as he gave me a dirty look. He was obviously quite angry with me and had been stretching out the material on that last slide for the past few minutes. However, the rest of the presentation went well, and

---

[12] This is an absolutely true story. I swear to it.

we sold an additional phase of work, but not an extension into Colgate. I vowed that I would never put myself through anything like that again and to this day, I test equipment and print documents well in advance as well as make it a policy to always wear a coat in winter.

The moral of the story is, despite having all content prepared, the logistics arranged, state-of-the-art equipment, and hired help, our presentation was done in because we didn't anticipate how long it would take to print a color slide. Seriously, who would have thought it? It's the little things that bite you!

Many, many years later, I had an interview with a CIO for a position for which I possessed all the requisite experience and skills. I had already passed screening interviews and prepared well for the interview. I even wrote up a few recommendations for some of the challenges that had been described to me. Overall, I was feeling very confident as the administrative assistant led me into an office where the CIO was wrapping up a meeting with another woman. That is, until I saw it—a large booger hanging from her nose. As I was about to mention, "You have something under your nose," I realized that the other woman was still in room and obviously had not mentioned it during their meeting. That would be awkward. As the woman collected her belongings, the CIO and her assistant had a quick conversation, and I was certain the booger would then be noted, but again, not so. Her assistant hadn't said anything, either. Aren't administrative assistants supposed to tell you things like that?

Now I was in a predicament. Normally, I tell people if something is wrong—if they have something caught in their teeth or their fly is unzipped—and would have done so in this case, but two people including the administrative assistant had not. Did they know something I didn't? Maybe I shouldn't say anything. While I was mulling over this booger decision, the CIO had sat down and was addressing me. I had no clue what she was saying. All I saw was this giant booger hanging from her nose caught in the light hairs above her lip, vibrating as she spoke, more white than green and pretty solid as boogers go. "Pay attention!" I reprimanded myself and asked her to repeat the question, not a good start to a job interview. As I recounted my background and relevant experience, I realized I couldn't look her in the face. Anytime I did, all I could focus on was "it" hovering over her lip. I chided myself for not telling her but felt that it was now too late to say anything.

As I answered more questions, I tried looking at her ear. Have you ever tried conversing with someone's ear? It's completely unnatural. Yet I couldn't make eye contact without getting completely distracted by the phlegm. Without eye contact, I was unable to generate any kind of rapport. Plus, I just couldn't concentrate on the discussion. This was absolutely the worst interview I had ever been on, and I couldn't wait to get out of there. My perfect job was done in by a piece of snot!

Beware of the killer bunny rabbits, the little, seemingly insignificant things in life that can have dire consequences. We may not be conscious of it, but much of our thinking has been shaped by Newtonian laws: for every action, there is an equal and opposite reaction, and a force needed to move an object is proportional to the size of its mass. In short, we expect that big objects require big forces and have big impacts while small objects require small forces and have small impacts. The stories in my life show that I am often defeated by the smallest things—boogers and melting acetates. In fact, that seems to be true of most catastrophes. Geese have been known to bring down jet airliners, a frozen O-ring caused the demise of the Challenger space shuttle, and substandard rivets caused the catastrophic failure of the Titanic's watertight compartments. It's chaos theory, not Newton's laws, that can explain how massive disasters are caused by little, seemingly insignificant things.

Overview of Chaos Theory

The study of chaos has shown that tiny changes can have huge impacts. A small effect can start a cascade of effects, and each in turn can start another cascade until the effects compound and cause a massive reaction. You may have heard of the butterfly effect, discovered in 1961 by Edward Lorenz, a meteorologist at MIT. He had programmed an early computer with a very simple weather forecasting model. He ran this program over and over, changing starting conditions to look for patterns in temperature, pressure, air currents, and other atmospheric factors that could be useful in weather prediction. One day he saw something interesting in the middle of a run and wanted to run the program again under the same conditions. In a hurry, he didn't start the program from the beginning. Instead he found a point on the computer printout before the area of interest and typed those in those parameters. Expecting the program to replicate the results he wanted to revisit, he went for a cup of coffee and let the computer crank. When he returned, the results were vastly different from the previous run.

Initially thinking that there was a mistake somewhere, he retraced the results of the program and realized that the printout displayed the parameters as only three decimal places, .506. The computer, however, was using six decimal places, .506127, a 1 part in 1,000th difference. At the start, the program produced a result similar to the initial program, but then the results grew farther and farther apart until there was no resemblance. The 1,000th difference change in starting conditions resulted in a completely different weather pattern, just as a butterfly flapping its wings theoretically creates minute changes in the atmosphere that can cause a chain of events culminating in a cyclone thousands of miles away.

Although there is no evidence that supports cyclones being caused in this manner, there are well-known situations in which one seemingly insignificant person's actions have far-reaching consequences. In January 2008, Jerome Kerviel flapped his wings at Sociét Générale, a French investment bank, causing the European stock market to crash, triggering the plunge of markets around the world, and eventually inducing the U.S. Federal Reserve to cut interest rates. A minor trader at the French bank, Kerviel had racked up $7.2 billion in losses on bullish positions in European markets at a time when fears of recession were causing markets to drop worldwide. When SociétGénérale discovered these unsanctioned positions, it was forced to sell them in a down market, causing an avalanche of sell orders and generating rumors that a big hedge fund was in trouble. This in turn caused more panic and more selling, affecting stock markets around the world. The market downturn on top of a fear of a recession and problems with mortgage lending in the United States led the Federal Reserve to cut interest rates. One person's bad decisions ended up affecting billions of people across the globe. Similarly, in 1995 a trader in Singapore, Nick Leeson, working for London's Baring Bank, managed to accrue $1.4 billion in losses by trading in futures. Single-handedly, he caused the oldest merchant bank in Great Britain, financier of the Louisiana Purchase and the Napoleonic Wars, to declare insolvency and be sold off to other banks.

Small things can have a big impact. What's even more amazing is how easy it is for small things to create chaos out of order. Just as we accept Newton's laws without question, we've also grown up believing in steady state systems, like supply and demand. When a product is in high demand, the price increases until the demand drops. As the price drops, demand rises again. This is the steady state system's self-regulating loop. Another classic steady state is the prey-predator relationship. As the predator population increases, the predators eats too many prey, causing their own decline from food shortages and allowing the prey population to increase, which allows more predators to survive—another self-regulating system. Or is it?

Since Lorenz's discovery, scientists have learned more about the butterfly effect and chaos theory in general. One fascinating finding is that a minor change in conditions can turn a stable, steady state system chaotic. Another pioneer of chaos theory, Robert May, used numerical computer models to study population growth. Before his work, many ecologists believed that animal populations converged toward a steady state in which birth rates and thus population growth were kept in balance by predation and starvation. Robert May used a computer program to graph the results for population growth when the population size and growth rate are dependent on each other.

What he found was contrary to common wisdom. For very low values of the growth rate, the population ended up extinct, as expected. For slightly higher values of the growth rate, the population reached a steady state, growing at a constant rate, also as expected. However, once the growth rate surpassed a certain point, the population oscillated back and forth between two values—boom and bust cycles that alternated each year. Continued increases in the growth rate increased the frequency of the oscillations until they became chaotic with no predictability at all. Even weirder, at some values within the chaotic region, the high growth rates resulted in predicable patterns while the surrounding points resulted in chaos. Small changes in the growth rate could lead to either an orderly sequence of population sizes or completely random population sizes.

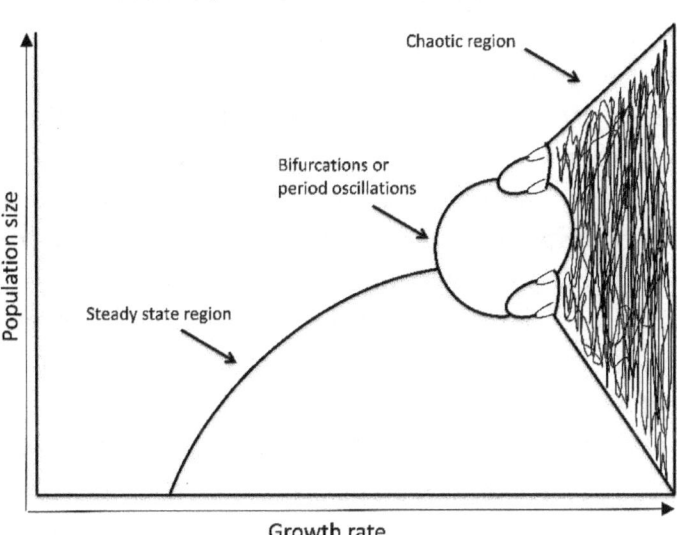

Plot of Population for Various Growth Rates

What was even more amazing was that other scientists recorded exactly the same findings for similar non-linear equations. These equations described cotton prices, income distribution, disease epidemics, and all sorts of unrelated phenomena found in science, the economy, and medicine. The steady state condition is just one among the many outcomes that can occur in a given system. Economies that appear to be self-regulating can end up wildly out of control if some of the conditions change. How many of our economic experts in the past decades professed a belief in the ability of free markets to regulate themselves? Essentially, there are no steady states, no self-regulating systems. The right combination of small changes can turn any system into chaos.

So what does this mean for business? First, because of the increased complexity of our world, we often make decisions on issues we don't fully understand and take actions without much thought for the long-term consequences. Congress didn't fully understand the potential consequences of deregulating banks. Coupled with the promotion of home ownership for the middle class, rising real estate prices, and the desire for better investment returns, Wall Street and the government created the conditions to push a steady state into chaos. In our quest for results, especially quick results, few people take the time to understand how these complex systems work. As Americans, we value action, not understanding. Of the many costly mistakes I've seen, like product recalls and production shutdowns, most happened because of a rush to get a product on the market. In that hurry-up mode, a seemingly simple change, such as a substitute inactive ingredient or a move to a slightly different manufacturing facility, caused a breakdown that could have been anticipated if people hadn't been rushing.

Another problem is that precious few people pay attention to details. In our rushed, action-oriented, overstretched world, we gloss over the intricacies of our plans and hope that the details will take care of themselves. We miss the small things because we are looking for the big things that could harm us. Most companies, especially since 9/11, have disaster recovery and backup plans in case of a disaster. Many of these same companies still use old password technology to secure their systems because biometrics and password management programs are expensive. As a result, many employees need to write their passwords down because they can't possibly remember them all, especially when the passwords change every four months. Which is more likely—a major terrorist event or natural disaster impacting the company or a disgruntled employee, competitor, or hacker causing major mischief?

We need to slow down, pay more attention to the little stuff, and spend more time understanding what we do. In other words, we need to supplement some of that action orientation with thinking. We may feel good if we've prepared for the major catastrophes, but it's the small things that bring us down, especially in the heat of battle. It's a little like our knights using their big, broad swords, meant for battling other armored knights, against a vicious, agile little rabbit.

Chapter Vocabulary

Burn-key solution   Contracting with a vendor for the installation only and not getting any kind of support afterward when things go drastically wrong.

Viscous circle   Same as a vicious circle, only much, much slower.

Viscoussion   Ad nauseam deliberation on the same old issues, which just ends up slowing progress.

15

Thou Shalt Count to Three, No More, No Less

Making simple things complicated

Arthur decides that a different method to defeat the rabbit is needed, and he calls for Brother Maynard to get the Holy Hand Grenade of Antioch. Not quite sure how to use it, they must consult the Holy Book of Armaments, chapter 2, verses 9 to 21.

> And the Lord spake, saying, "First shalt thou take out the Holy Pin. Then, shalt thou count to three, no more, no less. Three shalt be the number thou shalt count, and the number of the counting shall be three. Four shalt thou not count, nor either count thou two, excepting that thou then proceed to three. Five is right out. Once the number three, being the third number, be reached, then lobbest thou thy Holy Hand Grenade of Antioch towards thy foe, who, being naughty in my sight, shall snuff it."

Arthur reaches for the grenade, counts to five (oops), and throws it, decimating the area and, he hopes, the bunny.

Isn't this passage much the way we write in business, with way too much explanation (you gotta cover your ass) and the assumption that the audience is comprised of idiots? It's a little reminiscent of the email chain in the corporate communications quiz, which specified 15 minutes as being more than 10 minutes. I'd like to share an even more convoluted email taken from a very confusing set of emails that occurred after an acquisition, but first here is some background.

Like most large companies, Johnson and Johnson makes frequent business acquisitions. Historically, it would acquire a company and let it exist as a separate entity, the result being numerous operating companies, all considered separate legal entities and operating independently of each other. When J&J purchased the Pfizer Consumer Healthcare (PCH) business in December 2006, the combination of the two companies built some very strong product categories. Pfizer's Desitin was a good fit with J&J's baby products. Pfizer had Listerine; J&J had Reach. The combined wound care portfolio included Band Aid, First Aid, Neosporin, Cortaid, and Bengay. However, in order to realize the synergies between the product portfolios, it would have to combine its business units with the former Pfizer business. The fact that the J&J products resided in multiple operating companies complicated matters. So this is what happened:

Corporate Communications 101 Quiz, Part 2

From: JJGCC Communications
Sent: Wednesday, June 20, 2007 8:27 AM *(Note the date. The acquisition occurred in December 2006. - KP)*
Subject: Company and Division Names

Dear Consumer Associates,

Since the acquisition of Pfizer Consumer Healthcare and the formation of the Johnson & Johnson Group of Consumer Companies, many of you have been waiting patiently for what feels like basic information—the name of your business. Because Johnson & Johnson is a collection of over 200 operating companies, even seemingly straightforward information around naming is often complex, and we've had to work through a number of issues to arrive at final decisions. Well, that work has now been done. We're writing today to announce those decisions—including a new division name in the U.S.—to help you understand which company and division you belong to, and to provide guidelines on the use of company names for all colleagues.

But first I want to remind you of a few important distinctions:

a. Your business unit is a non-legal designation reflecting our internal management structure, and is not to be used externally.

b. Johnson & Johnson Group of Consumer Companies is a non-legal designation used to refer to the collection of Johnson & Johnson consumer operating companies, and is not to be used externally.

c. Your Operating Company is a legal entity (e.g. McNEIL-PPC, Inc.). Your Operating Company may have divisions within it, (e.g., McNeil Consumer Healthcare Division of McNEIL-PPC, Inc.).

In general, here's how business units match up with operating companies and divisions in the U.S. (outside of the U.S. you will have different situations in each country):

OTC GBU: employees are affiliated with one of the following legal entities: McNeil Consumer Healthcare Division of McNEIL-PPC, Inc.; McNeil Nutritionals LLC; or Johnson & Johnson-Merck Consumer Pharmaceuticals Co. For most legacy PCH employees in this GBU, you would be affiliated with the McNeil Consumer Healthcare division.

Beauty GBU: employees are affiliated with one of the following legal entities: Johnson & Johnson Consumer Products Company Division of Johnson & Johnson Consumer Companies, Inc.; Neutrogena Corporation; or OrthoNeutrogena Division of Ortho-McNeil Pharmaceutical, Inc.

Baby GBU: employees are affiliated with the Johnson & Johnson Consumer Products Company Division of Johnson & Johnson Consumer Companies, Inc.

CHC (Consumer Healthcare) GBU: employees are affiliated with one of the following legal entities: Johnson & Johnson Healthcare Products Division of McNEIL-PPC, Inc. (which is for most legacy PCH and all legacy Personal Products Company brands); Johnson & Johnson Consumer Products Company Division of Johnson & Johnson Consumer Companies, Inc. (really just for wound care brands); or OraPharma, Inc.

Sales organization: employees are affiliated with the Johnson & Johnson Sales and Logistics Company, LLC (although a number of new sales members may have a different opco at this time).

Employment is not always tied to the particular brand or global business unit (GBU) an employee may be performing some work on. For example, you could be performing some R&D work on the Reach® brand, which is marketed by Johnson & Johnson Healthcare Products Division of McNEIL-PPC, Inc., but you could be employed by Johnson & Johnson Consumer Companies Inc. in the R&D area. Similarly, if you are fully dedicated to marketing in the Woundcare business, your employer is likely to be Johnson & Johnson Consumer Companies, Inc., even though that franchise is globally part of the Consumer Healthcare

Who Moved My Holy Hand Grenade?

GBU. If you are uncertain of which specific Johnson & Johnson opco employs you, please contact your local Human Resources representative. [13]

Question 1:
According to the above guidelines, if you are a legacy Pfizer employee, you should be working for:
   a. Either OTC or CHC or PPC or GBU or OPCO or M-O-U-S-E
   b. McNeil Consumer Healthcare Division of McNEIL-PPC, Inc., or Johnson & Johnson Healthcare Products Division of McNEIL-PPC, Inc., or Johnson & Johnson Consumer Products Company Division of Johnson & Johnson Consumer Companies, Inc. or McDeal's Mismosh of Divisive Business Units
   c. The legal department as their jobs are obviously secure
   d. Another less confusing company

Question 2:
To be sure your business card has the proper legal identity, you should:
   a. Get about five different versions made and hope one of them is correct.
   b. Have it printed in Japanese, who'll know?
   c. Let your administrative assistant figure it out.
   d. Find a new less confusing employer.

Question 3:
An opco is a:
   a. GBU, only less focused
   b. Legal entropy
   c. Company that likes lots of options and can't make up its mind
   d. Painful surgical procedure

Question 4:
If you were to sum up the point of this email chain, it would be to:
   a. Clarify an essentially unclarifiable legal structure.
   b. Confuse everyone so thoroughly so they no longer ask what company they work for.

---

[13] The HR representatives were among the first to be laid off.

c. Ensure that no legal action can be taken because no one would know what company to name in the suit.
   d. Get as many people as possible to leave voluntarily to decrease the amount of severance to be paid out.

Question 5:
What's really most frightening about this narrative is that:
   a. Lots of other companies grow by acquisitions as well and probably have the same problem.
   b. It demonstrates how complicated merging two companies really is.
   c. It shows why lawyers, employees who don't make or sell products, are in higher demand than employees who actually create value.
   d. Given that J&J is considered to be one of the best companies in the world, what are the rest like?

While I poke fun at the confusion, 5d is very true – Johnson and Johnson is a well-respected company. Their handling of the Tylenol tampering incident in 1982 is often used as a best-practice case study in crisis management. For those of you unfamiliar with that tragedy, someone at a drugstore laced Tylenol capsules with cyanide, killing seven people. Fortunately for all involved, McNeil employees handled the crisis in an exemplary fashion by recalling all products from the shelves and instituting tamperproof packaging, which prompted the widespread use of this kind of packaging for all kinds of over-the-counter products.

This crisis had a huge impact on J&J's culture and continued to be cited 25 years later, as if it happened yesterday. One of the reasons for that impact was that J&J employees are indoctrinated in "The Credo", which is a stated set of values written by Robert Woods Johnson in 1943 that put the welfare of the customer before profits. The ethics espoused in the credo are supposed to guide all company decisions and are referred to often. Another part of J&J's heritage is that the company name is also the brand name for baby products and first aid supplies and has its own brand equity associated with purity. Employees knew that any scandal associated with J&J could taint the namesake brand, and this fear led to the desire to keep the other business units separate by using other legal names and structures. This tactic was successful in 1982 as the Tylenol scandal was associated with McNeil and not the parent company.

The Credo, the Tylenol crisis, and the fear of tarnishing the baby brand resulted in an unwritten rule of "do no harm" creeping into the culture, and this psychological component contributed heavily to the morass of legal entities and complicated organization structure. No one person could harm the company, no single team could tarnish the name, and no sole department could destroy the equity of the Johnson and Johnson brand because of all the controls and the multiple layers of reporting. Numerous operating companies helped ensure that any hint of bad press would be confined to a business unit with a dissimilar name.

However, this legal separation of operating companies meant that one project team, all working on the same project, would report to multiple companies. Sales, R&D, legal, IT, and marketing all reported up through different companies. When you tried to spend money as a team or get an approval for something, you had to navigate multiple accounting and legal entities, all with different policies and spending limits. Whose company should take the expense on its P&L? Which company had the budget? Which companies needed to sign off on an approval? To be honest, I worked at J&J for 17 months, and when I left, I still wasn't sure which company employed me. My paycheck was from McNeil, I worked on consumer healthcare products, my expense code was based on my office location, which was consumer healthcare, but my business cards said corporate IT.

But you don't need a merger or a crisis or even a credo to make things unnecessarily complicated. Any simple rule, written or unwritten, like a policy or a procedure, can take on a life of its own and begin to make life incomprehensibly complex. One of my favorite examples of this is SMART goals (SMART stands for Specific, Measurable, Actionable, Realistic, and Time-bound), the ubiquitous method for defining work tasks that is supposed to make work more manageable but sometimes does quite the opposite.

Let's revisit our pay-for-performance project with Sheila, the HR director. One of Sheila's new objectives was to implement SMART goals for the annual performance reviews because the SMART format makes rating goal achievement easier and more objective. For instance, "providing excellent customer service" is not a SMART goal, whereas "performing as the top one or two customer service centers on an annual customer survey" is a SMART goal. But the desire to put everything in a SMART format can be the cause of needless complexity.

Several years ago, I had a direct report whose job responsibility included giving employees on-site and telephone help with computer problems. I thought this was an important part of her job and allotted it as 20% of her annual performance. To rate her performance, my plan was to randomly contact people who had called for help and ask for their feedback. However, providing customer service help was not a SMART goal, and HR wanted me to rewrite the goal to conform to SMART standards. They suggested I add "helping x number of employees in a month," and I laughed. I only wanted her to help those who called and not have her solicit calls or be penalized if fewer people called. Then they suggested that we implement a customer satisfaction survey for everyone who called and establish a satisfaction index by which we could measure her performance. Everyone who called for help would now be burdened with filling out a survey, thus annoying people and inhibiting calls. Not to mention, tallying the survey results would be a new job responsibility for her and would have to be added to her goals. That wouldn't be a SMART goal and would need some kind of measurement to be SMART (unless you consider tallying 100% of the surveys as meeting the criteria.) After I mentioned these potential consequences, I prevailed with my original plan to randomly ask callers for feedback, but I was one of very few people who objected to creating these "measurable" tasks purely for measurement's sake.

In an earlier paragraph, I used the phrase "take on a life of its own" and therein lies the problem with business complexity. It doesn't take much effort to make things complicated. It does take much more effort, especially time and attention, to simplify things. Policies and procedures rarely get shorter over time unless someone specifically sets about to streamline them.

Like entropy, the fact that complexity seems to increase over time is an inherent part of life; species evolve and become more advanced and then branch into new species that evolve, on so on. Throughout my life, I've often heard how improbable the emergence of life is and that we on Earth must be the only life in the universe. The chances of a primordial pool of molecules and compounds combining spontaneously into self-replicating life, even with the addition of a bolt of lightning here and there, seem pretty slim. Yet, on Earth we have discovered life everywhere from the middle of active volcanoes to the bottom of the ocean. Just how improbable can life really be?

The ideas of Stuart Kauffman, one of the preeminent researchers in the study of complexity, on the emergence of life have shown that, far from improbable, the existence of some form of life is inevitable. Kauffman and others have worked on the theory of autocatalytic (catalysis of a reaction by one of its products) sets, combinations of molecules that reinforce each other and grow. In the primordial soup, before the origins of life, lots and lots of molecules moved about randomly. Some of them acted as catalysts for other molecules: the presence of molecule A increased the presence of molecule B, which increased the presence of molecule C, and so on. Of course, these same molecules could also have dampening effects on other molecules and prevent their growth. When the molecules reacted so that eventually molecule Z catalyzed the creation of A, the loop closed, and a self-reinforcing chain of molecules that replicated itself emerged. As this chain grew, it started reactions with other chains of molecules and grew more and more complex, eventually becoming a life form. Once a bunch of these autocatalytic sets were created, they began to compete for resources and started the process of natural selection. What a simple explanation for the emergence of life!

I am particularly enamored of another concept from complexity theory: the tit-for-tat rule to explain human behavior. Another pioneer in the study of complexity, Robert Axelrod, sponsored a contest for computer programmers to solve a classic game called "The Prisoner's Dilemma." Cops arrest two suspects for a crime for which they have no evidence. The police hope to get a confession from at least one of the suspects, so they tell each prisoner that if he confesses first, he will be granted immunity and be compensated for his cooperation. If he does not confess but his comrade does, he will serve the full prison sentence and have to pay the compensation to the confessor. If neither prisoner confesses, they both will go free. If both confess, they both will serve jail time.

This is a very interesting problem because full trust between the prisoners results in the optimal outcome (for the prisoners, not the cops): they both go free. Yet the price of trust by just one of the prisoners is high and unjust: jail along with a monetary punishment for that one person. A lack of trust on both sides leads to the least desirable outcome: both suspects are imprisoned. The program that won the contest was submitted by a psychologist named Anatol Rapoport. It was one of the simplest strategies submitted—tit for tat. Playing the game multiple times, each prisoner learned that if he ratted out his comrade this time, he would be ratted out the next. Staying quiet this time meant being in the clear next time. Eventually, using tit for tat, both prisoners learned to keep quiet so that they both could stay out of jail. Following tit for tat resulted in the optimal outcome. If you think about it, tit for tat governs a lot of human behavior. I'll scratch your back if you scratch mine. The best way to have a good neighbor is to be a good neighbor. Do unto others as you would have them do unto you. Just about every religion and every civilization has its own version of the golden rule.

There's a lesson for corporations in the tit-for-tat simulation about trust. When companies begin to mistrust their employees by implementing copious rules, regulations, oversight procedures, and worse yet, regular layoffs, they initiate a cycle of mistrust. In return, employees mistrust their company and perform work that meets only their self-interests, like getting promoted, earning a bonus, and adding to their résumés. As a result, employers implement more checks and balances to ensure that employees do what they are supposed to do to create value for the company and not for themselves. Employees respond by concentrating on their own welfare, doing the minimum of what is required and being dishonest about their workload. This is how a dysfunctional organization in which employees and management mistrust and work against each other is created.

Much of the complexity of corporate cultures can be boiled down to a few simple rules or beliefs. Like the convoluted organizational structure that resulted from "do no harm," policies, habits, and rituals grow out of simple rules. Organizations can follow the belief of "trust others until proven dishonest" or that of "don't trust until proven trustworthy." You can tell the difference by the emphasis on command and control and following procedures. Three of my four cultural dimensions in Chapter 1 have their roots in the judgment of whether people should be trusted: people versus process, hierarchical versus egalitarian, and collaborative versus competitive. You can trust people to do the right thing or put in processes to make sure they do. You can trust people to act appropriately on their own or add managers to ensure they do. You can trust people to work together on common goals or you can set up competitions rewarding those who achieve the goal first.

Another set of rules is "do it now" versus "do it later." Some organizations simply will not tolerate lead times on tasks. They do everything quickly, often without much thought or planning. In "do it later" organizations, everything takes days to complete, even the most minor of tasks, but the work is usually more thorough and better thought out. Some organizations can tolerate mistakes if they were well meaning, while others care only if the actions were correct and disregard intent ("mean well" versus "do right"). All sorts of rules that govern organizational behavior have their roots in values and beliefs.

Understanding the rules and beliefs that drive an organization is important, especially when embarking on any kind of initiative that requires behavioral change. The conventional wisdom is that change is hard, and change management programs are a big undertaking. Having run many change management programs, I disagree. The strength of the human race is its adaptability. We are the only species that thrives in the Arctic, the desert, the tropics, and so on. We adapt to our surroundings. I've found that people can embrace new rules quite readily as long as they don't conflict with their existing rules or values. This is why many companies' change programs fail. They try to institute a new rule that conflicts with an old rule, without first removing all the systems built up around the old rule. In the case of J&J, in order to build the premier brands in their new categories, they desired to be more innovative, and doing that required employees who were empowered. Everyone talked about how to empower employees, but nothing worked. The systems they already had in place to "do no harm" included very limited authority to spend money and numerous approvals for every action—both big obstacles to empowerment.

A company that has low cost as its rule but embarks on a quality and design improvement initiative will find it impossible to succeed if the systems built around cost controls take precedence. If budgets are constantly monitored, spending authority limited, and suppliers chosen based on low bidding, the behavior needed for high quality can never take root; employees are inhibited by the behavior promoting low cost. It is very easy to spot a company that has quality as its driving rule. The offices are well appointed, quality office supplies are easy to obtain, and conference rooms are stocked and well maintained with someone assigned to that responsibility. Companies driven by low cost have old or cheap furniture, office supplies under lock and key, and no flip charts and markers in meeting rooms because employees are hoarding them. Essentially, the primary driving rule governs every operation, and if you look closely enough you'll be able to discern it. Innovative companies look innovative when you walk in the door. Once, when I went for a job interview and entered the company's lobby, I found a ceramic dog curled on a rug and chunky rocking chairs with tree stumps as tables. I knew immediately I wanted to work there.

Detecting the driving rules of a company or system is the first step in understanding that system and being able to change it. I believe that for the last decade the financial markets have been driven by "find better returns." Led by competitive, domineer types, the search for better returns has naturally led to increased risk taking and to the complicated financial instruments and secret hedge funds that wrecked our economy in 2008. Imagine how the financial markets would operate if the driving rule was "seek long-term, stable gains." This, of course, would change the driving rule of many companies from "meet short-term earnings goals" to "meet long-term growth rates" or "pay a regular dividend." Imagine if these same companies could change their focus from "meet quarterly earnings" to "add value to society." If a company were adding value to society, wouldn't that almost guarantee a profitable business model? If everyone in a company were imbued with adding value, wouldn't that take a lot of the drudgery and meaninglessness out of work? Wouldn't it also put the focus back on people and away from the single-minded emphasis on profits? How can you create real value for the shareholder without creating real value for anyone else? Isn't "meeting customer needs" just a fancy way of saying "helping people"? Imagine waking up in the morning excited about contributing your small part to making the world a better place.

Behind our very complicated systems lie simple rules. The easiest way to change the system is to change the underlying rules. Work does not have to be a mindless pursuit of profits. Work can be meaningful and fun for both employees and society. If you are nice to those around you, they will be nice back. Distrusting others will send the message that you are not trustworthy. Subjecting an entire organization to rigid policies and procedures and a convoluted legal structure in order to prevent harm may prevent much of any action at all. Writing a complicated instruction manual for lobbing the holy hand grenade because you think people generally are idiots turns the readers into idiots because it is needlessly confusing. Just trust them to take out the pin and throw the grenade.

Chapter Vocabulary

Customer inquisition   Requiring that your online customers register with a whole slew of personal information before they can purchase anything.

Demongraphics   Finding the weaknesses of all your target markets and exploiting them in order to sell them more useless junk.

Elevator kitsch   The tactic of spieling off a short, rehearsed speech promoting yourself and your accomplishments whenever you take the elevator with senior management. *Related:* elevator leech

Iffyliate marketing   Being leery that your marketing partnerships will actually pan out.

16
The Grail Is in the Aaaaarrrrggggghhhhhhh

How to leave behind a concise, understandable message

After the knights blow up the killer bunny, they enter the Cave of Caerbannog, where the location of the grail is inscribed on a large stone. Well, sort of. The message says that the grail is hidden at the Castle of Arrrggggghhhhh. Is that the name of the castle? Or are those the last words of Joseph? Did he die while carving his message? Why would he bother to carve "Arrrggggghhhhh" in stone? As the men ponder how he died, they get a likely answer when they are set upon by a fearsome cartoon monster. Fortunately for the men, but unfortunately for the cartoonist, the cartoonist suffers a heart attack while drawing, and the monster just disappears.

Did you ever attend a good presentation, and when you went back to review the slides later, you couldn't make heads or tails out of the material? This has happened to me quite often. Or have you ever needed help with a certain step in a system or process, and the documentation is both indecipherable and unnavigable? What about the emails you wade through every day? How many of those are easy to understand? This chapter provides suggested formats for usually poorly written business documents: slides, emails, and manuals. I am also showing how graphics can be used in place of text to illuminate the intended meaning.

My biggest beef with business writing is that is it lengthy, overly verbose, full of jargon, and generally incomprehensible. Graphics are typically

Who Moved My Holy Hand Grenade?

used to pretty things up rather than aid comprehension. Because most business people are inundated with written material and cannot process it all fully, my single rule for writing is that the gist of the message should be understood at a glance. To demonstrate my point and to keep with the Monty Python theme, as this scene ends in a cartoon, I am using slides and graphics for the rest of this chapter.

Suggested Presentation Format

Start with a storyboard that tells a complete story without a voice over.

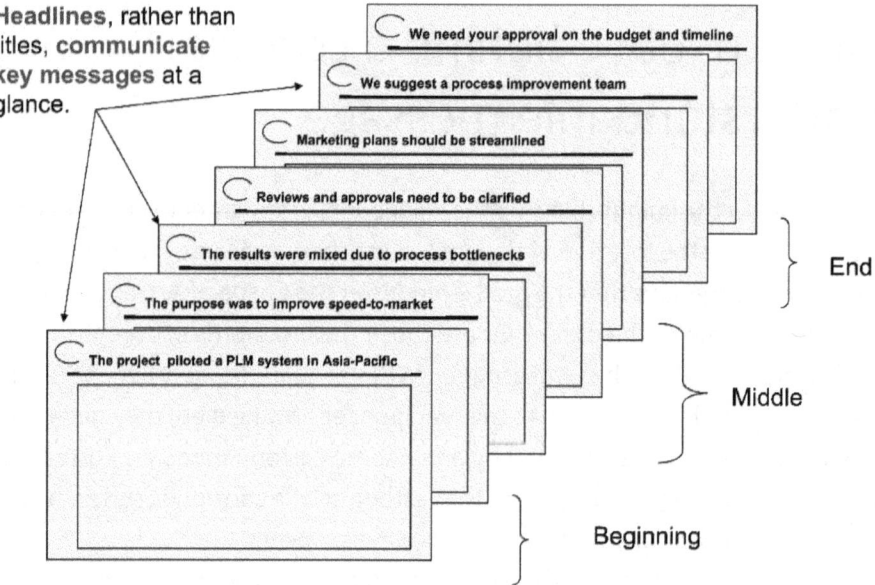

Then, structure your slides with a key point headline, supporting facts and data, and then an interpretation "kicker box."

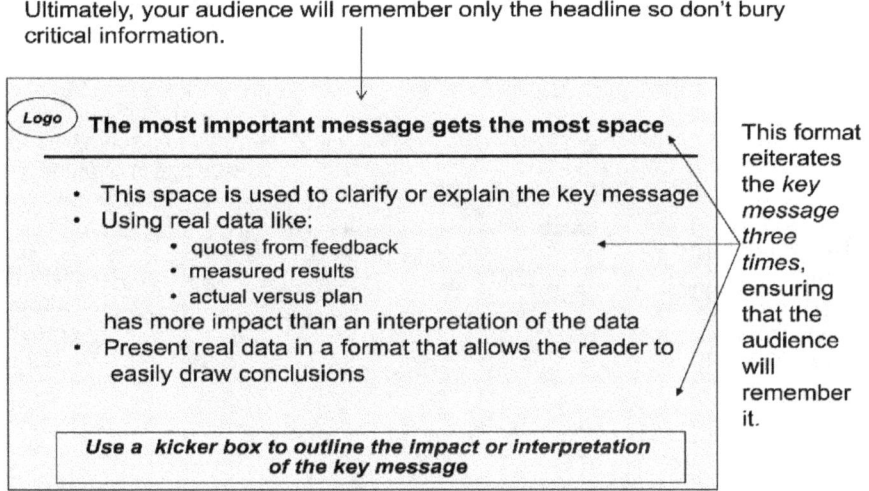

Suggested Email Format

Emails should follow the at-a-glance rule and use the structure of key message, background and/or explanation, and action required.

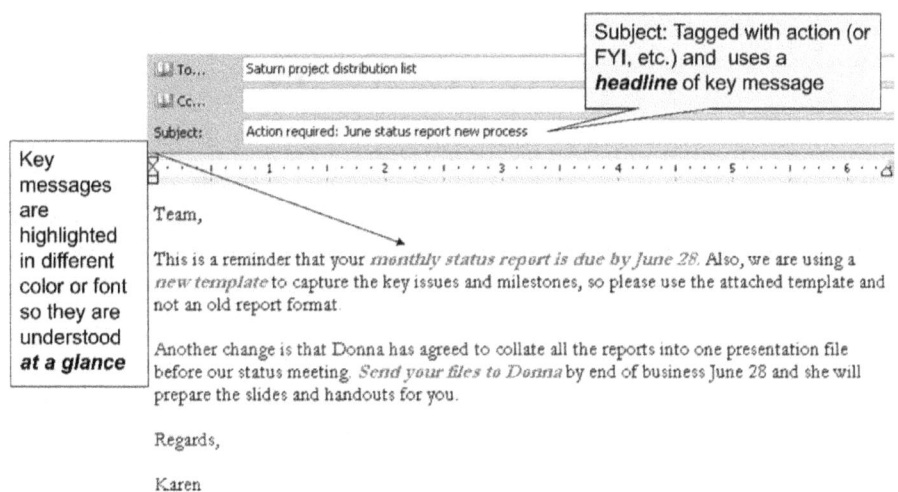

Suggested Documentation Format

Written documentation, especially instruction manuals, should organize and codify the text for easy assimilation by the reader.

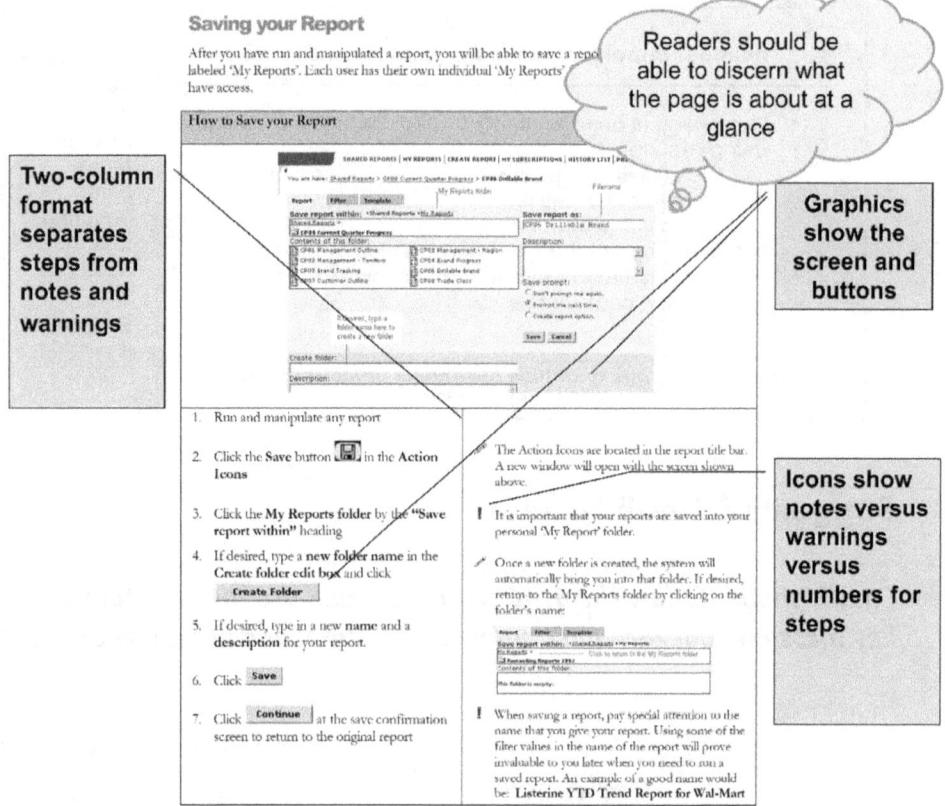

Using Graphics to Aid Understanding

Example 1: The Pearl Problem: you are allowed to pick one light and one dark egg in order to obtain a pearl. Which description do you prefer, A or B?

A – Text Only

> There are two barrels that contain both white and gray plastic eggs. In each barrel, 40% of the plastic eggs contain pearls, while the remaining 60% are empty.
> In barrel #1, 30% of the eggs with pearls are gray, and 10% of the empty eggs are gray. In barrel #2, 90% of the eggs with pearls are gray, and 30% of the empty eggs are gray. Try to find a pearl by picking one egg from each of the barrels—a total of two eggs, one white and one gray. From which barrel do you pick each color?

B – Graphic

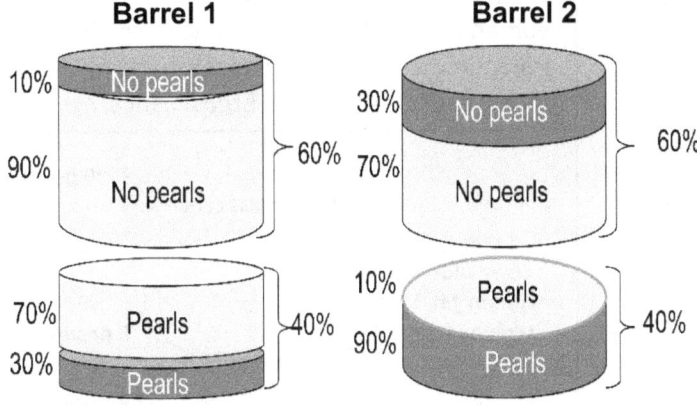

(Yudkowsky, *An Intuitive Explanation of Bayesian Reasoning*, 2006)

To get a pearl, would you choose a white egg or a gray egg from the first barrel? What color would you choose from the second barrel?

Example 2: The Breast Cancer Probability Problem described four ways. Which do you understand best?

1. Single-event probabilities format	The probability of breast cancer in a 40-year-old woman who gets a mammogram is 1%. A woman with breast cancer has an 80% probability of having a positive mammogram. A woman without breast cancer has about a 10% probability of a positive mammogram. If a 40-year-old woman has a positive mammogram, what is the probability that she really has breast cancer?
2. Relative frequencies format	1% of women at age 40 who get regular mammograms have breast cancer. 80% of women with breast cancer will have a positive mammogram. About 10% of women without breast cancer will also get a positive mammogram. If a 40-year-old woman has a positive mammogram, what is the probability that she really has breast cancer?
3. Natural frequencies format	10 of every 1,000 women at age 40 who get regular mammograms have breast cancer. 8 of every 10 women with breast cancer will have a positive mammogram. 99 of every 990 women without breast cancer will also have a positive mammogram. Of the women who received a positive result, how many do you expect really have breast cancer?
4. Graphic format	1,000 40-yr-old women get screened → 990 no breast cancer → 99 positive mammogram / 891 negative mammogram; 10 breast cancer → 8 positive mammogram / 2 negative mammogram

(Kurzenhäuser, 2005)

If you want people to remember your message, you need to spend the time and effort communicating it in a way that people can easily assimilate and retain. Otherwise, the only thing they will remember is along the lines of "aaarrrrggggghhhhh."

17

What's Your Favorite Color?

Attitude is everything

Now the only thing separating Arthur and his men from the Holy Grail is the Bridge of Death, which hangs over the Gorge of Eternal Peril. The bridge is guarded by a crotchety old bridge keeper. Just answer his three questions correctly and you can pass safely across the bridge. Answer incorrectly and you will be swept off the bridge and fall to your death in the gorge. Sounds like a good idea for a game show (Truth or Die?). Arthur nominates a very anxious Sir Robin to cross the bridge first, but Sir Robin begs off, offering Launcelot as a braver alternative. Sir Launcelot eagerly rises to the occasion and approaches the bridge keeper. Question one is "What is your name?" Question two, "What is your quest?" Question three, "What's your favorite color?" Easy-peezy. Sir Launcelot answers the questions and crosses the bridge safely. Now Sir Robin has a sudden surge of courage, and he approaches the bridge. Name. Check. Quest. Check. Question three: "What's the capital of Assyria?" Robin doesn't know and falls to his doom. Now that doesn't seem fair, does it?

It's Sir Galahad's turn next, and he doesn't know what to think. He answers the name and quest questions correctly. And the third question is—thank goodness, the one about favorite color. Blue, like Launcelot. Only, wait, Galahad really prefers yellow. Off he goes to his doom. Nonchalantly, King Arthur approaches the bridge. Again, the bridge keeper asks for his name and his quest, which Arthur answers correctly. For the third question, the bridge beeper asks for the air speed of an unladen swallow. Arthur needs more clarification. Does he mean a European or an African swallow? The bridge keeper doesn't know and so falls to his death. Hence, Arthur and the rest of his men (just Bedevere) cross the bridge to safety.

How would you fare passing the Bridge of Death? Would you survive like Launcelot and Arthur or would you be cast into the chasm like Robin and Galahad? Find out by taking the Knights of the Round Table Attitude and Personality Indicator (KRAPI)[14] to see which knight your personality matches. Just choose the answer that most reflects what you would do in the given situation.

KRAPI Test

1. You are woken from a deep sleep when a canvas sack is thrust over your head, and several people drag you to an awaiting car. You immediately think that:
    a. Your friends are dragging you to a surprise birthday party a month early.
    b. You are being abducted by aliens who will perform weird medical experiments on you.
    c. This could be the initiation rite for the country club you just joined.
    d. Maybe you shouldn't have missed the payment on the no-credit-check, high-interest loan you took out several months ago from Big Lou.

2. Your boss has suddenly taken some time off and sent you a message leaving you in charge. You discover that there is a meeting on your schedule with all the corporate executive officers to explain why your department did not meet any of its goals in the past year. On your way to the meeting you think:
    a. Yes, this is my chance to shine in front of all the company bigwigs!

---

[14] The KRAPI model draws from the Myers-Briggs Personality Type Indicator (MBTI); Life Orientations (LiFO) Communications Styles Profile; Dominance, Influence, Steadiness and Compliance (DISC) Assessment; Belbin Self-Perception Inventory; Thomas-Killman Conflict Mode Instrument (TKI); Fundamental Interpersonal Relations Orientation-Behavior (FIRO-B) assessment; California Psychological Inventory (CPI) instrument; 16 Personality Factor (16-PF) Questionnaire; Strong Interest Inventory; Keirsey Temperament Sorter-II (KTS-II); La Monica Empathy Profile (LEP); Power Base Inventory; Strong Interest Inventory; Emotional Intelligence (EQ) Test; and the Herrmann Brain Dominance Instrument (HBDI).

b. I'll just focus the conversation on how great our performance will be in the next quarter and let my boss handle the consequences of that later.
c. All I have to do is explain why the goals were unreasonable, and I am sure they will understand.
d. I can take ill suddenly and send my admin to the meeting.

3. You are in a third world country. After drinking the local firewater, you head back to your hotel but get lost. You mistakenly wander into a dark alleyway and find yourself surrounded by a group of foreign youth, urgently talking to you in the local language, which you don't understand. You:
    a. Ask them slowly and loudly to "P-L-E-A-S-E S-P-E-A-K E-N-G-L-I-S-H."
    b. Reach for your knife and start looking for their vulnerabilities.
    c. Pull out your pocket foreign language phrase book and try to figure out how you can help these poor people.
    d. Find your hidden track talent and run at a record-breaking speed.

4. Your new employee has become an impediment. He never writes anything down, forgets all the tasks he is supposed to accomplish, and has been the cause of several missed deadlines. You've given him this feedback several times to no avail. You would like to fire him, but he is the CEO's son and is being groomed for better things. So you:
    a. Take him out to lunch for a heart-to-heart with the purpose of winning him over.
    b. Write up a performance plan for him with all his key tasks and deadlines and make it part of a monthly review that gets reported up the chain.
    c. Convince another department how great he is and how much better he would fit in there.
    d. Begin applying for positions elsewhere.

5. It is 3 A.M., and you are woken by your phone ringing. You immediately think:
    a. My friend from Japan wants to chat.
    b. Hillary Clinton wants some advice in a crisis.

c. It's a wrong number.
d. Who died?

6. You receive a registered letter informing you that you have come into a great deal of money. The letter is not signed. Most likely it is from:
   a. Publishers' Clearing House
   b. The FBI rewarding you for breaking up a money-laundering ring
   c. The IRS refunding the massive overpayments you've made
   d. A Nigerian prince who needs your bank account information to reclaim his fortune

7. The medieval weapon on which you most rely is the:
   a. Broadsword, so you can slash and pound your enemies in hand-to-hand combat
   b. Battering ram to break down the doors of the unfaithful
   c. Bow and arrow, so you can pierce your foes at a distance
   d. Shield to protect yourself

8. The quest for the Holy Grail has been much longer and more arduous than you anticipated. You ran out of food and supplies several weeks back. If you don't take some action, everyone in your quest will likely die. You decide to:
   a. Muster all your resources and overthrow the nearest castle.
   b. Break up into scouting parties to look for provisions and report back in 10 days.
   c. Abandon the quest and return to Castle Anthrax.
   d. Eat the minstrels.

Give yourself 4 points for every A answer, 3 points for every B answer, 2 points for every C answer, and 1 point for every D answer.

Scores:

26–32

You are a Launcelot. Launcelots believe the world is kind to them because they have been gifted with extraordinary abilities. They rush about with all the confidence in the world, charging into things they know nothing about, completely unaware of or unconcerned with their own ignorance. Although they can cause incredible damage, in their own minds they've always been successful and will always be successful at whatever they choose to do. The anxiety and fears of other people are beyond their comprehension. When it comes to the Bridge of Death, it is only natural that the bridge keeper would give Launcelot three easy questions that he answers without hesitation.

20–25

Your score makes you an Arthur. Arthurs are more world-wise than Launcelots but still believe that they have to ability to overcome any obstacle in their path. All it takes is common sense, good leadership skills, and the right team—and success is guaranteed. Of course, Arthurs believe that they have above-average abilities giving them the advantage in any encounter or conflict. Hence, when Arthur gets a difficult question from the bridge keeper, his superior intelligence and royal abilities save him from certain death. You have to know these things when you are king.

14–19

You are a Galahad. Galahads don't believe that the world is against them, but they do think that they will screw up any opportunity that comes their way. In the Castle Anthrax, Galahad resists the young women's advances. On the bridge, he gets the easy questions but screws up the answers. The main problem with Galahad is that he doesn't trust himself or his own judgment. Are the girls in the castle good or evil? Should he give in to them or not? Is swearing chastity really a good idea? What is his favorite color? What should his favorite color be? If you find yourself second-guessing all your decisions, then you are certainly a Galahad. And don't go back and retake the quiz.

8–13

Hello Robin! Robins are the classic cowardly lions. They believe that the world is a very hostile place. In fact, it really does conspire against them, and Robins have no exceptional abilities for combating it. Thus, they try to avoid almost everything. They run away from anything that could potentially be difficult. Even if a situation has little potential for harm, they imagine ominous scenarios full of danger, just like Sir Robin's minstrels, who always sing of looming death and dismemberment.

Another way to analyze the personalities and attitudes of the knights is to use the Hofarti Window.[15] It is a model that shows how our beliefs about the world and ourselves shape our attitudes and behaviors. The x-axis plots how people view themselves and their abilities, either confidently or anxiously. The y-axis plots how people view the world around them as either an inherently friendly or hostile place. The resulting four quadrants are labeled with the corresponding personality of the knights.

HOFARTI Window

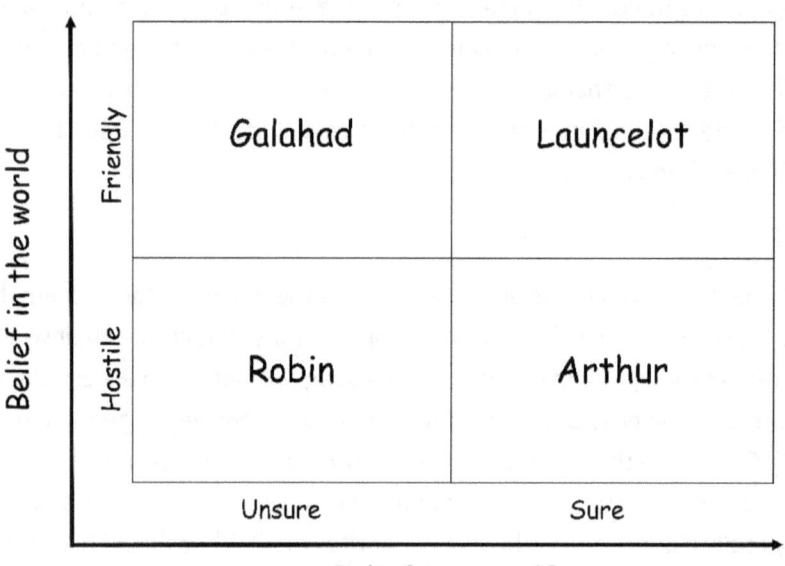

Okay, you got me. There's no such thing as the Hofarti Window. I made up the model. What can I say? I spent a decade of my life as a management consultant and thought the book needed more quadrant charts. The funny thing, though, is despite being total horseshit, it can still help you understand how you think, because that's pretty much what any model does. My purpose in creating the KRAPI test and the Hofarti Window is to show how the human mind loves models and automatically finds truth in them. I don't exactly know why, but somewhere in the language-processing part of our brains,

---

[15] Named after the creators, Howie, Farooq, and Tina.

we developed an affinity for narrative explanations (e.g., creation myths), pictorial descriptions (e.g., cave art), and symbolic representations (e.g., alphabets). How easily we can substitute a symbol for the real object!

This leads me to a discussion of paradigms. I mean, this wouldn't be a proper business book if I didn't discuss paradigms. Although the word "paradigm" technically means the same as "model," it has taken on a slightly different connotation in business to mean attitude and perceptions, and a huge industry of personal coaches and motivational speakers specializes in paradigm changes. In other words, paradigms have a different paradigm in business. Personally, I don't like the word "paradigm." It's too jargon-y and conceptual. I prefer the word "frame" because it represents the concrete as well as the abstract. A beautiful gilt frame on an amateurish painting can make it look like a museum piece. A poster framed in glass looks professional and expensive, whereas tacked to the wall, it looks, well, tacky. The right eyeglass frames can make someone look sophisticated and stylish, while the wrong ones can make the same person look downright ugly.

Frames have an enormous power to change how things are perceived and understood. The previous chapter showed the effect of changing the framing. Boldface, italics, color, and pictures all affect how we see and remember text. The ease of understanding the probability questions changes depending on how they are depicted. Framing, and reframing, is something we do all the time. Whenever we put a positive spin on something, we are changing what may be considered bad news to good news. This occurs all the time in politics and business, and in our personal lives. "You're not losing a daughter, you're gaining a son!" on marriage. "Just remember that he has moved on to a much better place" on death. "It's not an obstacle, it's a challenge!" on some daunting project. Changing frames can change our attitude.

Although some personality tests would have you believe that people exhibit set patterns of attitudes, in actuality changing your attitude is a very easy thing to do. With a little bit of effort, Robins can become Launcelots, Launcelots can become Arthurs, and Galahads can become unchaste. Here are some simple but powerful ways you can change your attitude and reframe your problems. These ideas aren't new, but if you use them regularly, you can change how you think about almost anything.

Take a Different Perspective

The advice to walk in another person's shoes is fairly commonplace, but to actually do so is typically relegated to movies and fairy tales. Mentally, we spend the majority of our time thinking about how to get what we want, often at the expense of others. There is even a huge industry built around assertiveness training, which teaches us how to persuade others, obtain our goals, and win. We may learn to beat our enemies, especially at their own game, but when we think like this, we automatically set up conflict. We may win one battle but ruin any chance of a long-term relationship. The real art of negotiation is not about winning but about finding common ground. We talk about "win/win" all the time, but in my experience a "win/win" solution is usually an accident or a convenient meeting of minds. Whenever a conflict exists, the normal operating mode is to prepare your arguments carefully, line up your allies to support you, and then insist on getting your way through persuasion. The real win/win approach is to learn what the other side wants and figure out how to match your goals to theirs. Mentally walking in their shoes and taking their perspective can open up a host of new opportunities based on new understanding. Don't you like people who can really empathize with your situation?

When I was younger and searching for a job, I noticed that I did better on interviews for jobs I didn't want. On those interviews where I tried really hard to be impressive and win the interviewer over, I wasn't as successful. (Of course, the booger hanging from the interviewer's nose didn't help.) When I analyzed the situation, I realized that during successful interviews, the interviewer did more talking than I did. Rather than trying to sell myself and all my wonderful expertise, as expected in an interview, I spent the time listening to the interviewer, trying to understand his or her problems and determining how I could help. In those sessions, I was unconsciously putting myself in the interviewer's shoes and found that I developed rapport with that person. As practice for other upcoming interviews, I once interviewed for a job for which I didn't have the requisite experience. In that particular interview, I asked a lot of questions about the problems the interviewer was experiencing and empathized with his situation. Although I explained that I didn't have the experience they were looking for, I offered suggestions on how to solve those problems. Happy with the practice session, I never expected to hear back. I was aghast when the headhunter called and said the company wanted to offer me the job. When I explained that the position wasn't what I was looking for, the company changed the job for me. Afterward, when I asked the person I interviewed with why he was so keen on me, he replied that I was the only person who had shown a full understanding of his issues and how to solve them. If I had spent the time selling myself, I never would have listened and gained that understanding.

Public speaking is another area where you should focus on others, contrary to conventional business wisdom, which dictates that you focus on yourself. Advice to stand up straight, use hand gestures, vary voice tonality are all suggestions to be self-conscious. But don't you just hate speakers who talk at you? Standing there at the podium with stagy hand gestures, following all the rules of good public speaking, they put you right to sleep. Good speakers constantly think about the audience—always checking the level of engagement, trying to fill expectations, and changing course when necessary. The best speakers and lecturers are those who care about you and about meeting your needs. The next time you give a speech or a presentation, stop thinking about how you are doing and concentrate on how the audience is reacting. What do they want to hear and how would they like to hear it? An engaged audience readily forgives less-than-perfect presentation skills. Forgetting yourself, not being self-conscious, is the best thing you can do in front of an audience.

On the flip side, becoming aware of yourself during occasions when you are fully focused on the events around you can be a huge learning experience. Video recording yourself is always an illuminating experience, though it isn't always practical. Asking others to give you feedback on your behavior or even just being conscious of your own body language, tone of voice, and breathing can help you to see yourself as others see you. I once received feedback that I had acted arrogantly in a meeting. This was a surprise to me as I spent a good deal of effort stopping myself from calling the other attendees "idiots." I thought I was acting like a team player when I disengaged from the discussion and composed myself. The next time I found myself in the same situation (which happens quite frequently), I paid attention to my body language and facial expressions. I realized that I had a scowl on my face, and my arms were crossed defensively. I verified the scowl in a mirror later. I thought I was hiding my feelings, but clearly I wasn't. For years, I had unknowingly been pissing off my coworkers with my body language.

Pretend

Some people find "What would Jesus do?" a powerful perspective. (Haven't you seen those bumper stickers?) Pretend for a moment that you are Jesus, and you want to find the righteous, selfless path. How does that change your thinking? You can take this technique and apply it to anyone you admire. What would Gandhi do? What would Einstein do? What would my cousin Vinnie do? A former actress shared her experience with me. She was looking for a job in business and was distressed because she had no business experience and didn't even know how to behave in a business environment. An acting coach suggested that she watch films about business and choose an actress to emulate. As instructed, she chose a character who was a successful businesswoman and watched that particular movie over and over until she had the character down pat. When she went on an interview, she acted the part (which she knew how to do well) and got the job. She acted as if she knew how to act in business!

"Acting as if" is a technique used often in NLP (neurolinguistic programming) therapy. It works amazingly well. Whenever someone says, "I can't do this," you ask that person to act as if he or she can. You can do this yourself by pretending to do the thing you believe you can't do. If you don't want to pretend, then you can do what the actress did and emulate someone who can.

If there is a skill you would really like to have, find a person or a character who has it and imitate that person. Pretending to be someone else is a fun way to try out new ways of doing things. It also quiets internal dialogues that often trip us up. Many of us have critical, internal conversations that prohibit us from acting foolish or taking risks. When we are pretending to be someone else, that conversation disappears.

I've used this technique to get around contentious business issues. "Let's pretend we all agree on the decision criteria for a moment. What would the next steps be?" Once I get people to see the steps needed to attain a desired goal, the contentious issue is now just a step in the process and not a huge obstacle no one can see past.

Set the Right Expectations

I get impatient waiting, especially when I have to sit in traffic. As a frequent commuter to New York City, waiting in traffic is a routine occurrence. Still, I would freak out when I hit a traffic jam. Even walking in the city or making my way through an airport, I would get upset when I encountered obstacles like crowds in my way. I just wanted to reach my destination as quickly and efficiently as possible. My expectation was that my path should be clear. Then someone gave me the advice not to view these delays as obstacles in the path to my destination but as part of the path. I started visualizing my journey full of all sorts of distractions and obstacles. Now when I travel, I don't think of the no-delay condition as my baseline. (Remember the planning bias in which we use the best-case scenario as our baseline?) I expect delays and handle them much more patiently. When there are none, I am pleasantly surprised.

Although businesses do a good job of setting goals, most businesses don't spend much time setting expectations. One company where I worked scheduled a meeting to set expectations in addition to one for setting performance goals, and it was incredibly helpful. Expectations encompass things like:

- Do your prefer voicemail, email, or instant messaging as the main mode of communication?
- Are you reachable 24/7?
- Are you expected to work late or start early?
- Do you use the morning to ease into and plan the day or are you gung-ho first thing?

- Conversely, do you use the end of the day for wrap-up or are you still raring to go?
- Does "on time" mean right on the number or a few minutes late?
- Do you want to be copied on all communications?
- Do you want regular status updates or just be alerted to potential problems?
- Do you expect tasks to be started within days of being assigned or do you care only about meeting the deadline?
- Are your deadlines real or do they contain contingency time?
- Are you meeting to resolve issues, determine knowledge gaps, or assign tasks?
- Do you expect to achieve consensus or are you okay with some discord?

Going through an expectations-setting process can eliminate much of the frustration that comes from misunderstanding each other's expectations. Just expecting things of others without being explicit can create conflicts. For instance, I am a night person. I like to plan my day in the morning and then use the end of the day to wrap up with my team. Unfortunately, once I had a team of early birds and they would be tired during the evening wrap-up, which was also the time period they liked for planning the next day. After we discussed this disparity, I switched my calendar. If I hadn't thought to talk about this simple matter, I would probably have been the source of much grumbling and discontent. Going through an expectations-setting process also helps people to set more realistic expectations. Unfortunately, unrealistic expectations seem to be the operating mode in business today; every project schedule is "aggressive," or nearly impossible to meet, and the deliverables promise to address every problem. Many of the headaches with slipping due dates and constant rescoping to scale back the project, would disappear if people set realistic expectations in the first place.

Setting the right expectations also applies to our personal lives. My arriving home from a weeklong business trip and expecting that the house will be clean is setting myself up for disappointment. Expecting that my husband and two teenage boys did some chores, but probably not many, is more realistic. Sitting down with them beforehand and talking about which chores they will do while I'm away, as a two-way conversation and not a lecture, is even better. We set ourselves up for bad feelings whenever we use an ideal condition as our expectation, whether that's a clean house, sunny weather on vacation, a 100% efficient work day, home improvements progressing smoothly, or following a diet perfectly. Sometimes I think most of us have an image of an ideal self who exists inside us and who will one day manifest itself as the perfect being we want to be. On that day we will become wealthy, eat right, exercise vigorously, learn to speak Spanish fluently, and floss regularly. Planning around imperfections and expecting some mishaps is a better way to go if you actually want to achieve some goals.

Travel in Time

In Chapter 2, I discussed the relativity of time. Now we can use that information to travel in time, not physically, but mentally. This is an exercise I used to do when my children were little. One of my kids would get very stressed over the slew of standardized tests. His teachers put great emphasis on doing well because of the No Child Left Behind Act, and my son would take the testing very seriously, so much so that he had difficulty sleeping. To help him relax, I would help him travel in time. We would pretend to travel to the future, to a few days ahead, when the tests were over and the weekend was beginning. He would imagine what it felt like to be finished with the testing, have no homework, and have the whole weekend to play. This helped him put the test in perspective. Instead of looming large, the tests became just a part of his week that would soon pass.

Whenever I am at work on a stressful project, I do something similar with the project team. I ask them to stop what they are doing and place themselves at the project's end, looking back at this stressful time. Then we describe what we are like from this perspective. Usually, the answers are along the lines of "making ourselves crazy over nothing," or "taking this job much too seriously."

Traveling into the past can also be helpful. I find that I tend to stew over incidents that don't go well, particularly those when I haven't behaved my best. Often, I find myself replaying the event in my mind. However, I discovered that there are two ways to replay past events. The first is to dwell on the things that went wrong and criticize yourself. The second is to change how you behaved and substitute how you wished it happened for what actually happened. Updating your memory with "better" information not only makes you feel better but also works as a past experience to draw from should a similar incident happen.

Choose Your Words

I've never studied linguistics formally, but I am fascinated by how our choice of words shapes how we think. I was recently negotiating a deal with someone I know well. He asked, "Why are you haggling with me? You know I would never cheat you." I replied, "I'm not haggling. I am negotiating terms that I can own, as well." He was okay with that, but not okay with haggling. His first assumption was that I didn't trust him. My agenda was that I needed to put my own thumbprints on the deal. Later in the negotiating process, he listed the terms in excruciating detail, which he wanted me to review and confirm. I asked him why he was nitpicking. He responded that he wasn't nitpicking; he wanted to get the specifics right so we would both have the same understanding. I was okay with that, but not with nitpicking.

So much of what we say has hidden assumptions, and often we don't realize that these embedded assumptions show through in our communication. In an environment of overworked, time-stressed coworkers, we often ask, "Will you be able to do this task for me?" That question implies that they can answer, "No." If you ask, "When will you be able to do this task for me?" then the implication is that they will do it at some point. Look at the differences verbs and verb tenses make:

- Can you do this for me? (Are you able to, given your time commitments?)
- Could you do this for me? (Is it possible, sometime in the future, that you will choose to do this?)
- Will you do this for me? (Decide now if you have the time.)
- Would you do this for me? (Will you work on this in the future when you have some time?)

Although we use different grammatical tenses and moods all the time, not many people understand the structure of grammar or use it to their advantage. For instance, the subjunctive mood is a verb form that expresses conditions contrary to reality, while the indicative mood expresses how things are. "If I were rich" is the subjunctive versus "I am rich," indicative. In a situation where you want to be creative, visionary, or future oriented, using the subjunctive can help overcome whatever obstacles you might have. "If the CEO were supportive, where would we begin?" However, when you are trying to develop or execute a plan of action, a firm grounding in reality is important, like "How do we proceed when the CEO is not supportive?" Although they are similar questions, the answers have a totally different context. I've been at many meetings where plans or decisions were derailed because people started to bring up hypothetical objections. "What if the suppliers were to go out of business?" "What if our patent were to be challenged?" These are good questions to ask if you are strategizing or contingency planning, but not when you are putting together action items. Action items and decisions need to be grounded in reality.

The past tense and the future tense can be useful, as well, and can help you travel in time. When dealing with a contentious situation or conflict, you can put it in the past by using the past tense. "At the last meeting, we had some objections to the plan," or "We used to have some heated discussions." Both sentences imply that we don't or won't have them anymore. As a complement, you can use the future tense to paint an optimistic version of the future. "We will have friendly discussions moving forward," or "We will be prepared to handle any objections."

I mentioned earlier that at Gemini Consulting, all new hires were indoctrinated with the phrases "I wish I knew" and "how to." We used these phrases so much that we had shorthand for them: IWIK and H2. The rule was that if someone had a concern or a complaint, it had to be phrased using IWIK or H2 so that it became an action rather than an obstacle. See the difference:

- We don't have enough information to make this decision. (Therefore, we can't make the decision.)
- I wish I knew more about the industry in order to make this decision. (We can still make the decision, but it would be better if we had this information.)
- How to get this industry information so we can make a decision. (Let's get this information and then decide.)

While your choice of words can change your assumptions, the converse is also true. Our assumptions can inadvertently shape our words. The words we use can reveal more than we want to if we don't choose carefully.

Who Moved My Holy Hand Grenade?

What's implied when you are told, "Please keep me updated with frequent status reports and notify me as soon as there might be a problem"? It sounds as if that person doesn't trust you to handle the project on your own. A less loaded way to say it is, "Please communicate regularly on all project-related status and issues." My pet peeve is calling a help desk and having to answer a barrage of simple-minded questions like, "Do you have the caps lock on?" This is because help desk personnel assume you're a moron, and it comes across. Several years ago, when I was working in IT, I attended a meeting to discuss how to improve cross-functional involvement on some high-visibility teams. A high-level executive with a marketing background had called the meeting and was soliciting ideas. After I suggested a novel approach, he commented to the group, "You see, this is what I mean. Even IT colleagues can contribute." He had no idea why I was offended by that generous compliment. What an attitude changer that was! I stewed for the rest of the meeting.

It amazes me how some words have a motivational (or as above, de-motivational) quality and can alter lives while most of what is said is just a bunch of jabbering. Most of the time, my advice falls on deaf ears, but every once in a while I manage to articulate a phrase that hits home. After attending a workshop on networking, I realized that many business networking events are like blind dating or speed dating and, justifiably, fill attendees with anxiety. This is because we feel forced to befriend people we don't really know and may not even like. My personal method and definition of networking is "filling your life with people whose company you enjoy." Whenever I share my perspective with the networking-phobic, they respond with a sense of relief and joy.

Another aphorism of mine that seems to resonate with people relates to teaching. Teaching is not the act of imparting your knowledge to others, but the act of leading others through a discovery process. When I managed a training department, I used to tell this to the guest speakers who would come in to lead sessions. Besides easing them of the burden of needing to have all the answers and thus allaying their nerves, this reframe of what teaching is all about led them to engage the group in lively discussions and more interactive, memorable sessions. An axiom that changed my life was, you should always do the things you want to do first, before the things you have to do; otherwise, you will never get to do what you want. When we give first priority to those things we don't like doing, we end up filling our lives with the things we don't want to do. When we do the things we want to do first, somehow we also manage to find the time to do the things we need to do.

I don't think anyone really knows why some words can alter the lives of some people some of the time. Language is processed in our neocortex, the same part of the brain where logic and reasoning take place. While the other two major areas of the brain, the hindbrain and the limbic system, are present in all animals and have evolved over 100 million years, the neocortex is limited to higher-level mammals, like primates, and has a much shorter evolutionary history. Because evolution, by its very nature, does not perfect its adaptations on its first few tries and requires many generations of natural selection, it seems logical to deduce that our neocortex—home of logic, reasoning, and language processing—is still pretty flawed. We already know that much of what passes for logic falls victim to a variety of cognitive biases. It seems likely we don't process language perfectly, either, leading us to confuse words and frames for reality at times, to both detrimental and beneficial effects. Hence, altering our reality can be as easy as altering our words.

What we need to keep in mind is how to use models, words, and frames to help us understand the world better and to achieve our goals. What's dangerous is when we confuse models with reality, and they start to limit our understanding and impede actions. I like personality tests and enjoy getting their insights. However, I can't remember if I am an ENTP or an ISFJ (Myers-Briggs) or a high dominance/low steadiness or a high influence/low compliance (Disc model), because I am neither an ENTP nor a DI. I am a person. Like my KRAPI test and Hofarti model, just because a model is useful or insightful doesn't make it the truth. My husband was asked to take a personality test as part of a interview process. He did well in the interviews and had the right skills and experience, but because he did not score high in the entrepreneurial category of the personality test, the company decided not to hire him. The irony is that my husband is an entrepreneur! He has started and run his own businesses for the last 25 years. A model trumped reality!

How we love to have tests, assessments, checklists, procedures, and processes tell us the answer. How often do we use these in place of judgment? I think we can blame this on our immature neocortex, which has an affinity for models and can stifle the other parts of our brain, such as those that control emotion or process purely sensory information. One thing our neocortex is very good at doing is providing a running commentary on our actions and our observations. There it is in the background, offering its interpretation of the proceedings around us, often without us even being aware of what it's saying. Instead of seeing some impersonal events that happen in conjunction with other events, we tend to create narratives about the events where we failed or succeeded or were helped or hindered. Sometimes we cast ourselves as heroes, especially the Launcelots and Arthurs of the world, and sometimes we cast ourselves as victims, like the Galahads and Robins. The truth is that when we cross the Bridge of Death, sometimes we get the easy questions, and sometimes we get the hard ones. How we fare, though, is less dependent on the bridge keeper than on what we think about ourselves and the world.

(This book is amazingly brilliant. Tell all your friends to buy it.)

Chapter Vocabulary

Critical business unctions Heavy reliance on those mandatory and meaningless utterances at all business gatherings like "Do less with more," "Think of it as a development opportunity," and "Work smarter, not harder."

Highly engaged workfarce Putting all sorts of superficial programs in place to make it look as if you care about your employees.

Paradigm shit Upon hearing yet another person lecture about the benefits of positive thinking, the reaction "Don't give me any more of that paradigm shit."

Positive platitude An upbeat jargon-y cliché to impart to your subordinates and peers, no matter how late you have to work, how menial your job, or how stressful your environment.

How to Put a Positive Spin on Everything

An essential core compretense (an attribute you need to pretend to have in order to advance your career) is to be able to put a positive spin on everything, and I mean everything, especially when you screw up. Here are some handy-dandy phrases you can use to spin less-than-desirable situations your way

Situation	Suggested spin
You're going to miss a deadline.	After finding out more about this, I realized that the deadline doesn't let me give this task the proper attention it deserves. At first look, it seemed straightforward, but after digging deeper I found a number of issues that still need to be addressed.
You screwed up big time.	In an effort to be more innovative and more risk taking, I did [big screw-up]. In hindsight, I realize that my action orientation could have benefited from more planning. However, this was a huge learning experience where I gained a lot of knowledge that I will certainly apply in the future.
You pissed off a customer.	Although my intention was to help them, obviously there was a misunderstanding that I am working hard to correct. I think in the long run, this will only make the relationship stronger.
You missed an important meeting.	I got some feedback that other people were looking for my lead and relying on my opinions, and I thought the team could benefit from an opportunity for other people to take the lead.
You bungled a presentation with the higher-ups.	Because I am new to this, I really didn't know what to expect and prepared for all the wrong things. Now I know exactly what not to do and what to focus on next time. Plus, I am taking this opportunity to follow up with them individually to personally address each of their concerns.

Okay, do you get the gist? You turn each screw-up into an opportunity. Generally, the formula is:
1. Acknowledge the screw-up, but gloss over it quickly.
2. Place the blame on some great leadership trait you possess, like bias for action or creativity, so you can use this as yet another opportunity to promote yourself. (Remember the validity effect from Chapter 5: repeat often.)
3. Offer a consequence of the mistake that makes you more valuable to the company.

18

I Unclog My Nose in Your Direction

The graceful art of negotiation

Arthur and his few remaining men, er man, are mysteriously transported by boat to the sacred castle wherein lies the grail. Arthur approaches the castle and begins to give thanks to God until he realizes that the keeper of the castle is the French guard from the previous scene. Again, the guard taunts Arthur in an exaggerated French accent and boasts of outwitting the English a second time. Furious, Arthur demands entrance to the castle as commanded by God. In response, the guard unleashes both a torrent of insults, "I wave my private parts at your aunties," "I unclog my nose at you," "You tiny-brained wipers of other people's bottoms," and a bucket of excrement. The row continues with more insults, more demands, and more excrement until Team English decides to regroup in the forest. We know Arthur won't back down, and so somehow he and Bedevere conjure up a huge army to attack the castle, replete with requisite battle preparation shots to build anticipation. Arthur issues the order to charge the castle and off they go to the film's climax.

Let's pretend this is English literature class and we are studying Monty Python and the Holy Grail as masterwork. Your professor suggests that the exchange between the French guard and Arthur is a metaphor for the Israeli-Palestinian conflict. Your reaction is:
  a. My professor has been smoking weed.
  b. This exchange could be a metaphor for any warring nations.
  c. This exchange is representative of all conflicts in general.
  d. My, how they've escalated to a full-out war so quickly.
  e. Perhaps we should call in some heavy-duty negotiators.

Correct!

Like Arthur, many people believe that the way to win a conflict is through the use of powerful persuasion, reasoned logic, forceful arguments, or just plain force. This is symptomatic of being stuck in the war paradigm. However, anyone skilled in the art of negotiation knows that the key to success is to find new ways to meet the objectives of both sides. Previously, I discussed finding the simple rules and/or objectives behind people's behaviors and perspectives. In this chapter, I'd like to explore misaligned objectives, how they create conflict, and how they can lead to lose/lose negotiations, sometimes called warfare.

A few years ago, I left a good corporate job to work for a software "start-up" company. Start-up is in quotes because it was an established business in Australia but was planning to use venture capital to open a U.S. office, which I was to lead and build. A large portion of my salary would be in equity. When the owner offered me 2% equity, I was not happy. Most of our communication had been by email, and we scheduled a time to negotiate my pay package via phone. Beforehand, I had sought out some advice and got some suggestions on what my percentage equity should be. Stuck in my own warfare paradigm, I had determined what minimum percentage would be acceptable to me and was prepared to stick to my guns.

However, during our call, a light bulb went on in my head, and I decided that we needed to talk about our objectives. While we discussed our respective positions, we each made sure that we understood the other person's perspective. In fact, we both used the words "so from your perspective, you feel that...." My concern was that I had quit my well-paying job and was ignoring my own business to expand someone else's. The small future upside did not offset the sacrifices and risks I was making now. Her concern was that she had already been in business for 14 years, used all her personal savings to invest in the business, and would be giving a large percentage to venture capitalists. I wanted a bigger future payout and she wanted to preserve her existing business. We ended the call without a resolution but with a better understanding of each other's rationale.

Afterward, I talked with another entrepreneur friend who had done something similar for his own business when he opened a European office. When I explained the situation, he suggested that the company incorporate separately in the United States, where I could get a larger equity stake, and she could keep her equity in the Australian company. It wasn't a compromise, and we both got what we wanted—a classic win/win negotiation. We never would have gotten there if we had started haggling over percentages, our first inclination. Plus, undoubtedly someone would have "lost," and that would have damaged our relationship. Skilled negotiators say that only way to reach a win/win solution is to understand what is important to the other side and to meet those objectives fully. I'll repeat that. A successfully negotiated agreement meets all, or at least most, of the objectives of both sides.

In business, we spend a lot of time writing objectives, reading objectives, and rating objectives, but not a whole lot of time understanding them. In many companies, part of the performance rating process is a feedback survey sent to peers to determine if you are, to put it bluntly, a nice person or a slime bucket in disguise. At one company where I worked, every year, once the feedback was collated, both HR and management expressed discontent at the lack of candid feedback. How can management really know what's going on and what the employees' development needs are if coworkers write only nice things? Each year, new requirements, like mandating that development needs must be filled in before submitting the survey, were implemented to force employees to write critical comments, but to no avail. Did anyone ever think about the objectives of the employees filling in the surveys? Each employee wanted a good rating for him or herself, and each employee was required to fill out a survey for peers. The same peers would be filling out a survey for that employee. Here the tit-for-tat rule overwhelms the need for candor. If you write something nice about me, I'll write something nice about you. If you expound on my development needs this year, I'll rip you a new one next year. Hence, everyone was nicey-nicey because the real objective was to get a good rating, not provide honest feedback. If a company wants honest feedback, it needs to decouple the feedback survey from the performance appraisal process.

Whenever you feel like you're banging your head against a wall trying to figure out why people aren't behaving the way they should, it's probably because of misaligned objectives. Here's an example that inspired a large amount of head banging. Several years back, I was asked to implement an inventory management system for our affiliate in Australia. The affiliate had outsourced its inventory management and distribution to a third-party distributor but was suffering from a large number of stockouts. Even after numerous discussions with the distributor and financial incentives to discourage stockouts, the problem persisted. The inventory manager thought that a shared information system would allow for better control of inventory. When I visited the distributor, I learned that a large part of its business was supplying information services to the numerous mom-and-pop retailers who were its main customers. This would lock in that distributor as the retailers' sole supplier. However, the distributor was heavily subsidizing these services at the time. To manage cash flow, it would often delay ordering inventory, leading to the large number of stockouts. No information system could possibly help. The distributor's goal was to lock in as many customers as possible to its information services. The manufacturer's goal was to sell and fill as many orders as possible. Their goals were at odds and would continue to conflict until one or both changed.

You don't need me to tell you that misaligned goals are the source of conflicts in business, personal life, and even diplomacy. Yet, in practice, few people take the time to uncover the objectives driving behavior. Instead, we usually implement new policies with a new set of artificial incentives on top of the current policies and incentives that don't work. In short, we spend most of our time addressing symptoms rather than underlying causes. My premise is that these conflicts are not exceptions to normal business operations but are the normal business operations, and many "improvement programs" create more conflicts. This is why so many of us are stressed out. Let's look at a business's supply chain and the typical metrics used to determine performance.

Typical Manufacturer Departments and Performance Measures

Department	Metric	Consequence
Sales	Quarterly sales quotas	Order volumes increase to meet quotas near end of sales periods, causing uneven demand cycles.
Customer service	Perfect order	Orders are held in customer service to be verified before processing, adding to order lead time.
Manufacturing	Uptime, capacity, cost per unit	Plants maximize volume of production regardless of actual demand. Disruptions to schedule are highly discouraged.
Inventory	Inventory turns, stockouts	Push to sell excess inventory created by maximized production results in sales promotions (which create spikes in demand) and lower profit margins.
Distribution	Freight cost	Shipments are bundled to maximize freight on board, adding to order lead time.
Entire supply chain	Delivery to promise Order lead time Customer satisfaction	Individual department metrics result in long lead times and inflexibility. Longer lead times require more inventory on hand to prevent stockouts.

Most manufacturers would prefer an even flow of demand to match an even flow of production, but the system of sales incentives creates artificial spikes and lags in demand. To make their bonuses, sales reps typically ramp up their efforts at the end of the accounting period. Add sales and marketing promotions, and demand becomes even more irregular. After customers have stocked up during the promotional period, their demand drops. Drops in demand usually lead to more promotions. To cover the spikes in demand, manufacturers carry more inventory in the form of safety stock.

Maximizing plant production and keeping the cost per unit low are at direct odds with keeping inventory levels low and filling orders as quickly as possible. Verifying orders to meet perfect order metrics and optimizing freight also add to the order cycle time. Of course, the longer the order lead times, the more inventory must be kept on hand to fill orders. The net result is that all these departments work at cross-purposes and rightly blame each other for their own poor performance on their individual metrics.

Optimizing each step of a value chain does not result in an optimized chain. I want to repeat this, because many people have difficulty grasping this concept. Optimizing steps within a process does not optimize the process. Often the entire chain suffers because of micro-optimization. It's like planning what to wear. You may have great accessories, great shoes, a great shirt, a great jacket, and great slacks, but you put them all together and the outfit stinks because the items don't work together well. The majority of reengineering projects I've been part of suffered from micro-optimization. After divvying up the value chain into its component parts, each part became its own project with its own goals, which were often at odds with the other projects.

Early in my career, I worked on a project to improve the supply chain of a large chemical manufacturer that needed to increase its profitability. This company had typical supply chain problems: excessive inventory, long lead times, delayed orders, shortages of some items, and lots of angry customers. Our job was to reengineer all the supply chain processes. Before the project even got off the ground, the flagship plant, the company's most modern and efficient facility, burned to the ground. Instead of working on the project, we were engaged to manage this crisis. During the weeks that ensued, we established a process for contacting customers, negotiating orders and due dates, working with contract suppliers, and ignoring shipping costs. As a result, the surplus inventory was eliminated, lead times decreased, orders arrived as planned, customers paid earlier, and both customer satisfaction and profitability improved.

Although the sales volume was down, the margins on those sales improved, and, helped by the decreased costs of carrying inventory and accounts receivables, the bottom line improved. These results blew me away. All the improvements we wanted without the process reengineering. What happened? The entire supply chain focused on one goal, filling orders on a timely basis, at the expense of some departmental goals, namely manufacturing and distribution costs. Although these costs increased, the customers were willing to pay more to get their deliveries on time in a crisis.

One of the biggest problems I see in business is that it wants to have its cake and eat it, too. Mission statements read "Provide best customer service at lowest prices" or "High quality at low cost." Employees are rated on their ability to think strategically while paying attention to details or on their ability to hit the ground running while establishing well-thought-out plans. Do the following comments sound familiar? "Great detail, but needs to be briefer!" "Great summary, but needs more detail!" It's very difficult to excel at two opposing abilities at one time. If you are a low-cost producer, then every department needs to act like a low-cost producer. If short inventory turns and low lead times are the goal, then allow that manufacturing and distributions costs will suffer. In other words, you really can't have your cake and eat it, too. Everyone needs to be aligned around the one goal.

One of the best analogies to illustrate the effects of micro-optimization is the triathlete. A triathlete cannot optimize his or her performance in all three events. A good swimmer has a well-developed upper body that is detrimental to a runner, as it adds heft. A good runner tends to be slight all over, lacking the muscle definition required for a high-performance swimmer and bicyclist. World-class cyclists have well-developed thighs that are detrimental for streamlined running and swimming. The key to excelling in a triathlon is to perform amazingly well in your strongest event and be good enough in the others. Trying to excel at all three will result in mediocrity.

Going back to the supply chain, when you look at the extended chain with suppliers and buyers, you'll often see cases of misaligned objectives. Picking a supplier based on low cost and then demanding that it meet your changing delivery requirements will result in higher costs, missed deliveries, or worse product quality. Picking a highly responsive supplier and then demanding lower costs will damage responsiveness. Yet squeezing suppliers is commonplace in business. Then we wonder why they go out of business or consolidate so that they have more negotiating power.

Part of the problem lies in an obsession with measures. Setting up metrics starts with parsing a process into discrete, "measureable" components. Then each component must be measured and monitored in hopes that optimizing each submeasure will optimize the overall process measure. I've already shown that this is not true. The worse part of these measurement systems is that they set up a conflict between self-interest and the interest of the company. If a consultant walks into your office and puts up a slide that says, "You can't manage what you can't measure," take a cue from our knights and "run away, run away." The more relevant aphorism is "People manage to the measures."

Let's look at sales targets. If a salesperson's compensation is some part salary and some part commission, then the more sales, the more he or she makes. If additional pay is based on meeting sales targets, then come hell or high water, that person will meet the sales target at the expense of the interests of the company. I know a regional manager who convinced his distributors to take on more product than they wanted so he and his team could meet their year-end sales goals. He promised that they could return what they didn't sell. He and his team met their targets and got their bonuses, and the company was flooded with returns two quarters later. This didn't just cost the company the bonus money; it also had to pay for the extra handling and storage, the increased product obsolescence, and the bad will that resulted from this scheme. Of course, in this manager's defense, the sales targets he was asked to meet had no grounding in reality but were the result of an executive's desire for stretch goals.

Other stories of metrics gone awry include a public transportation authority that decided to align the pay of bus drivers with their on-time rate. As a result, a lot of drivers skipped stops if they were running late, leaving passengers stranded. When postal workers couldn't meet their target processing times and error rates, at least one worker just hid huge quantities of mail. As a frequent flier for most of my life, I noticed that about a decade ago, stated flight durations lengthened. This coincided with industrywide measures of on-time arrival. Now it is commonplace for flights to arrive 30 to 45 minutes *early*—not a problem unless you arranged for a ride to pick you up at the arrival time, a rare occurrence with airline passengers. (Not.) When there is a conflict between their own interests and the company's interest, people will not only manipulate how they meet their measures, they will manipulate the measures themselves. Measures are not objective, not even financial ones. Finance is a matter of opinion; the rules are only generally accepted accounting principles (GAAP) and differ from country to country. What goes into a unit cost, or a capital expenditure versus an expense, or what qualifies as an earning can vary from company to company and can be manipulated to paint the desired picture. (Enron, anyone?) The same goes for almost any measure. I know someone who counted all the "neither approve nor disapprove" answers on a feedback survey as positive responses, resulting in a satisfaction rate in the 90th percentile.

This is why understanding and aligning objectives is more effective than implementing artificial incentives, which can easily be manipulated, and is essential in promoting win/win behavior. In any venture, the objectives of all key stakeholders need to be understood and then fulfilled. The main stakeholders of a business are customers, suppliers, employees, partners, shareholders, and community. Finding common goals to keep everyone happy is the key to success. This is Business Management 101. Most business people

I Unclog My Nose in Your Direction

have some inkling of it. Yet if you look around you, you'll see misaligned objectives everywhere. Some businesses believe that success is based on screwing suppliers or partners (by negotiating one-sided deals) or their community (by polluting.) Sometimes they even try to screw their own customers (by selling shoddy goods) or shareholders (by cooking the books). These strategies may work temporarily, but over the long-term? Never.[16]

*WARNING! *The following paragraphs concern two of the author's pet peeves. Beware of ranting*!

Take the airline industry. I'm talking about the big, old airline companies, like United and American, not the Southwests of the industry. These airlines have been around for a long time and at one time dominated the industry. I've been a frequent business traveler for much of my professional life and have seen that the policy of these airlines is to screw their best customers, frequent business travelers. We are the people who often travel every week with little advance notice of where and when we're going. How are we rewarded? Oh sure, we get frequent flier mileage (which is difficult to use because of restrictions) and the offer of business class upgrades. Ever try to use an upgrade? Business class is always full. Instead, I get to pay $1,600 for my seat in coach

---

16 Imagine the difference that "invest in long-term stable growth" could make as the basis for the financial industry rather than "meet short-term expectations," which encourages bad behavior.

while the person next to me who booked weeks ago and is en route to vacation, pays $250. What about that business traveler–friendly policy of requiring a Saturday overnight stay for a cheaper fare? And those expensive one-way fares? Why are the fares to Orlando and Las Vegas so much cheaper than fares to New York and Chicago?

The airline policies are designed to lure fickle leisure travelers, who often buy on price, and to saddle business travelers, their best customers, with the cost of subsidizing the cheaper seats. The airlines know they could get away with this because what is the alternative for the business traveler? Train? Bus? Rental car? Oops, what about private jet or charter flight? The last decade has seen a rise in the purchase and use of corporate and private jets. What a surprise! Now with higher fuel and other costs, fewer people to subsidize the cheap fares, and increased competition from lower-cost startups, all the big airlines are having financial troubles.[17]

Another industry that is suffering because of a past "screw your customers" business model is the music industry. When I was a teenager, I was a heavy purchaser of albums. (Yes, I know that I am dating myself.) At that time albums cost an average of $5 to $7. Most of my friends also bought albums, and we all had good collections. Record stores, a place to hang out and listen to new releases, were full of teens, a demographic with low earnings. Albums were not expensive items. If I waited, I could get the remainders for about $3 apiece. Every once in a while, there would be an album that cost more than the others, and those were the ones we illegally taped and shared via cassettes.

When CDs first came out, they were quite expensive. As the price lessened, I bought a CD player. I recall initially shopping at a big music store near me and buying CDs for about $10 to $12 each, more expensive than an album but promising better quality and more songs per disc. Over the next few years, I watched as everyone converted to the CD format, and the average price of a CD went to about $17. With tax, that was a nearly $20 purchase! And the discs now had only eight or nine songs, like an album! Extortion! Knowing how cheaply CDs can be manufactured, I felt exploited and stopped purchasing them, as did many of my friends. How could kids, traditionally big consumers of pop music, afford to enjoy music? With the new digital formats, they found a way with music-sharing websites and free downloads. Many newcomers

---

[17] I realize that this issue is more complex than I have relayed here, but my point is that airline industry chose not to meet the needs of its most profitable customers.

moved into the music business to meet the need for cheap music. Now individual song downloads are less than a dollar, and many of them can be found for free. Music has become cheap again. The traditional music industry is suffering, but how long did it expect it could continue to gouge its customers?

The moral of these tales of two industries is that when you exploit your customers, you are creating an opportunity for someone else to fill their needs. A business can stay in existence only if the goals of all the stakeholders are mutually beneficial. Screwing your customers is always a bad idea. It will be a short time before those customers revolt. Screwing your suppliers either forces them to look elsewhere for better partnerships or forces them out of business, creating a monopoly with excessive bargaining power. Screwing the community you reside in is one step removed from provoking the ire of your shareholders. Screwing your employees ensures you have the worst talent in the industry.

On every scale, within a company's department, across departments, across the supply chain, across different stakeholders, across different castles, and across different countries, the one and only way to ensure success is to understand and align everyone's goals for a mutually beneficial outcome. This is the essence of trade and diplomacy. Arthur demands that his needs be met and insists on getting his way until the conflict escalates into full-out war, much like the wars that companies wage on their suppliers, their employees, their competitors, and sometimes their customers. Much like the wars we wage on all our problems—the war on crime, the war on drugs, and the war on terror— without ever trying to figure out what caused the problem and whether there are ways to meet the same goal without going to battle. Arthur, you never asked what a castle full of Frenchmen was doing in the heart of England. Why wouldn't you want to know that?

Test Yourself!

Arthur must deal with many hidden agendas on his quest for the grail: Launcelot's need for heroics, Bedevere's desire to show off his intellect, the Knights Who Say "Ni"'s desire for free landscaping, the villagers' need to burn witches, Robin's desire for a continued life span, and so on. What is the best way Arthur can align the goals of his team members so he can meet his mission?

   a. Bring everyone together and have each share his most embarrassing moment.
   b. Do the trust exercise where one person falls and another has to catch him.
   c. Have everyone identify his strengths and weaknesses.
   d. Assign each person a specific "thinking hat" role that he must fulfill.
   e. Take turns "owning the pen" so that each has an opportunity to lead.

NARRATOR: *Now we are near the end of the movie and the end of the quest, as Arthur's army is about to charge the castle guarded by the Frenchmen. How do you rate Arthur as a CEO? He antagonizes his subjects (Dennis, the old woman), treats his knights as expendable (Bridge of Death), abuses his suppliers ("ni"-ing the shrubberer), ignores the advice of the sought-after expert (beware the fearsome rabbit), wreaks havoc on his community (killing the historian), and wages war on his competition (the French castle). Will he meet his strategic objective and obtain the grail?*

Chapter Vocabulary

Key performance undulators   The rise and fall in popularity of certain metrics.

Measuremental   Fixating on metrics to manage your business, often at the expense of items that are not so easily measured.

The French Guard's Guide to Negotiation

Here—from our expert negotiator, the French guard—are some tips to follow when negotiating an agreement.

PREPARATION: What? I blow Coca-Cola out my nose at you because preparation is for big, fat dumb-ass, bottom-of-the-dung-heap losers. There's no need to know what all your options are, because there is only one option—you get your way. Don't bother learning about their situation, either. They're big, fat, dumb-ass LOSERS. The only preparation you need is enough insults to use once you win.

ASSUMPTIONS: The only assumption you need to uncover is that the other side are IDIOTS! And that your mother was a bedpan and your father a square of the paper of the toilet. No one is bringing any baggage or has any biases or beliefs that need to be unearthed before an agreement can be made. Of course, only you are perfectly reasonable, and it is the other person who makes crazy demands and has crazy beliefs. And you smell like elephant dung draped on Limburger stuck to the bottom of a wet tennis shoe.

COMMITMENT: Go ahead; negotiate to WIN at all costs. It's not like your opponent will resent you or try to renege on an unfair deal or do everything in his power to sabotage it. You overbearing, empty-headed, not-a-single-thought-for-the-future, addled gimp, as long as you force your way on everyone else, you are the WINNER.

COLLABORATION: Oh yeah, in order to have a WINNER, you have to have a loser. It's a conflict, a war, not a partnership or a wussy brainstorming or a let's-hold-hands-and-sing-kumbaya-and-find-agreeable-options-to-meet-everyone's-needs-relationship-building session. I fart at you, a great big Mexican-food-for-lunch fart, you son of a dog groomer's assistant's assistant.

RELATIONSHIP: You will probably never need to negotiate again with this person you just tried to screw over. No need to build relationships. We French guards prefer to burn bridges. Relationships are for girly bed-wetters. In fact, it is unlikely you will ever cross paths even though you work in the same industry on the same projects in the same location. And no wants to build a relationship with you; my pimple pus is more appealing than you.

STRATEGY: Whatever you do, don't try to understand the other side's objectives and needs and create a solution that meets all goals. You don't care about those. They are more insignificant than the breath of flea on a titmouse. You want what you want and that's all that matters. Find your position and stick to it. Everyone will admire your stubbornness.

COMMUNICATION: Keep what you want close to the vest. Don't be honest about your options. Communicating openly will only make you appear WEAK—weaker than a membrane on a vacuole in an amoeba. And don't listen to anyone. You can't dominate a meeting if you listen to other people. I wave my unwashed armpit hair at your aunties.

19

Move Along, There's Nothing to See

The utter futility of grandiose journeys

Unfortunately, while Arthur's army is charging the castle, police cars pull up with sirens blaring. Out pops the historian's wife, who points out Arthur and his men as her husband's murderers. The police round up Arthur and the knights and put them in the back of a police van. The scene ends with a police officer telling everyone, including the movie crew in the middle of filming, to clear off. Then the screen goes black and the movie is over. No massive action scene, no comedic climax, no capture of the grail. Just black. No closing credits, no crazy outtakes, no finale music. Just round them all up and go blank.

Sigh.

It reminds me of employees arriving at work to find out that their company was sold or went bankrupt, and then everyone just packed up their offices and went home. All those unanswered emails, unfinished projects, unmet goals, and untested strategies became thoroughly irrelevant in an instant. Isn't this ending like reality? How often do companies actually obtain their grails? Chasing after grails wouldn't be so bad if it didn't involve stressed-out lives and overall misery. If the journey were fun and instructive, who would care about never finding the grail?

Sigh.

Isn't it about time we ended the Business Dark Ages and ushered in the Age of Business Enlightenment? How long will it take to refute corporate feudalism and bring about a renaissance in which workers can engage their employment with full hearts and souls and creative minds? When will we replace the mindless pursuit of profits and the torrent of excessive consumerism with the pursuit of meaningful goals that contribute to the betterment of humankind? Just as the irrational beliefs and ignorance binding peasants to their lords were finally cast off, we as modern business people must cast off the shackles keeping us in the Dark Ages—the modern management myths that are the foundation of our misinformed business dogma.

Management Myths

1. **We need to find and develop the right people**

    The personal life equivalent of this myth is "finding the perfect mate." Ever notice how people looking for their perfect mate never get married? Similarly, why does it take six to eight months to fill an ordinary job position? I'm always astonished when, after an exhaustive outside search turns up no viable candidates, the hiring manager selects someone from within who does not meet the stated experience and skills requirements. And that person works out fine.

    Companies already have the right people. They just are unable to recognize their talents or unable to let those talents flourish because of the fantasy of finding the ideal candidate or the ideal leader. You know, the one with "it." Different situations call for different skills and talents, and yet corporations tend to look for that one personality—that domineering type who is "biased for action," "risk taking," and "persuasive." We need to realize that the perfect candidate is completely undesirable. Persistent is stubborn; persuasive is domineering; take-charge is bossy; strategically oriented is careless about details; bias for action is poor at planning; assertive is aggressive. Our strengths are our weaknesses. We desperately need diversity in the workplace, not just of race or creed, but of thinking, skills, and values, to avoid the cultural biases and think-alike decision making that leads to disaster.

2. **Communication skills are critical in making yourself understood and motivating others to do what you want**

    I cannot believe how much time businesses spend on crafting communications. I think wordsmithing is the number one activity in business today. All the emails I included in this book as examples (with the exception of the one about the 10-minute screensaver (or was it the 15-minute screensaver?) were carefully hashed out by multiple people with multiple rewrites. Yet none of those communications achieved its goal. The truth is, no matter how carefully you choose your words, you cannot control what goes on inside other people's heads. What you can do is use all that effort and skill to *find out* what is going on in their heads. Listening is the most important communication skill and the most undervalued. We implore employees to speak up at meetings, to make themselves heard, and to be assertive. We rarely ask them to shut up and listen.

If you listen, you have a much better chance of understanding others and their needs and then of finding mutual goals. It's a much more productive place to start than constantly guessing how your words will be interpreted or what phrasings will motivate others to do your bidding. I hate nothing more than when I disagree with someone and then that person proceeds to "use communication skills" to try and get me do something I don't want to do. At its worst, that approach is manipulative and disrespectful. At its best, it's just plain ineffective. The reason there are so many misunderstandings is because we are all so busy trying to make ourselves understood that no one is trying to understand anyone else.

3. **We make rational decisions based on analyses, data, models, and measures**

Ha! I hope you are laughing at this one. Mostly, we use data and analyses to justify our points of view. We start with a thesis that we want to prove and then proceed to do so. We see what we are looking for and ignore what we are not looking for. That's how our brains operate. In those cases where we don't already have a thesis, we are likely to design the wrong analysis, misapply a model, or misinterpret the data because of our oversimplification of a complex situation. We need to recognize that mostly we make decisions based on ideology and emotions and to stop pretending that we are rational. When we recognize the simple rules and beliefs that bias our thinking, then we can start trying to be rational or at least start experimenting with different beliefs.

4. **Everything starts with a carefully crafted mission**

I envy people who knew as children what they wanted to be when they grew up and then grew up and did it. Of course, among my friends and acquaintances, hardly anyone fits that description. Most of us fell into our careers through some indirect pathway like taking a temporary job that turned into something else, changing careers based on the economy, or inadvertently finding something we love to do after years of doing something else. It's fantastic if we can create a mission for ourselves and then achieve it in a straight line. The reality, though, is that life often gets in the way. We can't control our fate, nor should we want to. Life offers some wonderful, unanticipated opportunities. Business works in the same fashion. It's great to work toward a mission. However, it's even greater to possess the wisdom to recognize unplanned opportunities and exploit them when they arise.

5. **Success depends on beating the competition**

From the outset, this is a very limiting view of the world. It means your competition gets to set the rules and define who you are and what you do. You can't be very innovative in this manner. It is also a never-ending, no-win cycle, because your competition also wants to beat you, and you need to retaliate, and on and on. Worse, this axiom is often used as the justification for bad behavior. All of our company's competitors are using cheap labor in China or raising prices or buying shoddy raw materials, so we have to do that, too. If all your friends jumped off a cliff, would you do it, too?

6. **We've got to manage to the bottom line**

When you break this sentence down, what it really says is that the ends justify the means. Do the ends ever justify the means? As long as we meet our quarterly projections and bring in profits, then anything is fair game. Isn't this the thinking that got so many companies into trouble in the first place? If we don't achieve the ends, and it is very likely that we won't, what have we gained or learned or contributed? Nothing. It all becomes a giant waste of time for all concerned, like so much of our jobs. Life happens in the journey, not the destination.

If there is one thing I've learned, it's that searching for the ideal candidate, developing the perfect leader, crafting the flawless communication, conducting the exhaustive, unbiased analysis, devising the game-changing strategy, defeating the competition, and aiming for straight-line growth in earnings are as futile as the quest for the Holy Grail. If none of these things are true, then what is the answer? Personally, I don't like right answers, just really good questions, but I know some of you need to have an answer. Here it is:

Businesses are people, silly!

As are customers, suppliers, shareholders, and community members! We need to treat business people as human people. Unfortunately, today's businesses treat their people as "human resources" or "human capital" that need to be "utilized," "managed," and "developed." Is it any wonder, then, that employees start to act like things with no passion, no creativity, no spark of initiative? As we codify, computerize, theorize, optimize, and standardize more and more of the interactions between humans, from performance plans and coaching checklists to customer service scripts and sales protocols, we lose the heart of human relationships: an understanding and appreciation of each other as unique individuals. The delusion is that, as business people, we think we are too busy to get to know each other, but how else can we motivate employees, get close to customers, be responsible members of the community, and meet the needs of shareholders?

How about this as the new management dogma?

Members of the business community, as full-fledged members of the human race, have a moral obligation to strive toward the advancement of life for their fellow community members—all of humankind.

Random Vocabulary That Didn't Fit the Chapters

New hire refuting process   In order to eliminate a massive number of résumés, the process by which interviewers strive to find reasons not to pursue the job candidates.

Adgenda   The agenda that grows and grows.

Corporate infrastricture   Technology limitations that restrict the ability to collaborate and share information, e.g., bandwidth for webcasts, size limitations on emails.

Cubicall   Shouting over or through the cubicle wall because you are too lazy to walk.

Ineffectual capital   The captured knowledge of a company that really only amounts to heaps of unread documents.

Meeting disbrief   Conducted after a meeting to disavow everything that was said in the meeting. *Related:* meeting rebrief

Meeting vacilitator   A meeting leader who constantly changes direction, ensures that every opposing opinion is thoroughly hashed out, and generally can't make a decision.

New project lunch   The only way to get people to your project meetings.

New project paunch   The result of all those lunch meetings.

Performance-miraged out   Pretending that an employee has performance issues in order to justify a layoff and replace that person with a cheaper worker.

Transitshun   When coworkers no longer talk to you or invite you to meetings because you have announced that you are leaving the company.

Refucturing   You f'd it up the last time, what makes you think this time will go better?

Answers to Exercises

You should know better. There are no right answers

Feedback Survey

Thank you for reading this book. In order to continually improve, the author would like to get your feedback. I know your time is important to you, but your feedback on this survey will help me to serve you better. Please circle the answer that most closely corresponds to the way you feel. Use the space provided to explain or expound on your answers.

1. The use of surveys to get feedback from customers, employees, etc. is
    a. A nice idea
    b. Sometimes inane
    c. Not a good use of my time
    d. Way overused
    e. Really pisses me off

2. The likelihood that the surveyors will read and enact your comments is
    a. I never thought about it
    b. Slim to none
    c. Well, we do skim them
    d. We put the surveys in a Scantron and get a report that gets filed
    e. We'd like to make changes, but that's above our pay grade

3. The likelihood that this author will read or even cares about your feedback now that you've already shelled out big bucks for this book is
    a. Slim to none
    b. There's no address to send this to
    c. At least it's only 11 questions
    d. The book's already written
    e. Ha, ha, ha, ha, ha!

4. Your overall impression of this book is that it's
    a. Brilliant
    b. Amazingly brilliant
    c. Either brilliant or amazingly brilliant
    d. Freakin' amazingly brilliant
    e. So brilliant I'm telling all my friends to buy it

5. Your overall impression of the author is that she's
    a. Brilliant
    b. Brilliant and beautiful
    c. Damn funny
    d. Funny, witty, brilliant, and beautiful
    e. A total egomaniac

6. Your reaction that the author is available for speaking engagements is
    a. That's awesome
    b. I'd pay any price to get her to speak at my company
    c. Get her contact information stat
    d. I'm putting that in my budget now
    e. I'm checking out her website at karengphelan.com

7. The likelihood that feedback surveys can be self-serving is
    a. Really?
    b. No way!
    c. Likely
    d. Highly likely
    e. How else can I justify my existence?

The following questions are designed to test your comprehension and retention of the material presented in this book.

8. Management consultants are
    a. Worth the price
    b. Often not as informed as they pretend to be
    c. Corporate psychologists who help us play nice
    d. Unnecessary if we just had a little common sense
    e. Evil incarnate

9. Academics who write business books
    a. Offer data-driven, impartial analyses with useful conclusions
    b. Start with a thesis that they then prove
    c. Are under pressure to write books so that they can get tenure
    d. Need to boost their income with book sales and consulting fees
    e. Never had a real job

10. Today's wealth of business management methods, measures, models, and methodologies provide
    a. Useful tools to manage my business
    b. An overwhelming array of often conflicting information
    c. Narrow slices of perspective that don't account for the big picture
    d. Oversimplified pictures based on "rational" thinking that doesn't account for the complexity of life
    e. Catchy gimmicks by which to sell services, seminars, and studies

11. The discovery that Monty Python and the Holy Grail really teaches everything a person needs to know about business management is
    a. A freakin' awesome coincidence
    b. A sign that God works in mysterious way
    c. A secret conspiracy by John Cleese to sell business videos
    d. A complete contrivance on the part of the author
    e. Further proof that people can be made to believe anything

Appendix A

Overview of LiFO (Life Orientations)

Probably the three most commonly used individual profiling tools are the Myers-Briggs Type personality indicator (based on the work of Carl Jung), DiSC (Dominance, Influence, Steadiness, Conscientiousness) assessment tool, and LiFO (Life Orientations). Psychologists will argue that each of these tools is very different and has particular applications, but I am not a psychologist, and I think that any of these assessments is a great place to start analyzing organizational woes. If you or your company are not familiar with any of these tools, you should contact one of the numerous companies that can do an assessment. The results will give your team an awareness of themselves in relation to their coworkers and supply you with a vocabulary to begin addressing fundamental differences in communication and work styles.

Overview of LiFO (Life Orientations)
(Adapted from *LIFO Training: Productivity Workbook*)

Because I am most familiar with LiFO, I'd like to give a quick summary of what this tool does and how corporations use it. Participants respond to questions or statements about situations and values by choosing the answer most or least like them. Here's a sample statement.

I feel the best way to get ahead in world is to:
a. Be a worthy person and count on those in authority to recognize that worth.
b. Work to establish a right to advancement and then claim it.
c. Preserve and build on what I have.
d. Develop a winning personality that will attract the notice of others.

Based on your responses, you determine which of four communication styles you rely on most heavily. These styles are "the four windows to the world," meaning that people's values and belief systems color their perspective of the world and the way in which they interact with it. The four styles are:

Supporting/Giving
PHILOSOPHY: "If I prove my worth by working hard and pursuing excellence, the good things in life will come to me." I value excellence.
GOALS: Prove worth. Be helpful.
STRENGTHS: Principled, cooperative, dedicated, pursues excellence

Controlling/Taking
PHILOSOPHY: "If I can get results by being competent and seizing opportunity, the good things in life will be there for the taking." I value action.
GOALS: Be competent. Get results.
STRENGTHS: Persistent, initiating, urgent, directing

Conserving/Holding
PHILOSOPHY: If I think before I act and make the most of what I've got, I can build up my supply of the good things in life." I value reason.
GOALS: Go slow. Be sure.
STRENGTHS: Systematic, analytical, maintaining, tenacious

Adapting/Dealing
PHILOSOPHY: "If I please other people and fill their needs first, then I can get the good things in life that I've wanted all along." I value harmony.
GOALS: Know people. Get along.
STRENGTHS: Harmonious, tactful, flexible, aware

Quick Differences Among the Styles

	Supporting/Giving	Controlling/Taking	Conserving/Holding	Adapting/Dealing
Default Pronoun	We	I	It	You
Default verb	Believe	Do	Think	Feel
Value	Fair	Fast	Factual	Flexible
Outlook on life	Idealistic	Opportunistic	Realistic	Optimistic
Fear Response	Fret	Fight	Frustrate	Flee

Appendix A

Now most people do not exhibit just one of these styles but rely on all of them to some extent, with one or two dominant styles. The reason for the double names, as in supporting/giving, is that the second name is the style used excessively.

Supporters work to ensure that everyone around them is included, treated fairly, and given the opportunity to succeed. Excellence means getting all the necessary help and expertise involved. Taken to excess, "giving" can turn into "doormat," with supporters always placing themselves below others or being busybodies by giving advice where none is wanted.

Controllers have the classic type A personality. They like to take the leadership role, love competition, exhibit confidence, and act and decide quickly. In excess, they can run roughshod over everyone else, take credit for others' work, and try to win at any cost. Although they have little time for niceties, they are the go-to people to get it done.

Conservers hate waste—wasted actions, effort, time, and materials. They prefer to take their time to thoroughly understand an issue before taking action and will create a methodology or system to perform a task before undertaking it. Conservers can get too detailed and are often accused of being uncooperative or withdrawn and stingy.

Adaptors are keenly aware of how to smooth others over and how to be perfectly charming and diplomatic. They are able to change plans quickly to adjust to the situation at hand. In excess, they are like stereotypical car dealers, changing their pitch, willing to do or say anything to make the sale, seeming to have no internal guiding morals. A common trait of adapters is to answer a question with a question. They usually want to know your opinion before they feel free to express their own.

Another component of style differences that I have found very helpful is the way people view the world around them. Some people believe that the world is an inherently hostile place with many dangers and do not trust others until proven trustworthy (controlling/taking and conserving/holding). Contrasting with this belief are those who think the world is basically benevolent and will automatically trust others unless that trust is betrayed (supporting/giving and adapting/dealing). You can see this trait played out in management styles. Some managers in a new role will micromanage everything until they feel comfortable that you can perform your job satisfactorily. Other managers never show up until a crisis occurs and then get involved. Similarly, some people believe that they can control the world around them and master their own destiny, either by taking action or influencing others (controlling/taking and adapting/dealing). Others believe that their fate is controlled by external factors and that the world will recognize them if they either prove their own worth or make sure they are right (supporting/giving and conserving/holding). This latter belief has helped me to understand the countless unproductive (in my view) arguments I've been part of about who was right when all I wanted to do was develop a course of action, not caring who was right or wrong.

Test Yourself!

Match these commonly heard phrases to the style that originated them.

Supporting/giving	Best in class
	Bottom line
	Just do it
Controlling/taking	Due diligence
	Stretch goals
	Achieve consensus
Conserving/holding	Fair process
	Whatever makes the client happy
	The numbers don't add up
Adapting/dealing	Be decisive
	Just give me the net/net
	Politically correct
	The customer is always right
	Excellence in everything we do

Appendix B

Strategy development tools

In 1980, Michael Porter published his now famous Five Forces Model in a book called *Competitive Strategy: Techniques for Analyzing Industries and Competitors.* The purpose of this model was to help companies analyze their industries so that they could develop strategies to maintain profitability and stay competitive. He identified five forces that shape an industry.

Five Forces Model

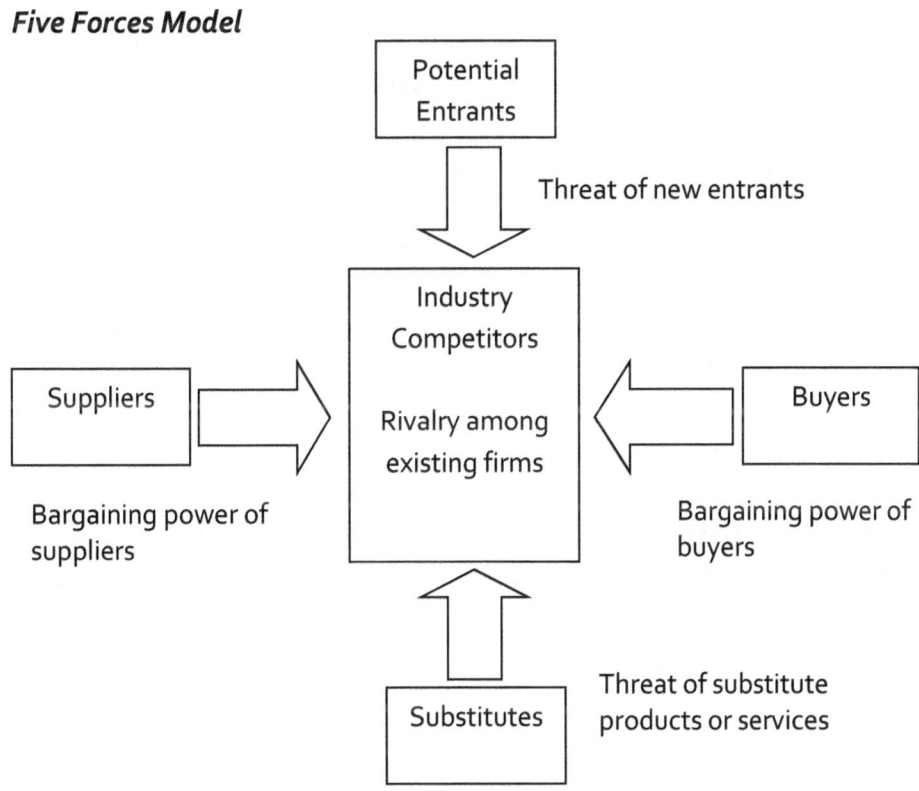

The first force is competition among industry rivals. Some industries, like consumer goods, have many competitors that constantly battle each other for market share. Highly competitive industries tend to have many new products and many price changes as incentives to buy. Other industries are more stable, with one or two major corporations dominating the industry. A company looking for new business opportunities may want to stay away from highly competitive industries and instead seek to exploit complacency within a stable industry.

This leads me to a second force, the threat of new entrants. How easy is it to enter this business? Web businesses are obviously very easy to start, but manufacturing requires quite a bit of capital expenditures. Regulation, proprietary expertise, specialized equipment, and restrictive distribution channels are all barriers to entry. Industries that are easy to enter will likely have a continuous stream of new entrants, increasing the competitive nature of the industry and also increasing the threat of substitute products, the third force.

How easy is it to supplant a product's demand with a different product? Remember the Palm Pilot? Smart phone technology made this once popular PDA obsolete. What about VCRs? Any high-tech product will become obsolete in a few years. Once their patents expires, propriety drugs are certain to be replaced by generics. This force is probably the most unpredictable because it comes from outside the industry and is often the result of a disruptive innovation.

The fourth force is the bargaining power of buyers. If you are a supplier to Walmart, then you have little bargaining power. Many governments and health insurance companies use formularies to purchase drugs. A drug must be listed on the formulary before it will be reimbursed, and governments often dictate the price they'll pay. The drug company needs to yield to the buyer in that instance, but when there is no formulary and a patient needs a life-saving medicine, the drug company can dictate the price. Most end consumers have no power, except their purchasing power, to determine the quality or cost of what they buy.

The last force is the bargaining power of suppliers. If the product is unique or of a particular quality, suppliers—especially if there aren't many—can wield a great deal of influence. If it's a commodity item that can be purchased relatively quickly and cheaply from multiple suppliers, then the

Appendix B

suppliers don't have much power. Labor unions, which supply employees, can also have varying degrees of influence. Some unions are reputed to be very strong while others acquiesce to most management demands.

The BCG Portfolio Analysis Model
(For analyzing your portfolio of businesses or products)

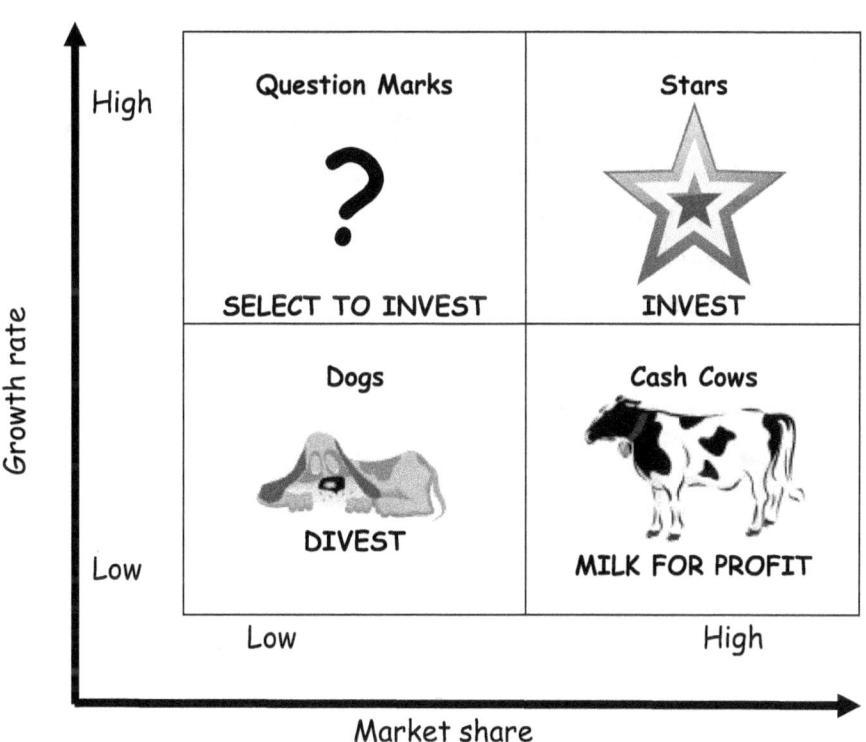

The four quadrants are referred to as stars, question marks, cash cows, and dogs, with dogs being the worst. Stars are the high-potential items that are consuming cash to grow but should eventually grow into cash cows. Cash cows are established, don't need much investment, and are highly profitable. Dogs don't consume investment or generate profits, and thus they should be liquidated or divested. Question marks are consuming investments to grow but don't generate revenue. They should be carefully monitored, with certain question marks selected for investment to become stars and the rest divested.

SWOT Analysis

Strengths (Internal) List your strengths, like: • Expertise • Product uniqueness	**Weaknesses (Internal)** List your weaknesses, like: • No technical experience • No financing available
Opportunities (External) List potential opportunities you can take advantage of, like: • Emerging markets • New technologies	**Threats (External)** List potential threats to your business, like: • Lower-priced competitors • No intellectual property protection

Acknowledgments

I'd like to thank my husband, Tom Hennigan, for acting as my sounding board and harshest critic. My gratitude goes to Mark Hurwich and Rich Catanese for being among the first to read my manuscript and provide feedback. I'd also like to credit Tom Hennigan, Jim Harris, and Paul Nurmi for contributing to the chapter vocabulary. Thank you to my family for putting up with my moods while I was writing this. Thank you, as well, to all the companies where I've worked for inadvertently providing me with an overwhelming amount of material.

Bibliography

Anissimov, Michael. "A Concise Introduction to Heuristics and Biases." June 2004. http://www.acceleratingfuture.com/michael/works/heuristicsandbiases.htm

Atkins, Stuart, Allan Katcher, and Eric Dahl. *LIFO Training: Productivity Workbook.* Los Angeles: BCon Lifo International, Inc., 2003.

Ayers, Michael S., and Lynne M. Reder. "A Theoretical Review of the Misinformation Effect: Predictions from an Activation-based Memory Model." *Psychonomic Bulletin & Review* 5, no. 1 (March 1998): 1–21.

Berenson, Alex. "A Long Shot Becomes Pfizer's Latest Chief Executive." *The New York Times*, July 26, 2006.

Bikhchandani, Sushil, David Hirshleifer, and Ivo Welch. "A Theory of Fads, Fashion, Custom, and Cultural Change as Informational Cascades." *The Journal of Political Economy* 100, no. 5 (October 1992): 992–1026.

Bruner, J. S., and M. C. Potter. "Interference in Visual Recognition." *Science*, April 24, 1964: 424–425.

Buehler, Roger, Dale Griffin, and Michael Ross. "Exploring the Planning Fallacy: Why People Underestimate Their Task Completion Times." *Journal of Personality and Social Psychology* 67, no. 3 (1994): 366–381.

Calcaterra, Nick. "Detailed History and Description of Transactional Analysis." July 2006. http://www.ericberne.com/transactional_analysis_description.htm.

Carroll, Paul B., and Chunka Mui. "Seven Ways to Fail Big." *Harvard Business Review*, September 2008: 82–91.

Christensen, Clayton M. *The Innovator's Dilemma.* New York: Harper Business, 2000.

Cleese, John, Graham Chapman, Terry Gilliam, Eric Idle, Terry Jones, and Michael Palin. *Monty Python and the Holy Grail Screenplay.* London: Methuen, 2002.

Cohen, Shoshanah, and Joseph Roussel. *Strategic Supply Chain Management.* New York: McGraw Hill, 2005.

Collins, Jim. *Good to Great.* New York: Harper Collins, 2001.

Davidson, Mike. *The Grand Strategist.* New York: Henry Holt, 1995.

Dodd, Dominic, and Ken Favarro. "Managing the Right Tension." *Harvard Business Review*, December 2006: 62-74.

Donohue, Thomas, president, U.S. Chamber of Commerce. "Enhancing America's Long-Term Competitiveness: Ending Wall Street's Quarterly Earnings Game." Keynote address, Wall Street Analyst Forum, New York, November 30, 2005.

Dresner, Howard. "The Gartner Fellows Interview: Clayton M. Christensen." *Gartners.* April 26, 2004. http://www.gartner.com/research/fellows/asset_93329_1176.jsp. (accessed 2006)

Dubner, Stephen J., and Stephen D. Levitt. "Unintended Consequences: Why Do Well-meaning Laws Backfire?" *The New York Times Magazine*, January 20, 2008: 18–19.

Evans, Jonathan St. B. T. "Biases in Deductive Reasoning." In *Cognitive Illusions*, edited by Rudiger F. Pohl, 127–144. New York: Psychology Press, 2004.

Fogg, Adam. "Monty Python Scripts." 1996. http://www.intriguing.com/mp/_scripts/cheese.php (accessed 2009).

Gleick, James. *Chaos: Making a New Science.* New York: Penguin, 1988.

Graham, John R., Campbell R. Harvey, and Shiva Rajgopal. "The Economic Implications of Corporate Financial Reporting." *Journal of Accounting and Economics*, vol. 40 (December 2005): 3–73.

Gribbin, John. *Deep Simplicity.* New York: Random House, 2004.

Hofstede, Geert, and Hofstede, Gert Jan. *Cultures and Organizations: Software of the Mind.* New York: McGraw Hill, 2005.

Johnson, Spencer. *Who Moved My Cheese.* New York: G. P. Putnam's Sons, 1998.

Kahneman, Daniel, and Amos Tversky. "Choices, Values, and Frames." *American Psychologist*, April 1984: 342–343.

Kahneman, Daniel, and Amos Tversky. "Prospect Theory: An Analysis of Decision under Risk." *Econometrica* 47, no. 2 (March 1979): 263–292.

Keiningham, Timothy L., Terry G, Vavra, and Lerzan Aksoy. "Managing Through Rose-Colored Glasses." *MIT Sloan Management Review* 48, no. 1 (Fall 2006): 15–18.

Kim, W. Chan, and Mauborgne Renee. "Blue Ocean Strategy." *Harvard Business Review*, October 2004: 76–84.

Kramer, Roderick M. "The Harder They Fall." *Harvard Business Review*, October 2003: 58–66.

Krehmeyer, Dean, Matthew Orsagh, and Kurt N. Schacht. "Breaking the Short-Term Cycle." Symposium Series on Short-Termism. CFA Institute and Business Roundtable for Corporate Ethics, 2006. 1–20.

Kruger, Justin, and David Dunning. "Unskilled and Unaware of It: How Difficulties in Recognizing One's Own Incompetence Lead to Inflated Self-Assessments." *Journal of Personality and Social Psychology* 77, no. 6 (1999): 1121–1134.

Kurzenhäuser, Stephanie. "What Are Natural Frequencies, and Why Are They Relevant for Physicians and Patients." *FB Erziehungswissenschaft und Psychologie 2005 Dissertation.* 2005.

Lambert, Kelly, and Scott O. Lilienfeld. "Brain Stains." *Scientific American Mind*, October-November 2007: 47–55.

Loftus, Elizabeth F., Daniel M. Berstein, and Jacqueline E. Pickerell. "Misinformation Effect." In *Cognitive Illusions*, edited by Rudiger F. Pohl, 345–361. New York: Psychology Press, 2004.

Lovallo, Dan, and Daniel Kahneman. "Delusions of Success: How Optimism Undermines Executives' Decisions." *Harvard Business Review*, July 2003: 56–63.

Markosian, Ned. *Time.* November 2002. http://plato.stanford.edu/entries/time/

Narayanan, V. G., and Ananth Raman. "Aligning Incentives in Supply Chains." *Harvard Business Review*, November 2004: 94–102.

Nickerson, Raymond S. "Confirmation Bias: A Ubiquitous Phenomenom in Many Guises." *Review of General Pyschology* 2, no. 2 (1998): 175–220.

O'Connor, Joseph and Seymour, John. *Introducing NLP.* London: Thorsons, 1995.

Oswald, Margit E., and Stefan Grosjean. "Confirmation Bias." In *Cognitive Illusions*, edited by Rudiger F. Pohl, 79–96. New York: Psychology Press, 2004.

Pearlstein, Steven. "The Compromise Effect." *Washington Post.* January 22, 2002. http://www.washingtonpost.com/ac2/wp-dyn/A41329-2002Jan26

Pohl, Rudiger F. "Hindsight Bias." In *Cognitive Illusions*, edited by Rudiger F. Pohl, 363–378. New York: Psychology Press, 2004.

Poidevin, Robin Le. *The Experience and Perception of Time.* The Stanford Encyclopedia of Philosophy (Winter 2004 Edition), Edward N. Zalta (ed.) http://plato.stanford.edu/entries/time-experience/

Porter, Michael. *Competitive Strategy: Techniques for Analyzing Industries and Competitors.* New York: The Free Press, 1980.

Rachlinski, Jeffrey J. "Rulemaking Versus Adjudication: A Psychological Perspective." *Cornell Law School Legal Studies Research Paper Series.* February 21, 2005. http://lsr.nellco.org/cornell/lsrp/papers/18/

Reicher, Stephen D., S. Alexander Haslam, and Michael J. Platow. "The New Psychology of Leadership." *Scientific American Mind*, August-September 2007: 22–27.

Bibliography

Renner, Catherine Hackett. "Validity Effect." In *Cognitive Illusions*, edited by Rudiger F. Pohl, 201–213. New York: Psychology Press, 2004.

Repenning, Nelson P. "Theory Building with Causal Loops." *MIT Sloan School Executive Series on Management & Technology.* 2006.

Repenning, Nelson P., and John D. Sterman. "Nobody Ever Gets Credit for Fixing Problems that Never Happened." *California Management Review CMR* 43, no. 4 (Summer 2001): 64–88.

Rhoads, Kelton. "Loss Aversion, Risk, & Framing: The Psychology of an Influence Strategy." August 2007. http://www.workingpsychology.com/lossaver.html

RIAA. "2007 Music Shipments." http://76.74.24.142/81128FFD-028F-282E-1CE5-FDBF16A46388.pdf

Savitt, Steven. *Being and Becoming in Modern Physics.* The Stanford Encyclopedia of Philosophy, September 2006, Edward N. Zalta (ed.) http://plato.stanford.edu/entries/spacetime-bebecome/

Schein, Edgar H. *Organizational Culture and Leadership.* San Franciso: Jossey-Bass, 2004.

Senge, Peter and de Geus, Arie. *The Living Company.* Boston: Harvard Business School Press, 1997.

Senge, Peter M. *The Fifth Discipline.* New York: Doubleday, 1990.

Shermer, Michael. "The Prospects for Homo Economicus." *Scientific American.* June 17, 2007. http://www.sciam.com/article.cfm?id=the-prospects-for-homo-economicus

Spreier, Scott W., Mary H. Fontaine, and Ruth L. Malloy. "Leadership Run Amok: The Destructive Potential of Overachievers." *Harvard Business Review*, June 2006: 72–81.

Staff. "Company News; Pfizer Promotes 3 Executives To Vice Chairman Positions." *New York Times*, February 25, 2005.

Staff. "Short-term Thinking Damaging Long-term Growth Potential, Investment Managers Told." *BIV Daily Business News.* May 1, 2007.

http://www.bivinteractive.com/index.php?option=com_content&task=view&id=75&Itemid=47

Sutton, Robert. *The No Asshole Rule.* New York: Warner Business Books, 2007.

Tierney, John. "Diet and Fat: A Severe Case of Mistaken Consensus." *The New York Times*, October 9, 2007.

Waldrop, Mitchell M. *Complexity: The Emerging Science at the Edge of Order and Chaos.* New York: Simon & Schuster, 1992.

Ward, David, and Elena Rivani. "An Overview of Strategy Development Models and the Ward-Rivani Model." *EconWPA Papers Archive.* June 7, 2005. http://129.3.20.41/econ-wp/get/papers/0506/0506002.pdf (accessed 2009).

Wikipedia. "Loss Aversion." March 2009. http://en.wikipedia.org/wiki/Loss_aversion.

Wikipedia. "Sunk Costs." February 2009. http://en.wikipedia.org/wiki/Sunk_cost.

Wittmann, Marc, and Martin P. Paulus. "Decision making, impulsivity and time." *Trends in Cognitive Science.* January 2008: 7-12.

Yudkowsky, Eliezer. "An Intuitive Explanation of Bayesian Reasoning." June 4, 2006. http://yudkowsky.net/rational/bayes

——. "Overcoming Bias: Planning Fallacy." September 17, 2007. http://www.overcomingbias.com/2007/09/planning-fallac.html

Zook, Chris. *Unstoppable: Finding Hidden Assets to Renew the Core and Fuel Profitable Growth.* Boston: Harvard Business School Press, 2007.

Outtakes[18]

(If movies can have them, why not books?)

I have my own hypothesis about intuition and heuristics. As a mother, I loved to watch the behavior of my children and quickly realized that infants and toddlers can be amazingly intelligent. Even though they haven't mastered language, they have complicated thought processes going on in their little heads. When both my boys started walking at age one, I taught them not to go in the street and not to touch the furnace, burners, and electrical outlets. By showing them the dangers involved, they immediately understood how harmful these activities could be and avoided them (without fail!). One of my sons, at age two, could play a software game in which he had to pick out the right words to complete a meaningful sentence. Seemingly this task required reading, but he could do it without being able to read. Curious, I observed my kids' playmates and noticed that other very young children were able to master tasks of great complexity. I concluded that they must possess a sophisticated way of thinking that is independent of language. As we age, we become more and more language dependent to code both our thoughts and our memories. In doing this, we forget these non-language methods of thinking and call them our "subconscious" because we can no longer access them easily.

Of course, this hypothesis is the first one I adopted and I didn't really consider any others. I thought I should test it before I included it in this book, but then I realized that I would be subject to selection bias in choosing the tests and would only end up trying to confirm my hypotheses. If I did test it, I would probably take note of only the evidence that verified my theory. Even if I didn't do that, I've never conducted psychological studies before so I would likely be subject to the incompetence effect and inadvertently develop invalid findings. So I decided not to bother.

---

[18] You're still here? Haven't you had enough?

We sit at the meeting table
Make excuses when we're able
We review pie charts and graphic arts
From PowerPoints illegible
That's life in the big corporation
We hate to take vacations

Based on its contextual use, the process of "unlocking value" is to "disembowelment" as:
    a. "Organizational de-layering" is to "decapitation"
    b. "Rightsizing" is to "amputation"
    c. "Outsourcing" is to "amnesia"
    d. "Change management" is to "Prozac"
    e. "Performance metrics and monitoring" is to "myopia"

Corporate Thermodynamics

There are some simple rules governing everything in the work world. Like relativity, the laws of thermodynamics apply to the workplace, and, like relativity, many people are unfamiliar with how they work at work. In an effort to help, I've put together a quick synopsis of the three laws of thermodynamic and describe how companies often try to work contrary to these laws.

The field of thermodynamics originated during the early industrial age as engineers tried to create more and more efficient heat engines to power the factories and machinery that were taking hold everywhere. The holy grail of thermodynamics was the perpetual motion machine that could power itself on its spent energy. These early engineers learned that, in a closed system, you cannot create or destroy energy. In other words, you can't get something for nothing. This is the first law of thermodynamics, and it did not preclude a perpetual motion machine. However, these engineers also learned that in an energy conversion, say, from heat to motion, a certain amount of energy is lost to entropy.[19] The second law of thermodynamics states that the entropy of any system will always naturally increase. For example, if you have three distinct gases in three compartments in a container and then open those compartments, the gases will mix until all resemblance to the initial three ordered

---

[19] Entropy is defined as the randomness or disorder of a system and also as unusable energy.

gases is gone. Once mixed like this, they do not unmix naturally. Still bent on finding a perpetual motion machine, the early engineers tried to create a system in which there was no entropy. This led to the discovery of the third law, which states that a temperature of absolute zero—the state where there would be no energy loss, no motion, and thus no entropy—can never be reached. Atomic motion and energy loss will always exist, albeit in small amounts.

What this meant for our industrial-age engineers is that they could never develop a 100% efficient engine. Some amount of energy would always be lost to entropy. The more times energy is converted, such as heat energy into kinetic energy into electricity, the more energy is lost. Each conversion exacts an energy loss. Hence, a Rube Goldberg device is not very efficient. Although this was disappointing, the second law showed them that they could use energy to decrease entropy, and so the idea of refrigeration was born. However, it is important to remember that it takes more energy to cool things to an ordered state and decrease their entropy than it does to heat them to a disordered state because they will naturally tend to disorder.

All this is well and good for heat engines, but how do these laws apply to corporations? The amazing thing is that these laws apply to any closed system, even the universe! With the addition of Einstein's discovery that mass can be converted into energy, the first law of thermodynamics is also the Law of Conservation of Mass and Energy, which applies to the universe. Physics has also confirmed the second law. We know that the universe is continually expanding into a less ordered state. The second law of thermodynamics determines why time runs only in one direction and why we can't unbreak an egg. The third law also applies to the entire universe: there is no place that has no entropy or no energy.

Corporations are closed systems as well, and these laws apply to all closed systems. Because corporations require a large amount of work to keep running, let me also include the definition of work, which is related to energy. Work is the transfer of energy (or mathematically, force × distance × angle applied). Like our early engineers, corporate management is also on a quest for greater and greater efficiency. To this effect, they often initiate improvement programs. However, you cannot get more energy (or work) out of a closed system unless an external force or energy is applied. Therefore, a company cannot become more efficient on its own. It needs help from the outside through consultants, new hires, or new training programs. All the effort that takes place in internal initiatives just creates more entropy! Plus, it is thermodynamically and physically impossible to do more with less.

Many companies are also trying to find efficiencies and cost savings through outsourcing and shared services. The important thing to remember when reorganizing in this fashion is that you often need to create a layer of middlemen to manage the shared or outsourced function, and thus you create more hand-off points. Each work transfer means more lost work. In addition, you need to consider the relationship between work and distance; the more distance you are forced to traverse, the more work for everyone involved.

It is no surprise that, over time, the entropy of a company's organization increases. We see this occur as departments expand and spawn new departments, and generally the complexity and disorder of the organization increases. However, what is surprising is how much effort it takes to keep an organization in an ordered state. Reorganizing requires much more energy than any other activity without the proportionate increase in efficiency! And the third law tells us that no matter how hard we try, we can never find the perfect, efficient organizational structure. Applying these three universal and simple rules should help companies conserve both work and energy.

Index

"I feel..." statements, 95
Action/results versus thought/wisdom culture, 14
Adams Confectionary, 23
Adapting to Scale, 138
Adding Stretch Goals Causal Loop, 110
Amazing Vision-o-matic, 128
Amos Tversky, 53, 265
Art of War, 163
Asian flu problem, 53
Axelrod, Robert, 194
balancing loop, 109, 111
Baring Bank, 183
BCG Portfolio Analysis Model, 259
Behind-the-Times Corporation, 105
Berkshire Hathaway, 22
Berne, Eric, 92
Berra, Yogi, 126
Bextra, 122
BKG (Bunnies, Knights, Grails) Priority Portfolio Analysis, 169
Boston Big Dig, 101
Breast Cancer Probability Problem, 204
Bridge of Death, 205, 206, 209, 222, 236
Bruner, Jerome, 66
BTC, 105, *See* Behind the Times Corporation

Cap Gemini, 23
Cap Gemini Ernst & Young, 23
Carl Jung, 253
Cave of Caerbannog, 199
Celebrex, 121, 122
Chantix, 122
Chaos theory, 182
Characteristics of the Domineer, 42
Chrysler, 22
cognitive bias, 63, 66, 74
Colgate-Palmolive, 173
Collaborative versus competitive culture, 10
Competitive Strategy: Techniques for Analyzing Industries and Competitors, 162
confirmation bias, 66, 67, 68
Daniel Kahneman, 53, 266
Deloitte & Touche, 23
Deloitte Haskins & Sells, 23, 127, 162, 173
DH&S. *See* Deloitte Haskins & Sells
Dimensions of corporate culture, 10
DiSC, 253
domineer, 41, 42, 55, 165, 197
Dunning, David, 70
Eisenhower, Dwight D., 126
Endangered Species Act of 1973, 104
Enron, 43, 232

273

Executive Committee Song and Dance, 78
Exubera, 122, 157
Fatalism, 28
Five farces model, 168
Five Forces Model, 257
four stages of learning, 71
Futurism, 29
Games People Play, 92
Gantt chart, 109
Gates, Bill, 127
GE, 24
Gemini, 23, 120, 121, 122, 219, *See* Gemini Consulting
Gemini Consulting, 23, 120, 121, 219
General Motors, 22
generally accepted accounting principles, 232
Gorge of Eternal Peril, 205
Grant, Ulysses S., 127
Hierarchical versus egalitarian culture, 11
Hills Pet Products, 173
hindsight bias, 64, 68
Hofarti model, 221
Hofarti Window, 210
Holy Book of Armaments, 187
homosocial reproduction, 42
IBM, 127
Idiot Village, 135
incompetence effect, 70, 269
informational cascade, 72
J&J. *See* Johnson & Johnson
Jack Welch, 24
Jerome Bruner, 66
Jim Collins, 39

John F. Kennedy, 44
Johnson & Johnson, 23, 188, 189, 190, 192
Kahneman, 53, 265
Karen Katen, 157
Kauffman, Stuart, 193
Kerviel, Jerome, 183
Kindler, Jeff, 154, 157
Knights of the Round Table Attitude and Personality Indicator, 206
Kongo Gumi, 24
KRAPI, 206, 221, See Knights of the Roundtable Aptitude and Personality Indicator
KRAPI test, 210
Kruger, Justin, 70
Leadership abilities, 40
Leeson, Nick, 183
LiFO, 206, 253
Lipitor, 121
Lorenz, Edward, 182
loss aversion, 53, 63
management by objectives, 105
Management by objectives, 104
Mary Potter, 66
Maslow, Abraham, 71
May, Robert, 184
McKinnell, Hank, 121, 155, 157
McNEIL-PPC, 189, 190
Merck, 122, 189
metaprograms, 82, 85
    General/specific, 84
    Internal/external standards, 83
    Match/mismatch, 85
    Options/procedures, 84
    Proactive/reactive, 82

Toward/away from motivation, 83
Microsoft, 127
Ministry of Funny Walks, 79
misinformation effect, 68
MIT Sloan School of Management, 109
MS-DOS, 127
Murphy's Law, 101, 103
Myers-Briggs, 206, 221, 253
Neurolinguistic programming, 80
NLP, 80, 82, 214, 266, *See* Neurolinguistic Programming
No Child Left Behind Act, 217
Ode to a Corporate Three-Headed Knight, 116
On War, 163
paradigm, 161, 167, 211, 223, 226
pay for performance, 105, 108, 111
Pearl Problem, 203
Pfizer, 23, 120, 121, 122, 138, 153, 154, 157, 188, 190, 263, 267
Pharmacia, 23, 121
Philosophy of time, 27
Physics of time: Some basic laws to remember at work, 27
planning fallacy, 100, 103
Planning Fallacy, 100, 263, 268
Porter, Michael, 166, 257
Porter,Michael, 162
Possibilism, 28
Potter, Mary, 66
Presentism, 27
Prisoner's Dilemma, 194
Process versus people culture, 12
Psychology of time, 29, 31
Rapoport, Anatol, 194
reinforcing loop, 109, 111
Repenning, Nelson, 109
Repenning, Nelson, 139
Rezulin, 122
Richard Wagoner, 22
Rosabeth Moss Kanter, 42
Schick, 23
Shedlarz, David, 157
SMART, 107, 108, 192, 193
SMART goal, 193
SMART goals, 106, 107, 192
Sociéte Générale, 183
Sterman, John, 109, 139
Suggested documentation format, 202
Suggested email format, 201, 203
SWEAT Analysis, 169
SWOT Analysis, 260
Sydney Opera House, 101
system dynamics, 108
systems dynamics, 103, 104, 139, *See* systems thinking
systems thinking, 108
Systems thinking, 103
TA, 92, *See* transactional analysis
The Cheese Shoppe, xii
The Dark Ages—Sadlibs Version, 1
the domineer, 41
The Innovator's Dilemma, 166
Tips for writing effective presentations, 200
Tit for tat, 194, 195
Touche Ross, 23, 127, 162
Transactional analysis, 92
Tversky, 53
unintended consequences, 100, 104

275

Unintended consequences, 103
United Research Company, 23
VAK, 80
validity effect, 64
Viagra, 121
Vioxx, 122

Warner-Lambert, 121
Warren Buffet, 22
Wason, Peter, 66
Waxman-Hatch Act of 1984, 104
Who Moved My Cheese?, xi
Winston Churchill, 44

About the Author

Karen Phelan is a business consultant, author, evangelist, and humorist. Because you have to have a sense of humor to work in business these days, right? Plus, she definitely wants everyone to know just how funny business really is (that's the evangelist part.) Karen uses humor and a touch (okay, more like a smack) of sarcasm to shed light on common but inane business practices like, hey, let's spend six weeks every year doing  nothing but assessing employees against a checklist, assigning them a number, conducting a series of meetings to argue over the numbers so that they fit on a shape, all the while pretending that a subjective process is actually objective, and, even though most of the year is spent coaching people to excel, insisting that most everybody is mediocre, and then expecting everyone to be happy and motivated at the end of this time-consuming, exhausting, emotional, and yet non-value adding ritual.

In contrast, Karen believes that people aren't broken and don't need to be computed, diagnosed and fixed in order to function as productive members of an organization. Karen believes that organizations have a choice – to do things in the most complicated, painful, and systematic manner possible or find the easy, fun and human way. And who could be better to illustrate the most complicated and painful way of executing a plan than Monty Python on their quest to find the grail? Who Moved My Holy Hand Grenade is a fun way to learn everything you need to know about business.

Karen Phelan is a co-founder of an organizational development consulting firm, Operating Principals LLC, which is built around finding the easy, fun, and simple solutions to business problems. Karen has over a dozen years of consulting experience at Gemini Consulting and Deloitte & Touche and has held several management positions at Pfizer and Johnson & Johnson. Karen started her career in a military think tank and holds a B.S and M.S. in engineering from MIT.

www.ingramcontent.com/pod-product-compliance
Lightning Source LLC
LaVergne TN
LVHW061213060426
835507LV00016B/1906